# Freud's Jewish Identity

# Freud's Jewish Identity
## A CASE STUDY IN THE IMPACT OF ETHNICITY

Jerry Victor Diller

Rutherford • Madison • Teaneck
Fairleigh Dickinson University Press
London and Toronto: Associated University Presses

© 1991 by Associated University Presses, Inc.

All rights reserved. Authorization to photocopy items for internal or personal use, or the internal or personal use of specific clients, is granted by the copyright owner, provided that a base fee of $10.00, plus eight cents per page, per copy is paid directly to the Copyright Clearance Center, 27 Congress Street, Salem, Massachusetts 01970. [0-8386-3374-9/91 $10.00+8¢ pp, pc.]

Associated University Presses
440 Forsgate Drive
Cranbury, NJ 08512

Associated University Presses
25 Sicilian Avenue
London WC1A 2QH, England

Associated University Presses
P.O. Box 39, Clarkson Pst. Stn.
Mississauga, Ontario
L5J 3X9 Canada

The paper used in this publication meets the requirements of the American National Standard for Permanence of Paper for Printed Library Materials Z39.48-1984.

**Library of Congress Cataloging-in-Publication Data**

Diller, Jerry V.
    Freud's Jewish identity : a case study in the impact of ethnicity / Jerry Victor Diller
      p. cm.
    Includes bibliographical references.
    ISBN 0-8386-3374-9 (alk. paper)
    1. Freud, Sigmund, 1856–1939.  2. Psychoanalysts—Austria—Vienna—Biography.  3. Ethnicity—Austria—Vienna—Psychological aspects. 4. Jews—Austria—Vienna—Cultural assimilation.  5. Jews—Austria—Vienna—Ethnic identity.  6. Vienna (Austria)—Ethnic relations.
I. Title.
RC339.52.F733D55    1991
150.19′52—dc20
[B]                                                        89-45621
                                                                   CIP

PRINTED IN THE UNITED STATES OF AMERICA

To my father, Max Diller
and
my uncle, Ed Diller;
two very different, yet special connections
to the Jewish past

**SARA F. YOSELOFF MEMORIAL PUBLICATIONS**
In Judaism and Jewish Affairs

**This volume is one in a series established in memory
of Sara F. Yoseloff,
who devoted her life to the making of books.**

# Contents

| | |
|---|---:|
| Acknowledgments | 9 |
| 1 The Politics of Ethnicity | 13 |
| 2 The Assimilated Jews of Vienna | 28 |
| 3 The Dynamics of Jewish Identity | 45 |
| 4 Growing Up Jewish | 54 |
| 5 Freud's Jewish Identity | 90 |
| 6 The Jews and Gentiles of Psychoanalysis | 147 |
| 7 Psychoanalysis and Its Jewish Connection | 209 |
| Notes | 219 |
| References | 234 |
| Index | 238 |

# Acknowledgments

This odyssey into Freud's life and Jewish identity turned out to be far more than a dry, academic exercise. It became instead a journey into my own roots, my own self, my own unconscious processes. In the interim Freud taught me much about Jewish genius, Jewish suffering, and Jewish dignity, and for these insights I shall be eternally grateful.

I wish to thank, first of all, the Memorial Foundation for Jewish Culture, New York, whose fellowship grant to me for the academic year 1986–87 supported a majority of the preparation of the present manuscript. I am also appreciative for the help and support given to me by Harry Keyishian and the editorial committee at Fairleigh Dickinson University Press and Lauren Lepow, Julien Yoseloff, Cynthia Perwin Halpern, and others involved in this books' production at Associated University Presses. Thanks also to Julie Greenstein for her early substantive and editorial comments on the manuscript. And most importantly, my sincere thanks to Carole who so tolerantly endured my obsessive pursuit of Freud's identity and to Becca and Rachel who will always remain convinced that this book should have been called "How Dad Spent His Summer Vacations."

Grateful acknowledgment is made to the following for permission to reprint previously published material:

Basic Books, Inc., The Hogarth Press, and the estate of Ernest Jones: excerpts from *The Life and Work of Sigmund Freud* by Ernest Jones. Copyright © 1953, 1955, 1957 (volumes 1, 2, and 3 respectively), by Basic Books, Inc., Publishers, New York.

Basic Books, Inc. and The Hogarth Press: excerpts from *The Letters of Sigmund Freud*, translated by James and Tania Stern, edited by Ernst L. Freud. Copyright © 1960 by Sigmund Freud

Copyrights Ltd., London.

Princeton University Press and Routledge Ltd.: excerpt from *Collected Works of C. G. Jung* by C. G. Jung, Volume 10, *Civilization in Transition*. Copyright © 1964 by Princeton University Press.

Joseph Wortis: excerpt from *Fragments of an Analysis with Freud* by Joseph Wortis. Copyright © 1954 by Joseph, published by Simon and Schuster, Inc., New York.

# Freud's Jewish Identity

# 1
# The Politics of Ethnicity

The history of psychoanalysis is inextricably bound up with the ethnic identity of its founder, Sigmund Freud. To the majority of the citizens of turn-of-the-century Vienna, in fact, psychoanalysis was all but indistinguishable from its Jewish origins. Freud was after all a Jew, as were all of his early Viennese followers, and he first presented his radical theories not before some august medical body but instead in lectures to the B'nai Brith, a Jewish fraternal order. So strong were these associations that in time psychoanalysis came to be known as the "Jewish science."

It is not surprising then, given this stigma, that psychoanalysis quickly became a popular target for anti-Semitism. Emerging as it did at a time of growing anti-Jewish sentiment in Vienna, it served as a favorite subject for anti-Semitic slurs and diatribes. Jokes and aphorisms, such as the following published by Karl Kraus, himself a Jew, in his popular Viennese newspaper *Die Fackel*, were typical. "Psychoanalysis is the newest Jewish disease; the older people are still suffering from diabetes. . . . They reach into our dreams as though they were our pockets. . . . According to the latest research, the unconscious appears to be a sort of ghetto for people's thoughts. Apparently many are now homesick for it."[1] To its critics the "Jewish science" was just that, a body of teachings and practices applicable only to the Jewish psyche and therefore unworthy of serious consideration.

With the rise of National Socialism and its institutionalization of anti-Semitism, the campaign against psychoanalysis intensified. Freud's books and those of his followers were publicly burned in Berlin for their "soul-destroying overemphasis on the sex drive,"[2] and as Nazism spread, Jewish analysts were systematically harassed, driven out of scientific and psychological associations, replaced by Aryan counterparts, and eventually forced to flee for their lives. By 1938, the year Freud was finally given permission to leave Vienna for London, the Nazi plan for liquidating the "Jewish science" in Germany was virtually complete.

Freud, himself an irreligious yet prideful Jew, vacillated in his reaction to the ever-present anti-Semitism. At times he responded openly and with defiance—opposing anti-Semitic political candidates, speaking out against the complicity of the Catholic church and even, when directly confronted, standing his ground in the face of anti-Semitic mobs. On other occasions he remained surprisingly Stoic, unperturbed by personal affronts and even able to respond with humor and wit. When, for example, he was forced to sign a certificate stating that he had been well-treated by the Gestapo as a condition of his family's release from Vienna, he added the following quip to the document: "I can heartily recommend the Gestapo to anyone."[3]

As Freud grew older, however, the escalating anti-Jewish hatred began to take its emotional toll, causing him first concern and eventually paranoia over the future of psychoanalysis. Increasingly, he came to see anti-Semitism as the source of his career frustrations and setbacks. He grew fearful that his creation was in danger of becoming a "Jewish national affair,"[4] and in response he tried desperately to attract non-Jewish followers and support. Even in one of his last major works, *Moses and Monotheism*, he sought to soften anti-Jewish sentiment by rewriting Jewish history so as to invalidate its historic claim to special chosenness, the doctrine Freud held responsible for Christian anti-Semitism.

While the importance of these ethnically related events seems rather obvious, most biographical portrayals of Freud tend to overlook or at best to underplay their significance. In a recent hour-long PBS "Nova" presentation on psychoanalysis, for instance, only a single passing reference was made to Freud's ethnic background and that in the context of his being limited in his career choices because of anti-Semitism. For reasons that will be explored shortly, there seems to be a widespread tendency among biographers to gloss over ethnic issues, that is, to see them as unimportant and to underestimate their impact. While this is not universally the case and there are those who concur with Paul Roazen's assessment that "it is impossible to overemphasize Freud's Jewishness, since it was the single most important part of his background,"[5] biographers who see this represent a clear minority. Thus, it is not surprising that of the well over one hundred thousand books and articles currently listed in *The Index of Psychoanalytic Writings*, only a handful, at most forty or fifty, deal in any direct way with Freud's Jewishness or with the relationship between Jews and psychoanalysis.

But this is only part of the picture, for even within these works, Freud's ethnicity and that of the movement is more often than not seriously distorted or misrepresented. Dennis Klein is quite correct when he describes the literature on Freud's Jewishness as suffering from "an overextended acrobatics of either disguising or magnifying the meaning and impact of the movement's unmistakable sectarian quality."[6] By sectarian, Klein is here referring to psychoanalysis' connection to Jews and Judaism. While Freud clearly intended his ideas to be universal in character, their obvious connection to his own Jewishness cannot help but raise some doubts in this regard.

A brief look at some of this literature is revealing. Biographers who disregard Freud's Jewishness entirely typically portray him as a devout atheist, indifferent and unattracted to tradition, having somehow heroically, yet mysteriously, transcended the impact of his origins. His ethnicity is seen as nothing more than a minor irritant, easily overcome and of little real significance in the development of his revolutionary ideas. While Freud did at times portray himself in a similar manner, thus devaluing the impact of his ethnicity, this fact is interpreted in the present work as symptomatic of his own ambivalence over being Jewish. Where these writers err is first in their assumption that Freud's contempt for religion led to a rejection of all things Jewish (which is clearly not the case) and second, in the belief that he could have with so little difficulty severed his connections to Judaism.

The fact of the matter is that Jews of Freud's day, even when they most fervently wished it, could not so easily shed the yoke of the past and escape the reality of who they were. To assimilate meant making oneself acceptable to mainstream society, and this required not only rejecting Jewish tradition, but also meticulously changing one's appearance, behavior, language, and general demeanor to mimic gentile ways. But even these efforts were no guarantee of social acceptance, for anti-Semitism pervaded all levels of Viennese society and to many gentiles a "Jew was a Jew," and nothing, not even conversion, could alter this fact. Consequently and as a matter of personal survival, the majority of Viennese Jews chose to live life among their coreligionists, be they Orthodox, totally secularized, or somewhere in-between. The few who did cut their ties completely paid dearly for it, taking on the status of pariahs and having to accept constant ridicule and abuse for the priviledge of remaining within gentile social circles. It is well-established that Freud adopted the former path, remaining throughout his life a self-consciously identified Jew, working and living out his years in almost the exclusive company of fellow Jews. In 1926 he wrote to Marie Bonaparte: "My merit in the Jewish cause is confined to a single point: that I have never denied my Jewishness."[7]

Other biographers err not in their willingness to focus on Freud's ethnicity, but in their tendency to distort it. Take, for example, the case of Gregory Zilboorg. Zilboorg, an eminent American psychiatrist, took violent exception to Freud's ideas on religion and argued that the rejection of religion was not an "essential component of psychoanalysis"[8] but rather a caveat introduced by Freud to justify his own atheism. Zilboorg further hints, though rather subtly, that Freud's antipathy actually masked an attraction to Christianity.[9] "Even the casual reader," he wrote, ". . . could not fail to notice that Freud saw a natural continuity, a spiritual unity, in the religious road from Moses through the prophets to Christ."[10] While such an accusation is not totally out of the question given the vicissitudes of Jewish identity in Freud's day, the facts in Freud's case do not support it. Quite to the contrary, he never relented in his criticism of the church and was in turn widely perceived as a dangerous enemy in clerical circles. Nor did he ever seriously or consciously consider conversion.

One can however discern a possible motive for Zilboorg's minimizing the discrepancy between psychoanlysis and religion and for softening Freud's hatred of Christianity by referring to Zilboorg's own biography. Born of Orthodox Jewish parents in Russia, he abandoned Judaism soon after maturity in order to pursue enlightened ideas and ultimately training in psychoanalysis. He distinguished himself early as a psychopathologist, but with age turned his attention increasingly to matters of religion and faith, ultimately setting for himself the task of creating a "satisfying synthesis between psychoanalysis and religion."[11] That Zilboorg's preoccupation may have in reality masked a deep inner conflict over his own Jewishness and represented a projection of his own desires onto Freud becomes clear when one considers the final days of Zilboorg's life and his deathbed decision to convert to Catholicism.

Finally, there are biographers who have tended to blur the facts of Freud's life and career in order to make of him either a Jewish champion or villain. Mortimer Ostow, for instance, in what is otherwise a very insightful analysis, refers to a study of Freud's *Moses and Monotheism* in just these terms. "Dr. Gershom D. Cohen," he writes, "discerned an esoteric message in *Moses and Monotheism* alongside the familiar exoteric thesis. The message is an equally vigorous assertion of the virtues and strengths of the Jews."[12] Certainly an unusual interpretation of a work widely recognized as Freud's most vigorous attack on the Jewish religion.

Or consider at the other extreme Theodore Lewis's analysis of Freud as a self-hating Jew. "The melancholy fact is that Freud was a Jew only by the accident of birth.... He hated violently everything Jewish. The 'accident' gave him a group of complexes which prevented him from thinking objectively about his people, about religion in general, and about Judaism in particular."[13] In order to support his diagnosis, Lewis selectively presents only those details that demonstrate a negative attitude toward Judaism and he simultaneously disregards well-documented facts that reflect an equally strong Jewish chauvinistic bent in Freud's character. In so doing, he manages to overlook the important phenomenon of Jewish ambivalence, a psychic state in which the individual is both drawn to and repelled by his or her own Jewishness. Such ambivalence, while no doubt bothersome and in the extreme pathological, does not in any way necessarily imply the kind of deep psychological flaw suggested by Lewis. It was in fact quite common among assimilated European Jews.

Some of the silence around Freud's Jewishness is no doubt related to the politics of anti-Semitism. Intergroup contact can be by its very nature frought with strong emotions, and people learn early, especially if formally educated, to mask prejudices and to speak of ethnic matters in a cautious and guarded manner, if at all. Where levels of mistrust are particularly high, it is often most prudent to remain silent on the subject and to avoid the possibility of conflict or of saying the wrong thing altogether. For the non-Jew, such avoidance is a preferable alternative, for not only does it avoid the possibility of uncomfortable encounters, but is also avoids a continual reminder of the unjust system in which one colludes. The gentile thus has the luxury and motivation to step outside the ethnic drama and in this way to deny its reality. Not so the Jew, for whom ethnicity and anti-Semitism can be an ever-present filter through which life is experienced. In such cases denial is often the only way to find distance from the hurt, the continual reminder of supposed inferiority, and the anger that cannot safely be vented. Often, however, the racial prejudices of majority group members and the sensitivities of minority group members are just too powerful to remain hidden. Instead, they gain expression unconsciously through the distortion of personal perceptions of oneself and of others. The anti-Semite, for example, may see all Jews acting in a stereotypical manner, while the self-hating Jew may minimize anti-Semitism or blame Jews themselves for its occurance. The fearful Jew in turn may see anti-Jewish sentiment everywhere, even in situations where it does not in fact exist. Nor would it be uncommon for either Jew or gentile to project their own racial conflicts onto others or portray them in their own work.

Such dynamics are clearly evident in the biographical studies of Freud just described. They will in addition be encountered within the drama of psychoanalytic history itself and it will become obvious that an appreciation of their impact is necessary in order to make sense out of much of the information and many events that may at first appear contradictory, misleading, or illogical. It is only against this background of inner ethnic politics that the reader can begin to grasp the complex forces at work in Freud's life, in the lives of his Jewish and gentile contemporaries who struggled daily with the ramifications of the "Jewish Question,"[14] and among the writers who have attempted to chronicle this history.

A second source of the confusion surrounding Freud's ethnic identity has its roots in his position on religion. As an assimilated Jew in turn-of-the-century Vienna, he identified strongly and passionately with the values of the Enlightenment. Enlightened thought and the social and political change that accompanied its emergence promised and to some extent provided nineteenth-century Jews an opportunity to leave the ghettos of Europe and to move into the modern world. The principle of universalism and its accompanying rejection of particularistic doctrines were especially vital because they affirmed the Jews' common humanity and their right to equal citizenship. It is thus not surprising that Freud's theory with its heavy emphasis upon the universality of human behavior (that of the Jew included) would echo a strong condemnation of particularism in all its various forms, especially that practiced by the church, the historic bastion of anti-Semitism and the traditional enemy of enlighted thought. To be fair, Freud was equally vehement in his rejection of ritualistic Judaism, but he was able internally to separate Jewish ethnicity from religious doctrine and thus to retain a strong personal identity as a Jew.

Frued's position on religion was quite clear. Religious belief has is roots in the child's need to appease and control the overwhelming forces that surround it. It is modeled after the father complex. And it represents a primitive and transitional stage in the evolution of the individual. Repeatedly Freud drew a parallel between religion and neurosis. In *Totem and Taboo*, for instance, he pointed to a similarity between the customs and religious practices of primitive peoples and the obsessive actions of neurotic patients, and in a later work, *The Future of an Illusion*, he argued that to become fixated upon religion and to indulge in the kind of illusory thinking upon which it is based was to court neurosis. Freud's ideas on the place of religion in the history of the human species were equally dismal. "If we attempt to assign the place of religion in the evolution of mankind, it appears not as a permanent acquisiton but as a counterpart to the neurosis which individual civilized men have to go through in their passage from childhood to maturity."[15]

Given this rather bleak assessment, it is not surprising that so many of Freud's followers shared his antipathy toward religion and that as a consequence, there would be so few efforts to define psychoanalysis in terms of religious origins, Judaic or otherwise. To trace the roots of psychoanalysis back to what is seen within the movement as a regressive and destructive force would be to taint it irrevocably. Freud instead chose to define his ideas and work in relation to the Enlightenment tradition, and in contrast to the dearth of studies linking psychoanalysis to Judaism, one can find numerous analyses of the philosophical roots of various analytic concepts as well as of Freud's development as a German thinker. Freud predicted that humanity would ultimately give up its neurotic dependence on religion and replace it with a *Weltanschauung* more squarely grounded in the rational tradition, and he saw his own efforts in the creation of psychoanalysis as a first step in this direction.

But this is only one side of the picture, for Freud's contempt for religion had personal and emotional as well as intellectual roots. Born into a newly assimilated family, barely one generation out of the ghetto, he like most young Jews of the day quickly developed a strong ambivalence about Jewish tradition. Anti-Semitism was a fact of daily existence and to be a Jew in a predominantly Christian world meant to be less than acceptable, both professionally and socially. Thus stigmatized, assimilated Jews of turn-of-the-century Vienna found themselves caught between worlds: trying, often frantically, to disassociate themselves from the past, yet at the same time barred from full entry into mainstream culture.

This untenable psychological situation drove many to self-hatred, that is, to a denial and rejection of their identities as Jews as well as a devaluing and hatred of all things Jewish. A frequent endpoint of this process was conversion to Christianity. Others, however, Freud included, who were far too prideful and defiant ever to adopt such a self-rejecting course, managed their negative feelings toward Judaism by displacing them elsewhere. In Freud's case, for example, they were projected onto Jewish ritual, Orthodox Jewry, Christianity, and religion in general—all particularly unpleasant reminders to him of an unenlightened and restrictive past. Thus it was possible to resolve the tension and ambivalence psychologically, unconsciously rejecting the religious component of Judaism while at the same time retaining a strong identification and attachment to other aspects of Judaism, such as its ethnicity and its messianism. Such psychic acrobatics were typical of the Jews who were drawn to psychoanalysis. One finds few instances of real self-hatred and identity-rejection among its ranks, however. Freud in fact looked upon Jewish identity-rejection and the decision to convert with some contempt, as will become evident in the case of Alfred Adler.

Psychoanalytic theory holds that such accommodations are at best precarious and that too much self-insight can upset the balance. This was the situation with Freud himself, whose self-analysis served to bring to awareness powerful feelings of Jewish ambivalence. Only through an analysis of these feelings, as well as by means of his subsequent identification with the biblical figure of Moses was he able to move toward some resolution and eventually to a more positive attachment to Judaism. The possibility of similar psychic upset and the inner havoc it would cause is perhaps another reason for the reluctance of many Jewish analysts to look too deeply into the ethnic roots of their profession. Of this hesitancy, Mortimer Ostow writes: "When I was a student at the New York Psychoanalytic Institute, there was an unspoken gentlemen's agreement that in psychoanalysis one does not discuss Jewishness, except to demonstrate to an occasional religious patient that his piety is a sign of neurosis."[16] To ask such questions, even at the level of theory, might well disrupt the inner censoring process and thus bring to consciousness old memories and accommodations best left hidden. Besides, the association of Judaism with psychoanalysis might well prove an embarrassment or at least a source of discomfort for those who may long ago have severed family and religious ties in order to pursue professional careers.

Freud's own ambivalence led him to make a number of omissions, distortions, and contradictory statements about his experiences as a Jew. Taken at face value, such statements have served to confuse biographers and lead many to underestimate the importance of his ethnicity. On various occasions, for example, he claimed ignorance of the Jewish religion. In the preface to the Hebrew edition of *Totem and Taboo*, he referred to himself as "ignorant of the language of the holy writ" and as "completely estranged from the religion of his father,"[17] and in the Yiddish translation of another work he expressed regret over never having learned either Hebrew or Yiddish during his student days. Yet a reconstruction of the religious curriculum to which he was exposed as a youth, his frequent use of Yiddish in his correspondence, and the text of a Hebrew inscription written in the family Bible and presented to him by his father on his thirty-fifth birthday challenge the complete veracity of these statements. Similarly, in a letter to his wife Martha, written after visiting the catacombs in Rome, Freud claimed unfamiliarity with the very common Jewish term *menorah* (a seven-branched candelabra), and in a letter to Wilhelm Fleiss he misquotes a well-known biblical quotation.[18] It is unclear whether these statements were made intentionally or unintentionally What is clear is the fact that Freud felt great negativity toward the religion to which each of these items points, and to distance himself from them psychologically would not represent an illogical unconscious ploy.

Freud in addition made several well-analyzed parapraxes, that is, unintentional yet meaningful slips of the tongue or omissions, related to Jewish themes. One was his omission of Theodor Herzl's name in the analysis of a dream stimulated by the writer's play *The New Ghetto* and another was his surprising lack of reference to Karl Abraham's very relevant work in *Moses and Monotheism*. Both will be discussed at greater length later, but for now it is sufficient to suggest that the former is related to Freud's early mistrust of Zionism and the latter to Abraham's role as Freud's primary Jewish confidant. Such omissions and errors are not uncommon in cases of strong emotional ambivalence and with enough data they can be related directly to specific underlying conflicts. What they do not reflect, however, as some biographers would suggest, is Freud's indifference to Judaism.

Of equal interest are the seemingly unintentional distortions of ethnic materials on the part of biographers themselves. Several interesting examples emerged during my research for the present book. The first grew out of a comparison of two translations of Freud's letters to Wilhelm Fliess. The earlier translation, by Eric Mosbacker and James Strachey, was published in 1954; the more recent one by Jeffrey Masson in 1985. In comparison to Masson's work, Mosbacker and Strachey's translation seems almost sanitized of Judaic material and references. Many personal events with Jewish significance communicated by Freud to Fliess and included in Masson's translation are edited out of the earlier version. The use of Yiddish expressions is also excised in the Mosbacker and Strachey version. Thus, "Farewell, and let me soon have a sensible answer to this *meschuggene* [crazy] letter" (3 December 1897) becomes "Kindest regards, and let me have a sensible . . . answer."[19] Or "I am afraid it is *stuss* [bunk]" (6 September 1899) becomes "but I am afraid it is rubbish."[20] The experience of reading the two translations in their entirety is also quite different. Masson's translation portrays a warm and homey friendship and correspondence between two Jews; Mosbacker and Strachey's a more professional distant relationship between colleagues.

A second example of editorial distortion occurs in relation to Lionel Trilling and Steven Marcus's abridgement of Ernest Jones's famous biography of Freud, that is, its condensation from three into one volume. A careful reading of the discarded material shows that much of it, certainly more than one would predict merely on the basis of chance, concerns Jews, Judaism, and Freud's ethnic identity. While Jones himself was clearly well aware of and at peace, if not totally comfortable with, the movement's sectarian nature, his abridgers may not have been so disposed. The orthodox inner circle of psychoanalysis has strived to protect Freud's personal life from public exposure and to present him and the movement in the most positive light possible. This has been accomplished through prudent editing and the selective release of private documents. Perhaps a similar motive fueled the editing of Jones's biography.

A final factor contributing to the confusion around Freud's ethnicity was the existence of very real yet seldom acknowledged tensions between Jewish and non-Jewish analysts within the movement itself. Ernest Jones, for instance, Freud's foremost biographer and the first non-Jew to enter the inner circle, repeatedly hinted at his own discomfort and feelings of exclusion at being an outsider in an exclusively Jewish group. In his history of Freud he emphasized the movement's decidedly Jewish character, describing Freud as "Jewish to the core" and as having "very few friends who were not Jews."[21] Later Jones suggested that after Jung's defection, Freud never trusted another non-Jew. Freud, clearly sensitive to the rebuffs of non-Jews, fanned the flames of interethnic discord within the movement through his own chauvinistic attitudes. He believed, for instance, that all gentiles harbor anti-Semitic feelings and that "as long as Jews are not admitted to Gentile circles, they have no choice but to band together."[22]

Most explosive in this regard was the involvement of Carl Jung and his Swiss followers' in psychoanalysis. Due to growing insecurities, Freud desperately craved non-Jewish validation for his theories and actively sought Jung's participation in the movement to allieviate his fears. As long as the Swiss continued to profess his ideas, he felt assured that his work was universal in character. His obsession with international recognition and the steps he took to ensure it upset his Jewish Viennese followers who had remained loyal to him from the beginning and now felt preempted by the newcomers. These tensions reached the boiling point with Freud's choice of Carl Jung as heir-apparent and president of the International Psychoanalytic Society, passing over his Jewish disciples from Vienna who had far greater seniority in the movement. The conflict over Jung became particularly ugly during the Nazi years when accusations of anti-Semitism and collaboration were leveled against Jung for his activities as editor of the Aryanized journal *Zentralblatt für Psychotherapie* and for statements emphasizing differences between Jewish and Aryan psychologies.

These racial undercurrents, in spite of their intensity, were seldom acknowledged or discussed prior to the accusations made against Jung. There was, first of all, the fear of exacerbating already precarious rifts within the movement and of stimulating further anti-Semitism from the outside. Second, airing such dirty laundry in public was not only undignified but it could also detract from the status of psychoanalysis and provide further justification for its rejection.

For the past several years, I have as a scholar knowledgable in issues of minority identity and a student of psychoanalytic history, sifted through this morass of confused and contradictory information. What I have found, I believe, is a clearer and more accurate portrayal of the impact of Freud's Jewishness upon his life and work. The case study that follows offers a more comprehensive understanding of Freud's identity as a Jew and of the role of Jews and Judaism in the creation of psychoanalysis than has been previously available. My method is psychodynamic and to this end I have tried not only to enumerate in some detail the conscious and unconscious aspects of Freud's identification as a Jew, but also to trace these back historically through his adolescence to certain critical early events. In order to give greater depth to my case study, I have included chapters on the Jews of Freud's day, the psychological dynamics of Jewish identification and group membership, and the relationship between Jews, Judaism, and psychoanalytic theory. The present work is not intended as an exhaustive biography or history. Such efforts already exist far better than I could ever accomplish. What I intend rather is to highlight the ethnic aspects of Freud's life and those of the movement and show how this Jewish dimension has interacted with a variety of other factors to create the body of knowledge known as psychoanalysis.

The present study also provides an unprecedented glimpse into Jewish existence in postemancipated Europe. The period in question witnessed nothing less than the birth of modern Jewry and, as such, lays bare the basic psychological forces that have come to define contemporary Jewish life. Chief among these is the Jews' status as an oppressed minority. The varied reactions to this social and psychological fact, as witnessed in the lives of Freud and his associates, offers a unique opportunity to observe at first hand the workings of the contemporary Jewish psyche.

Freud's biography is instructive in this regard, first because of its setting: turn-of-the-century Vienna, a veritable microcosm of Jewish hopes and frustrations, described by Juliet Mitchell as "the most Jewish city in Europe."[23] The Vienna of that period was in fact the birthplace of both Zionism and modern anti-Semitism—two movements that would come to define much of subsequent Jewish history. It was in addition an unparalleled haven for Jewish productivity and genius. In 1910, for example, the year Freud published *Five Lectures on Psychoanalysis* and the year he received his first international recognition, three-quarters of Vienna's journalists, a third of its university students, and an overwhelming majority of its artists and intellectuals were Jewish. Crucial to an understanding of the time is the fact that Vienna was a society in transition, caught in the throes of radical social and political change. The resulting chaos and unrest proved a very mixed blessing for its Jewish population. On the one hand, the crumbling of institutions and practices long-responsible for restricting Jewish activity meant, initially anyway, greater freedom and mobility. At the same time growing frustration among Vienna's gentile majority increasingly found expression in anti-Semitism with the Jew emerging as an unwilling symbol and target for all that was objectionable in the new order. The net result was a psychic complex marked by ambivalence toward tradition, neurosis, and unprecedented creative energy, qualities clearly evident in Freud, his followers, and in many of those who sought treatment from him.

Second, Freud's biography is of interest as an ethnic document, not because it offers any unique insights into the psychology of genius but rather for just the opposite reason: because it is so very typical of the times in which he lived. Freud does not easily fit the image of the lonely visionary, out of sync with his culture, marching to the beat of a different drummer. Quite the contrary. His life in fact closely personifies the two faces of postemancipated Jewish existence, what Hannah Arendt has called the "parvenu" and the "pariah."[24]

Freud's "parvenu" side, like that of other middle-class Jews of the day, involved an early interest in liberal politics, a strong attraction to German culture, and a strong contempt for Eastern European Jewry. The first Freud abandoned rather quickly in order to pursue a career in medicine, joining a medical profession that numbered over fifty percent Jewish. The second he disavowed only reluctantly and in the waning years of his life, as anti-Semitism and then Nazism spread across Europe and as it became increasingly difficult, even for the most deluded, to believe in the high ideals of German culture. The last, his contempt for Eastern European Jewry, he never lost, and it found its ultimate expression in his scathing critique of religion and ritualistic observance. Ironically, Freud came to the study of the mind quite indirectly, making his choice of a specialty not out of some compelling passion or calling but rather almost purely on the basis of the potentials for future career advancement. Hungry with ambition and plagued by perpetual insecurities—a combination not uncommon among newly emancipated and aspiring minorities—he experienced enormous frustration over various delays in his academic promotion, even coming to believe that anti-Semitism would ultimately destroy his life's work and rob him of his well-deserved acclaim.

At the same time Freud was very much the pariah and the outsider. Through his theories and at times through his personal behavior, he showed an obstinate refusal to bow to gentile society. In this regard he surreptiously took revenge upon the society that would not allow him to enter, painting it in the darkest possible terms and creating for it an understanding of human nature that made no distinction between Jew and non-Jew. In sum then, the impetus for the discovery of psychoanalysis grew not out of Freud's disengagement from the world, as the image of the analytic therapist might imply, but instead from an intense involvement with it: the involvement of a frustrated and nakedly ambitious Jew gifted with uncanny insight into the very heart and soul of his times.

Freud's biography is also unique in the vast array of materials available for analysis. Freud was himself a prolific writer and correspondent and in time became the center of a cult of followers who religiously collected his every word. Add to this an almost endless series of biographies and personal accounts of interactions with him, most noteworthy for their variable quality and accuracy, and one can begin to appreciate the extent of the literature that now exists. This prodigious amount of information is not without value, however, for it can afford the possibility of multiple verification of facts, a near-necessity in the study of such highly charged topics as ethnicity and race relations, where personal projections and distortions are commonplace, even among the most respected scholars.

Finally, there is the value to be derived from the use of psychoanalysis itself as a tool in the study of ethnic identity. Until quite recently, sociologists and anthropologists dominated research in this area. What resulted in the main was a series of demographic studies of assimilation patterns, voting behavior, and residential and migration trends. Such efforts, while no doubt useful, tell little if anything of the inner life of ethnic peoples: of their hopes, fears, frustrations. Were it not for the novels of writers like Ralph Ellison, James Baldwin, and Richard Wright[25] and the isolated voices of early psychologists, such as Franz Fanon and Kurt Lewin,[26] we would know little of the impact of discrimination and racism, the pressures to assimilate, and the conflicting demands for allegiance and conformity that the minority group itself exerts. Recent research in these areas testifies to the complex nature of ethnic identification and to the formidable challenges to healthy mental adjustment that minority group members must face.

To underemphasize or overlook this subjective element, as has so often been the case in previous research, is to rob ethnicity of its richness and complexity and to reduce it to mere charicature. Perhaps Freud's greatest contribution was the discovery of a language and method for exploring this inner world. That he willingly and unrelentingly turned his tools inward upon himself, immersed as he was in a desperate struggle with his own Jewishness, served as testimony to his enormous personal courage. What emerges from his self-analysis and from other analytic studies of the Jewish dimension in Freud is an invaluable legacy of insights into the dynamics of ethnic psychology. It is in the hope of illuminating this legacy that I have undertaken this work.

# 2
# The Assimilated Jews of Vienna

The Jewish world as Freud knew it had its origins only a generation or two before his birth in a radical historic discontinuity known as Jewish emanipation. Before delving into the specifics of Freud's psychological legacy as a Viennese Jew, it is useful to develop a broader picture of European Jewish history in order to better appreciate the powerful forces that were at work in the lives of his grandparents and parents, transforming all aspects of their world, including and perhaps especially the meaning and substance of their Jewish identity. It is with this in mind that the following piece of psychohistory is offered.

\* \* \*

The closing decades of the eighteenth century marked a profound turning point in Jewish history and psychology. After thousands of years of cultural and religious stability, and after having withstood numerous dislocations and atrocities committed in the name of Christ and Christianity, the Jews of Europe were torn by the roots from their traditional ghetto existence and dropped, largely defenseless, into the strange world of modernity. This process, hard as it may be to conceive, required only a handful of decades for completion. At its end, an ancient lifestyle, medieval in its character and structure, had been largely undermined, and a people long dependent on each other for survival and sustenance were left fragmented and set adrift to fend for themselves, isolated in a hostile environment. Ironically, and in misguided anticipation of a final end to Jewish suffering, this period has been called Jewish emancipation.

Put simply, the term emancipation has come to reflect a sequence of historic processes: the Jewish encounter with modernity and Enlightenment thought, the resulting destruction of the ghetto lifestyle and its hold on the individual Jew, and efforts by those who exited the ghetto to gain entry into mainstream Christian society. The radical ideas of the Enlightenment two centuries earlier had slowly eroded the archaic political systems of Europe, finding their initial major expression in the French Revolution of 1789. As successive waves of democratization, scientism, and rationalism beat against the old order of the church and the monarchy, cracks appeared in its foundation. Jewish ghettoes, unchanged since medieval times and located in various geographic domains across Europe, suffered a fate similar to that of their Christian neighbors. Not unexpectedly, these winds of change stimulated very mixed reactions among ghetto residents. Some saw within the humanistic, democratic, and liberal strains of Enlightenment thought hope for the future and the end of an antiquated system of oppression that had kept Jews isolated for a thousand years—a nation within nations, unwanted guests, pawns to be used socially, economically, and politically. Others envisioned a new order that would allow for personal freedom and escape from the oppresive demands of religious ritual and the theocracy that sustained it. And still others feared for the future of Judaism in the wake of the intruding Enlightenment consciousness, which defined religion as the ultimate enemy.

Emancipation was a process, not an event, occurring at varying times and with differing intensities in Jewish communities across Europe. In general the Jews of Eastern Europe, armed as they were with a more isolated and rural lifestyle, a culture recently revitalized by Hasidism and Haskalah, and a world as yet undisturbed by political liberalism or intellectual awakening, remained largely untouched by the effects of the Enlightenment during this period. Most would receive their baptism into modernity in the new world. Forced out of their homes at the turn of the century by increasing waves of anti-Semitism and bewildered and confused by the ordeal of emigration to America, the Eastern European Jews would fall prey to similar forces in their new homeland.

The Jews of Western Europe, on the other hand, and especially the German and Austrian Jews, received the full effects of continental emancipation, being literally catapulted into the modern world by a combination of forces from both outside and within the ghetto world. The rulers of Austria, for example, whether because of anti-Semitism and the desire to drive Jews out of the empire, or out of a growing sympathy with the ideas of Enlightenment, or out of fear that failing to develop such a sympathy would ultimately lead to their overthrow, began in the late 1700s to institute a series of anti-Jewish laws (such as compulsory school attendance and military service) whose net effect was to integrate Jews into the Austrian citizenry and simultaneously to eradicate their differences from it. While such edicts were often cleverly avoided, Enlightenment ideas eventually found their way in. At the same time the inner life of the western ghetto had become stagnant and ingrown, progressively losing its vitality and ability to withstand threats from the outside. It thus became an easy target for the forces that loomed ominously at its door.

The Jews of the ghetto were unprepared for the radical changes brought on by modernity and could only respond with shock and disbelief. There were few preliminary hints of what was to come, and the arrival of the change was so rapid that immediate adjustment was all but impossible. Parents, for instance, found their children surreptitiously reading Enlightenment works that had been smuggled into the ghetto. Empassioned and swept away by the new ideas, youth no longer saw the need to bow to the will and authority of the past. The situation was further confused by the fickleness of local governments, who in the spirit of liberalism granted a Jewish community certain rights of citizenship one day, only to retract them a year or so later when more reactionary attitudes or elements took control. This pattern of revolution and counterrevolution, of gaining and losing freedom, typified the Jewish movement in the modern era. Neither the few Jews who had exited the ghetto earlier (primarily through economic pursuits) nor those who remained and were conscious of what was occurring offered much help. The former had cut themselves off from tradition by choice and in so doing had turned their backs on it forever. The latter, feeling the need to respond, tried desperately to modernize and accommodate the Jewish religion and lifestyle, but they often did so in such an ill-advised and naïve manner that it actually weakened rather than strengthened the ghetto's staying power. In time, and after assimilation had become more commonplace, such efforts would in fact become more thoughtful and substantial.

External threat had always been a key contributor to Jewish group cohesiveness. People huddled together out of fear and for mutual survival and in the process insulated Jewish ritual, custom, and belief from outside encroachment. Even those who wished to escape the confines of ghetto life had nowhere to turn. Emancipation ameliorated the external pressures by making the gentile world accessible to Jews and thus turned them into free and mobile individuals. When the floodgates lifted, the reaction was immediate. Jews began living where they chose, behaving as they pleased, and remaining loyal or indifferent to the group, depending upon personal choice.

Jewish theology was the core around which all aspects of ghetto life revolved. Ritual, social intercourse, family structure, beliefs, and superstitions all oriented the Jew to God. As each new idea of the Enlightenment swept through the ghetto, it chipped away at traditional conceptions of God and patterns of belief and practice. New philosophies beat against the religious worldview, transforming biblical figures into abstrctions and undermined faith in them. The growing rationality dealt a death blow to core concepts of an historic God, the chosenness of the Jewish people, the belief in the coming of a messiah, and the literalness of the Bible, making them all totally unacceptable. Traditional practices ceased as their theological underpinnings lost credence and the social pressures to observe them weakened. Thus, as the cornerstone of Jewish life crumbled, the various elements that reinforced it lost their power, disassociated themselves from each other, and ceased being integral parts of Jewish self-expression.

Interactions between Jews and gentiles became more frequent and when they occurred the process of social comparison began to loom larger and larger. Jews became fascinated by and drawn to non-Jewish ways, and subtly, and at times not so subtly, they began to imitate them in the hope of gaining entry into mainstream culture. No longer interested in fulfilling their ambitions within the Jewish world, they looked to bigger arenas. It was clearly felt that to be successful one had to become like the gentiles. Equality would be forthcoming only when the Jew had become indistinguishable from the non-Jew.

In sum, Jewish emancipation radically undermined the ghetto world by permanently disrupting its interrelated totality. What was once an integrated and self-reinforcing whole quickly deteriorated, as unnatural distinctions were made between its various aspects. Economic pursuits were no longer tied to the community. Education ceased to be synonymous with Torah and Talmud study. Ethnicity became distinct from religiosity, and the family gave up its function as the inculcator of ritualistic Jewish life. Where religious belief remained, it too came to be transformed. Alternative sects, emphasizing a more personal and accessible God as well as humanistic and ethical values, grew and gained followers. Those who could not adjust in this manner found increasing fulfillment not in new visions of God or tradition, but in humanistic causes (such as socialism, communism, Zionism, and psychoanalysis) in the case of intellectuals, and in affluence for the growing middle class. The enormous energies that had once been channeled into religious pursuits were now being redirected toward very different and secular ends.

As chaos reined supreme within the ghetto, it simultaneously intruded itself into the inner psyche of the assimilating Jew, rupturing previous bases for self-understanding and identity. The internal consequences of this chaos were staggering. One major symptom was a fragmentation in the way people thought. Mind increasingly came to function independent of emotion and intuition, and the integrity of the Jewish self fell prey to self-consciousness and compartmentalization. With the Enlightenment, Jews became self-conscious about their own Jewishness and in time they grew alienated from it. In the ghetto, being a Jew was a given, a fact of life that required no further exploration. Jews uncritically followed customs and habits thousands of years old and participated in a lifestyle that defined all aspects of their existence. They questioned the fairness of God, the reasons for their sad plight and exile, but never the fact of who they were.

A given becomes a matter of debate, an absolute becomes relative, only when there is an alternative available. Emancipation provided Jews with that alternative in the form of potential escape and assimilation, the possibility of no longer being Jews. In so doing, it forced them to inquire into the nature of their Jewishness, thereby objectifying it and setting them apart from it. By asking the questions: "Why am I a Jew and what does that mean," by tasting of the tree of Knowledge as Adam had, post-emancipation Jews set into motion a process which would eventually and permanently alienate them from the past.

Differentiation of the ghetto into various parts also led to a compartmentalization of the meaning of Jewish identity. As aspects of the traditional lifestyle lost hold, they were dropped, and what remained became the basis for one's Jewish identity. Being Jewish thus came to mean very different things to different Jews. Some remained religious Jews; others became ethnic Jews; still others cultural Jews and so forth. In the intact ghetto, such distinctions had been meaningless. In the aftermath of emancipation, however, each of these dimensions gained the potential for autonomously defining Jewish self-understanding. Judaism lost its centrality in human affairs, its ability to function as the core around which the individual's life was organized, and it was thus relegated to a peripheral or at most a secondary position in the world of most Jews.

Exit from the ghetto created enormous emotional turmoil as well. Increased tension and heightened inner conflict were commonplace. Some of the tension resulted naturally from the dissolution of the ghetto itself. As the culture collapsed, so too did its ability to provide the individual Jew with psychological support and safety. Kurt Lewin writes the following of the changing psychic situation.

> If we compare the position of the individual Jew in the Ghetto period with his situation in modern times, we find that he now stands much more for and by himself. . . . In the Ghetto period a Jew may have been exposed to especially high pressure when acting outside his group, but on the other hand there was for him some region in which he felt "at home," in which he could act freely as a member of his group, and did not need to stand by himself against pressure from without. . . . With the intermingling of the Jewish and non-Jewish groups, the Jew has relatively more often to face as an individual the pressures against Jews.[1]

The growing personal isolation and its resulting psychic pressure were further compounded by the demands of civilized society. In the emancipated world, unfamiliar patterns were expected of the Jew. The prototype for proper behavior was stranger meeting stranger, not intimate interacting with intimate. Civility required the proper social distance, aloofness, the creation of an appropriate facade, and subtle and guarded dialogue. Such rules must have mystified and confused the newly liberated Jews, so antithetical were they to the habits of ghetto life, with its physical contact, nonexistent privacy, and heated and emotional interactions. At times the new immigrants to modernity must have felt themselves doubly isolated: repulsed by the strange and unfamiliar world they craved, and secretly yearning at least in their loneliest moments for a return to the oppressive familiarity of the ghetto.

Two final factors exacerbated the emotional picture. First, a return to the ghetto, even where it remained physically intact, was seldom an option for those disgruntled Jews who discovered in retrospect that emancipation demanded too high a personal price. In the process of freeing themselves from the traditional lifestyle, most had so radically changed themselves—their basic style of thought, behavior, tastes, and sensibilities—that they were no longer the same people. Thus modified, they would have been as ill-at-ease in the ghetto as they were in the emancipated world. In general, enthusiasm for and trust in the enlightened Christian world tended to dampen with time, while disassimilation, that is, a return to a more traditional identification, tended to increase in direct proportion to the growth of anti-Semitism.

Second, and perhaps most critical, Jews were never afforded full access to gentile society as they had hoped. Full emancipation and assimilation never occurred anywhere. As one barrier fell, a new one seemed to be erected. As legal sanctions were lifted, for example, social ones took their place. The insidious and deeply rooted anti-Semitism of Europe overshadowed the dream of equality, keeping it a fantasy that was never to become fully realized. And this fact only created more desperation and confusion, especially in those most bent upon escape from the ghetto. Some, as a final gesture, sought conversion; others desperately attempted to erase the vestiges of their Jewish past and in their place mimicked Christian ways. But no matter what they did to become more acceptable, it was never enough, and they found themselves still outsiders, excluded and barred from full entry.

In race relations rationalizations always develop to justify overt discrimination, and those related to the anti-Semitism of this period were particularly complex and contradictory. Some gentiles feared and hated Jews because they would not assimilate, but rather insisted on retaining and flaunting their differences. Others despised Jews for just the opposite reason: because they sought to make themselves indistinguishable from gentiles. To succeed in "passing" was as much a reason for rejecting the Jew as was the refusal to become fully German. There was no way out of such logic. In short, Jews were damned if they did and damned if they didn't. The hotly debated "Jewish Question"—the question of whether Jews were truly capable of changing themselves sufficiently to be acceptable to civilized society—symbolized the plight of the assimilated Jew. Its rhetoric became a polite forum for the not-so-polite or subtle aspirations of many Jews and for the not-so-hidden agendas of anti-Semitic gentiles. For the latter it meant finding new justifications for keeping Jews out of the Christian world. The myth of the Christ-killer and blood rituals were too crude for Enlightenment sensibilities, and there now existed, often only on paper, legal sanctions against overt political, economic, and professional exclusion. To the former the "Jewish Question" meant critical self-evaluation and, where necessary, radical self-transformation. It was hoped that if one could only tear away that last vestige of the past that betokened a difference, one would finally be allowed to enter the promised land.

Such conflicts typified and defined the experience of newly emancipated Jews. They left the Jewish psyche sharply split into two warring factions and heavily conflicted over the value of being Jewish. One side yearned for freedom and an end to a troublesome past. Many Jews in fact felt embarrassed and limited by their heritage and actively sought means of leaving it behind. The religion and ways of the ghetto were anachronisms, out of place in the rational world, and only provided gentiles with a further excuse for denying them access to full citizenship. A contrary inner impulse, however, recoiled at such inner feelings. Jews had after all good reasons to feel suspicious and even contemptuous of the world of modernity. It had not proven to be the panacea first envisioned. Many of its ways seemed barbaric and regressive, clearly no improvement over life in the ghetto. And most importantly, it had duped the Jews into believing in the possibility of equal status and had subsequently never fulfilled the hope that had first drawn them out of the ghetto: the promise that self-transformation would be rewarded with social acceptance. After meticulously destroying all aspects of the ghetto within, Jews still found themselves denied full entry into mainstream culture. In reaction, and often out of nothing more than pure defiance and anger, they clung to vestiges of the past, to some connection with tradition no matter how flimsy, refusing to turn their backs totally upon their Jewishness. Such ambivalence and the enormous tension it produced was part and parcel of Jewish assimilated life.

\* \* \*

This then was the legacy of emancipation and Jewish assimilation. In turning attention back to the specifics of Freud's world, one finds these dynamics acted out on a daily basis among the Jews of Vienna. What is unique about the Austrian experience, however, is its extreme intensity. Because of the unusual circumstances surrounding Vienna's entry into the modern world, its Jews experienced an unparalleled period of liberalism and openness to assimilation, followed in short order by the emergence of an anti-Semitism so fierce that it rivaled any in European history. Turn-of-the-century Vienna thus offers a unique microcosm of assimilated life, one in which the extremes of Jewish hopes and frustrations were dramatically acted out. What Jews did elsewhere, they did with greater fervor and desperation in Vienna. It is not surprising that Freud's Vienna could boast of a small Jewish minority (a mere 5 percent of the population) who produced the vast majority of its artistic, cultural, and scientific achievements, many of which were destined like psychoanalysis to have international impact and influence. It produced as well not infrequent suicides by Jews who could no longer live with the fact of their Jewishness.

Before emancipation Austria's Jews had been distributed among several very different lifestyles and conditions. There were, first of all, the tolerated families of Vienna, a small group of Jews who had returned to the city after several bans on Jewish citizenship, the most recent in 1670. Since their return they had prospered economically, primarily by means of textiles and grain, and they now played a prominant role in the city's economy. Also residing in Vienna was a group of Sephardic Jews, immigrants from Constantinople and Salonika. Rather insular as a community, they tended to keep to themselves, to practice Judaism in their own manner, and to reject the advances of other Jews. Other Jews lived in the ghettos of towns in the region. Limited to the strict confines of the ghetto's perimeters, they worked primarily as merchants and shopkeepers. Competition was intense, and they toiled long hours with their only diversion being the religion of their ancestors, which was practiced in a strict and authoritarian manner. The primary life experience of these Jews was fear—fear of some authority: be it parent, spouse, rabbi, or God, and above all, fear of the non-Jew. For obvious reasons this group would prove the most responsive to the lure of emancipation.

The majority of the Jewish population of Austria, however, lived in the small towns and villages *(shtetls)* of Galacia.[2] In close contact with their peasant neighbors, these Jews worked primarily as traveling merchants, craftspeople, innkeepers, and small farmers. Although their economic lives, especially their comings and goings, were carefully monitored by local and national officials and regulated by edicts, their communities functioned rather autonomously, without intrusion from the outside. With periodic exceptions, they retained generally good relations with the gentiles who surrounded them. Their religious life, unlike that of the urban ghetto Jew, was particularly vital and engaging. Galicia in that era was in fact a center for various completing Jewish religious sects: Hasidic, Rabbinic, and Haskalah.[3] It was in just such a setting, Tysnemitz by name, that Freud's father Jacob was born and raised. Finally, there were certain locales where Jews were not allowed permanent settlement. Freud's own birthplace, Moravia, was an example. Prior to emancipation, Jews wishing to be in such a district, typically for commercial reasons, were granted only temporary residency permits that had to be renewed every six months. To further discourage their presence, they could reside only in certain inns. Jews desiring private quarters had to formally apply for them and, if accepted, pay a special tax.

In 1867 the Jews of Austria were awarded the right of full citizenship. This event ushered in a period of political liberalism and in its wake widespread Jewish emancipation and assimilation. Jews migrated in large numbers both from rural areas to towns and from the provinces of Austria and even neighboring Russia to Vienna. As they came they underwent the full range of assimilationist transformations. In varying degrees these Jews took on the ways of the gentile, adopted German in the place of Yiddish, and softened or jettisoned religious observances altogether. A few, obliged as all citizens were to classify themselves according to faith, even registered as Catholics or Protestants.

While there was some resistance from the traditionalists within the ghetto, it was largely ineffectual. Pockets of Orthodoxy remained, but they were clearly on the defensive, doing what they could to guard against the further intrusion of Enlightenment ideas. It goes without saying that these were times of enormous conflict within families and between generations, and it was not uncommon to find Orthodox parents saying the "prayer for the dead" over wayward children.[4] Nevertheless, young and not-so-young Jews came to Vienna in increasing numbers, hoping to find a new and less encumbered life for themselves. In 1860 Jacob Freud, his young wife, and his children joined this flow.

The ensuing two decades, a period of substantial liberalism and limited anti-Semitism, strongly reinforced the hopes of the newly emancipated. In appreciation for the enormous freedom they had been afforded, this first generation of transplanted Jews developed deep and unabiding attachments to the state.

They became supercitizens, and in the words of Theodor Herzl "attached themselves with all of their heart to the German nation."[5] Assimilation, thus validated, ran even more rampant, with many Jews attempting to become even more Germanic than their gentile countrymen. Paralleling this fierce nationalism was a love for German culture and for that matter for all things German. So strong were these feelings, so deep these attachments, that when anti-Semitism once again began to rear its ugly head in Vienna, there was a widespread refusal on the part of Jews to recognize and acknowledge its existence.

The reemergence of anti-Semitism in the 1880s and 1890s was clearly a traumatic and demoralizing event, especially for Vienna's older Jewish population. In spite of the initial protection afforded by denial, they soon came to feel conspicuous and different as the realities of anti-Semitism slowly crept into consciousness. The enormous contrast between the good will they had experienced over the past two decades, a clear manifestation of their innermost hopes and dreams, and what was now emerging sensitized them to even the slightest anti-Jewish comment or act. Fearful of being confronted directly in an anti-Semitic incident, they became less publicly visible and more hidden, avoiding whenever possible situations that would identify them as Jews. Rather than facing the facts, many merely redoubled their efforts at assimilation. The growing Eastern European immigrant population in fact provided a safe target for their frustrations. They both blamed the newcomers for their plight and went to greater and greater lengths to distinguish themselves from these unwanted Jewish brethren. To their children, this first generation of Jews out of the ghetto, so squarely caught in the dilemma of assimilation, must have seemed almost comic-tragic figures. The next generation, less committed than their parents to the assimilationist dream yet more assimilated in manner and sensibilities, would themselves begin to disassimilate, even finding a renewed interest in their ethnicity in response to the growing anti-Semitism. As a Jew, Freud straddled these two generations, exhibiting a fierce pro-German attraction in his youth, which in time waned and even turned sour as the events of pre– and post–World War I Vienna unfolded before his eyes.

Austrian anti-Semitism was more virulent and deeply rooted than that practiced in other parts of Europe and as such it proved particularly problematic. By the end of the 1880s, for instance, not only had anti-Jewish sentiment become racial in character (that is, visited equally upon established and highly assimilated as well as upon immigrant Jews), but it had in addition become a major element in Austrian politics. Ironically, the liberalism and democratic reforms of the 1860s and 1870s had merely served to worsen a deeply fragmented Austrian political scene. When the conditions supporting this Enlightenment era disappeared, the suppressed anti-Semitism reemerged stronger than ever and became a rallying point for various political groups. In time the factions coalesced into the Christian Social Party, and on 8 April 1897 Emperor Franz Josef, reluctantly and after several unsuccessful efforts to depose its leader, appointed Karl Kuegar, an avid anti-Semite, mayor of Vienna.

The Jews of Vienna and their very sense of self could not help but be effected by this turn of event. As one chronicler of the period wrote. "The way people expressed themselves toward Jews had plainly changed. Even if there was absolutely no occasion for it, they would stare in an unfriendly way—everywhere, wherever they turned up. . . . Gentle conversation . . . ceased all at once. There was an invisible distance between the tables where Christians sat and those where Jews sat."[6] The fact of one's Jewishness came to overshadow all other realities. Thus Freud's creation became "Jewish psychology," Einstein's efforts "Jewish physics," and the compositions of Mahler written "with a Jewish accent." Interestingly enough, none of the three saw what they had created as particularly Jewish. So deep were Vienna's prejudices against its Jews that they can still be felt, even today. Hendrik Ruitenbeek recounts the experience of his first visit to Vienna in 1973. While being driven to Bergasse 19 to visit what had been Freud's apartment, he told the driver about his mission. The driver in turn responded coldely: "Ah, Freud, he was a Jew, wasn't he?"[7]

Being the object of such hatred took its toll psychologically. There was, first of all, the ever-present anxiety, (sometimes experienced directly, at other times lurking just outside of consciousness), that one might be recognized or singled out as Jew and ridiculed. It could happen anytime or anywhere, when least expected. It was never very far from the surface, emerging when one was most vulnerable. There was also the suspiciousness, hypersensitivity, and cynicism that inevitably developed. Arthur Schnitzler, a Jewish novelist, contemporary to Freud, expresses it well through one of his characters. "Do you think there's a single Christian in the world, even taking the noblest, straightest and truest one you like, one single Christian who has not in some moment or other of spite, temper or rage, made at any rate mentally, some contemptuous allusion to the Jewishness of even his best friend, his mistress or his wife, if they were Jews or of Jewish descent."[8] Finally, there was the perpetual restlessness and seemingly limitless energy, both consequences of the Jew's inevitable frustration at trying to succeed in a hostile environment.

If one adds to this complex the consequences of Jewish marginality as described earlier in the chapter, one can begin to approximate the set of characteristics, many of them clearly unhealthy, that typified the Jews of Freud's world. Included also in what Frederic Grunfeld has called a "family resemblance,"[9] were the Jews' fierce concentration, compulsive work habits, chronic irritability, vacillation between calm and anger, boundless faith in the future, and unrelenting drive to prove themselves. These characteristics were especially prominent among the intellectual and visionaries, many of whom walked the thin line between neurosis and creativity, but who nevertheless, like Freud, Kafka, Marx, and Einstein, left indelible marks upon the world.

The Jews of Vienna varied markedly in their responses to being Jewish. Not unpredictably, dramatic extremes were commonplace. At one end of the continuum was the phenomenon of *Selbsthass* or Jewish self-hatred, which has been defined as a "frantic urge to escape the burden of one's Jewishness not merely by renouncing but by denouncing Judaism."[10] Such Jews, and there were many of them, actively denied and tried to escape the fact of their identities in every manner possible. Often they were highly anti-Semitic in their own right, belittling all things Jewish and internalizing the values and ways of the majority down to the smallest detail. Trapped in an unwanted ethnic status and desperately desirous of joining the majority, self-hating Jews turned the resulting frustration and hostility inward, against the self and their ethnicity.

Freud's world was full of dramatic examples of such individuals. Take, for example, Hermann Levi,[11] the famed German conductor and son of a rabbi, who freely participated in the anti-Semitic slurring and joke-telling of the day and, even worse, who subjugated himself to continual racial abuse in order to sit at the feet of and serve the virulent anti-Semite Richard Wagner. Or the Austrian writer Otto Weininger, whose book *Geschlect und Charakter* argued for the natural superiority of men over women and of Aryan over Jew, and who was so fearful of his own femininity and hyperaware of his own Jewishness that he solved both problems at the same time by killing himself. While such extreme measures were perhaps unusual, few Jews of that day could honestly boast of being totally free of self-hatred. More typically, such self-rejection took the form of subtle and often unconscious reactions, such as, to quote Peter Gay, "a feeling of shame and rejection that would overcome them as they witnessed what they identified as a 'Jewish' display in public places, in business dealings, in political controversy, in the gutter press."[12]

This tendency to deny and reject one's Jewishness was not limited to the individual, however. It was a shaping force, as was suggested in chapter 1, not only in the development of psychoanalysis but also in various other social movements that gained widespread followings among Jews after the demise of the ghetto. Nowhere is there a more telling example of this dynamic than the case of Zionism, especially that form we know as labor Zionism.

According to anthropologist Stanley Diamond, the early kibbutz, the culmination of the Zionist dream, could best be understood as a reaction against the Jewish background of its first settlers. Its institutions and values were in fact purposefully, although perhaps unconsciously, chosen in order to create a society that was antithetical to the Jewish life they had left behind in Europe. The high value the kibbutz placed on strict equality, on asceticism, on manual labor, and the rejection of materialism and religion, as well as its institutions of communal dining and child-rearing all represented a rejection of traditional Jewish forms. The Jewish ambivalence of the early kibbutzniks was nowhere more evident than in their feelings about their children, the products of their lifelong experiment. Diamond quotes one mother as saying. "The Sabra does not have a 'Yiddisher' heart. He is not complex. He is not deep. He is not like us at all. He is a straight, simple man."[13] The children were in fact compared to *goyim*, the somewhat pejorative Yiddish term for gentile. It is worth quoting Diamond a bit further on this point, for by equating the Sabra with the gentile, the early Zionist was engaging a very telling and self-effacing stereotype.

> Within the parents' particular European frame of reference, a Goy was considered a physically competent, physically courageous, rather cold, insensitive, simple-minded person, a person to be feared, envied, and condemned at the same time. But, almost above all, Goy was considered a "normal" man, as opposed to the "abnormal, alienated" Jew. The use of the term Goy to describe the children indicates . . . that the parents are proud of them, consider them "normal" and "healthy," but also feel estranged from them. It is pertinent that the Sabras themselves, prefer to be called Israelis rather than Jews, and their image of the Jew is a highly stereotyped one, negatively toned.[14]

On close examination, however, the existence of such anti-Jewish sentiment at the very heart of a movement so obviously dedicated to Jewish continuity is perhaps not so very surprising, given the Jewish identity of its founder, Theodor Herzl. Herzl, a contemporary of Freud in Vienna, almost singlehandedly transformed the idea of a Jewish homeland into a political reality. His motivation for doing so can be traced back not to some unabiding love for the Jewish people, but rather to a personal need to make sense out of his own conflicted Jewish identity. Born in Budapest, he moved to Vienna in 1876, quickly falling under the lure of its spell. Coming from a highly assimilated German family, he knew little of his heritage other than its limitations. He would in fact have coverted but was afraid of offending his parents. As a youth, he fell under the sway of writers like Duhring,[2] who argued that uncultivated Jews should not be allowed to live in Europe. Sensitive to rejection, especially after being excluded from Albia fraternity at Vienna University because of his defense of the Jews, he anxiously aspired to Vienna's aesthetic elite, the only aristocracy open to those of the Jewish persuasion. Unconsciously mimicking those who he secretly admired, he became quite the dandy, both in manner and dress, insisting later in life that those who attended the first Zionist International Conference in Basel be adorned in frock coats. He in time became quite proficient in the literary forms of the day and was hired as Paris correspondent for the *Neue Freie Presse*. His coverage of the Dreyfus trial had an enormous impact upon him, convincing him of the need for a radical solution to the Jewish problem in Europe. He fantasized a number of romantic alternatives—for example, dueling as a means of protecting Jewish honor and the mass conversion of Austrian youth in exchange for Papal protection—before attaching himself finally to the idea of a Jewish homeland. In each potential solution he saw himself in the role of the aristocrat, leading his people in the creation of a new society.

At the other extreme of Jewish identification was the need to lash out at the oppressor, to defend the race and take pride in one's origins (no matter how vague they might have become). This tendency took both overt and covert forms. As Austrian anti-Semitism grew more violent, some young Jews responded in kind, defending themselves physically when insulted or provoked. Many Jewish university students in fact became expert fencers as a means of gaining satisfaction against members of the highly anti-Semitic dueling fraternities. A gentleman was after all allowed to defend his honor. Unfortunately, this avenue of redress was eventually closed when a new dueling code was introduced, clearly specifying Jews as unworthy of such considerations. As will become apparent in the case study of Freud that follows, the matter of defending one's honor as a Jew was a critical one to him.

More in character with Jewish tradition and temperament was the indirect and well-camouflaged assault with words and ideas. After the destruction of the second temple, the Jewish presence in the world became more passive and inner-directed, with the model of the warrior king and avenging god giving way to that of the scholar and teacher. Jews learned to sharpen their wits in endless hours of study and debate and to lash out when necessary with ideas and not fists. Postemancipated Jews were heir to this psychic legacy and were drawn in large numbers to the great social movements of the day (psychoanalysis included) whose critiques of society served as unconscious vehicles for their rebellion against the status quo. Many Jews of Freud's day found in these visionary movements a respondent chord, an avenue for catharsis, and a means of retaining a modicum of pride in an anti-Semitic world.

While a minority of the Jews of turn-of-the-century Vienna might have been appropriately classified as either completely positive or negative in their Jewish identifications, most stood somewhere in-between, experiencing simultaneous tendencies toward Jewish affirmation and rejection. The two coexisted furthermore in a precarious state of balance. Such ambivalence was typical of assimilated Jewry, and as we shall see, it was a central organizing factor in Freud's own Jewish development. But to point out the widespread existence of psychological ambivalence is merely a first step. What is of real interest, as Martin Bergmann suggests, is "the creative use to which the ambivalence was put." With this question in mind we can begin to move toward a detailed exploration of Freud's own experiences and his identity as a Jew.

# 3
# The Dynamics of Jewish Identity

In order to better appreciate the nature and importance of Freud's Jewishness a basic knowledge of the workings of ethnic identity is necessary. While much of the material that follows is based on recent research, there is no reason to believe that these dynamics and their impact on Jewish life were any different in turn-of-the-century Vienna. Fictional descriptions as well as early studies of postemancipated European Jewry[1] show patterns of widespread Jewish ambivalence and identity confusion quite similar to those reported in more recent explorations of Jewish identity.[2] While there is clearly less overt anti-Semitism impacting upon the lives of Jews today, the various psychological circumstances that gave rise to difficulties in identity formation that were described in chapter 2 still remain. Added to these are new sources of dissatisfaction and alienation, for example, Israel's increasingly negative image in the world community and the unsatisfying quality of much of organized Jewish religious activity today; these continue to make Jewish identification problematic.

By way of definition, an ethnic group is any definable people whose members share both a common culture (language, values, personal characteristics, family patterns, and so forth) and a sense of themselves as different and separate. Typically, the boundaries that set them apart are asserted both from within the group itself, through an emphasis on differences and the need for group cohesiveness due to perceived threat, and from outside via prejudice and differential treatment. When an ethnic group becomes the object of collective discrimination, we refer to it as a minority. Members of different minorities often exhibit similar psychological characteristics in addition to the unique cultural patterns of personality and temperament they share within the group. This is due to similarities in their status as devalued outsiders and to the manner in which such circumstances are dealt with intrapsychically. Within this general schema, the Jews of Freud's day would be considered an ethnic minority.

The term *identity*, first introduced by Freud, refers to a particular level of ego development in the maturing individual. As typically used, it implies the existence of a stable inner sense of who someone is, and it is formed by the successful integration of various experiences of the self into a coherent and largely positive self-image. Ethnic identity in turn refers to that portion of personal identity that contributes to one's self-image as a member of a minority group, in this case, as a Jew. Thus, when we speak of Jewish identity, we refer to the individual's subjective experience of his or her own Jewishness, that is, what he or she feels about it both consciously and unconsciously, how it is conceived and how he or she reacts to it. Jewish identity formation, like that of personal identity, results from an integration of the various experiences one has had as a Jew. Being a part of a broader psychological whole, it is not surprising that difficulties in ethnic identity formation should be reflected in personal identity formation. Recent research[3] has in fact shown that Jews with positive ethnic identities tend to be more psychologically healthy and well-adjusted than those with more conflicted feelings about their Jewishness.

While ethnic identity formation (like its personal counterpart) is not typically completed until after adolescence, the experiences that contribute to it begin quite early. Jewish children become cognizant of being group members as early as three years of age and they are certainly aware of it by five or six. What this awareness includes is a perception of differences in appearance and actions between Jews and non-Jews, an ability to apply ethnic labels appropriately, and the emergence of simple emotional reactions to Jews and non-Jews. Of course, such emotions tend to parallel and be based upon those of their parents. Like other minority children, young Jews tend to be more knowledgeable about their group than their majority counterparts. This knowledge as well as the child's understanding of Jewishness itself tends to follow closely the development of intellectual capacities, moving from very concrete to more and more abstract knowledge. Thus, a very young child might think of being Jewish in terms of concrete objects and rituals, for example "being Jewish is lighting candles," while in time he or she may speak of "talking Jewish" and eventually of "being Jewish," finally using the term as a personal attribute.

The focus of what is psychologically important about being Jewish does however change with age. The younger child (ages seven to eight), in search of ways to define the self and make it special and unique, tends to exaggerate differences, prefers associations with other Jewish children, and looks to parents for values, beliefs, and cues to group affiliation. Since he or she is only mildly aware of racial injustices such as ethnic name-calling, such things tend to be overlooked and reassurance is gained from feelings that "our group is best." By preadolescence (ages ten to twelve) the child's preferences have begun to shift away from the in-group and one can begin to discern a growing tension between the Jewish and non-Jewish aspects of life. For example, pleasure in observing Jewish customs and rituals may be interspersed with sensitivities as to what others might think if such unusual behaviors were observed.

By adolescence (ages thirteen to seventeen) such conflicts tend to reach their peak intensity, for at this stage of development to be different is to be horribly tainted. Research has in fact shown that Jewish children of this age (in comparison to younger ones): show significantly more fears, sensitivities and insecurities about being Jewish; are more likely to reject and derogate the Jewish group; are less hostile toward the majority and are more desirous of contact with it.[4] Such reactions are not altogether surprising, however, given the nature of adolescent rebellion and the fact that this is a time when young Jews must first face the realities of their minority group status alone and without the protective support of the family. They must personally decide what sense to make out of their differences from others; how to respond to prejudice and discrimination when faced with it; how to order conflicting loyalties and role demands; and how much to accentuate or hide their Jewishness. For those Jewish adolescents whose identity has not been overwhelmed by negativity or ambivalence, this period of heightened uncertainty and conflict will slowly fade and give way to the demands of young adulthood—finding work, a partner, and starting a family—all circumstances that tend to bring about a closer Jewish connection. For those who are more deeply conflicted, the uncertainty about their Jewishness will continue throughout life, a source of frustration and embarrassment.

While Jewish children develop psychologically in much the same manner as all other children, certain developmental tasks are made more difficult because of their minority status. The formation of a positive ethnic (and thus personal) identity is one of these tasks. Jewish and other minority children are both more likely to have unpleasant experiences associated with their ethnicity and also internalize the negative perceptions society holds toward them and their group. As such negative experiences accumulate, it becomes increasingly difficult to integrate them into a coherent and positive sense of self. Instead, negative self-images are either actively rejected and disowned and thus experienced as "not me," or they are allowed to remain as part of the self, but unintegrated, and therefore a source of strong ambivalent feelings about the self. In chapter 2 both alternatives were seen to be dramatically acted out among the Jews of turn-of-the-century Vienna in the form of self-hatred and Jewish ambivalence.[5]

Inner conflicts of this sort ultimately find expression in some form of overt behavior. In the case of negative identification, there is a tendency to deny, avoid, or escape group membership and simultaneously to take on the attitudes and habits of the majority (including prejudices and stereotypes against Jews and Judaism). Thus a figure like Gregory Zilboorg, born of Orthodox Jewish parents and likely privy to strongly negative experiences related to his ethnicity, might unconsciously find himself drawn to the study of the Christian religion, might see his own inner conflicts acted out in the life of Freud, and ultimately might convert to Catholicism as a means of escaping his unwanted Jewishness. While the lure to Christianity might well be motivated by genuine religious intent, such an act on the part of a Jew especially in times of rampant anti-Semitism cannot help but be tinged with some inner conflict.

For the ambivalent identifier, the same alternatives are possible but they coexist with positive feelings about being Jewish, leading to either a vacillation between love and hate or to the simultaneous expression of contradictory attitudes and behaviors. Thus, Freud, as will be seen in much greater detail, was able to reject vehemently Jewish ritual and Orthodox Jews yet at the same time associate almost exclusively with fellow Jews, identify strongly with biblical characters, and attribute the personal strength necessary to found psychoanalysis to his Jewishness. Of course, the compartmentalization of Jewish identity described in chapter 2 encourages the possibility of such inner structuring.

Accommodations of this sort are precarious at best and tend to fall apart or at least grow fragile in relation to all forms of emotional upheaval and change. In this regard it is perhaps most accurate to conceive of Jewish identity formation as an ongoing process, as a series of accommodations to an ever-changing network of underlying Jewish experiences. Generally, core conflicts established early in life that continue to feed basic feelings of Jewish negativity or ambivalence are difficult to resolve completely, but even here significant movement is possible. Freud's own Jewish biography reflects such a dynamic and ever-adapting picture. In the case study that follows, several critical early events that laid the foundation for Freud's ambivalent identification as a Jew will be described. In turn, his various unconscious efforts to resolve these early conflicts will be traced. One can however discern across the years some movement in the nature of Freud's Jewish identity, primarily in the form of a softening of his negativity in response to the death of his father, the break with Jung, and his growing identification with the figure of Moses.

While problems in positive identity formation seem to be a common consequence of growing up for minority individuals, it should not be assumed that conflicts are inevitable. Though less typical, one can always find in every era Jews faced with similarly oppressive circumstances who manage to emerge from their formative years with healthy and well-integrated Jewish identities, that is, positive in their feelings about Judaism and themselves as Jews, psychologically grounded in this aspect of their identity, and able to draw from it as a source of strength and knowledge. This fact leads one to inquire into the specific life circumstances that might have served as buffers against the stresses and forces that disrupt ethnic identity development. Three factors seem to be critical in this regard: individual differences among minority group members, characteristics of the group itself, and the role played by the family in mediating between a hostile world and an impressionable child. Each of these realms will have significant implications for the development of Freud's Jewish identity.

Recent research on stress and coping in minority group members has pointed to certain personal characteristics that seem to facilitate the individual's ability to handle stressful conditions like those that are part and parcel of growing up as an ethnic minority.[6] Included are the following: an ability not to overreact to stress; specific coping and problem-solving skills; a history of success in coping with race-related situations; a perception of oneself as capable of manipulating the world and of controlling one's destiny; and a healthy and well-integrated sense of self. Obviously, such factors do not work in isolation but rather reinforce each other. Success in coping leads to personal empowerment and feelings of competency, which in turn increase the probability of future successes in adapting and coping. Successive failures, on the other hand, tend to be internalized and taken as proof of one's shortcomings and inability to cope. This in turn leads to greater feelings of impotence and helplessness and to greater susceptibility to stress. Such vicious circles in time come totally to color the individual's experience and expectations of the world and can in fact lead to self-fulfilling prophecies. It is interesting to note here that minority group members who feel in control of their lives tend to blame external circumstances (especially racism) for their failures, while those who feel more helpless and at the whim of forces beyond their control tend to blame personal inadequacies. In this regard it will become evident how Freud's own inner strength, determination, and unwavering energy as well as special intellectual gifts, all obvious from an early age, allowed him to withstand and even redouble his efforts in the face of anti-Jewish sentiment and attacks.

The ethnic group itself can also play a major role in buffering the individual from the inner ravages of racial hatred and anti-Semitism. It has even been suggested by some theorists that minority groups routinely evolve their own survival mechanisms to allow them to cope better with the ill treatment they receive at the hands of the majority.[7] The extended-family system of American blacks as well as their immersion in religious life provide excellent examples of such coping mechanisms. In the first instance, the extra resources and support necessary for the survival of the often economically and socially beleaguered black family are mustered and institutionalized; in the second example a psychological buffer zone that acts as a more positive socializing agent (in place of majority culture) is created. Such mechanisms do not always act in the psychological interest of the individual, however. Where the threat of physical harm and death to overly assertive minority males existed, for instance, families unconsciously developed methods for breaking the spirit or curbing aggression in sons in order to ensure their physical survival.

Jews for their part have over time developed their own cultural means of gathering communal resources and withstanding hostility. Within the traditional ghetto for example various practices and institutions evolved to care for the needs of its residents. Shunned or at best tolerated by their gentile neighbors, ghettos by necessity became self-sufficient communities with their own legal, commercial, and welfare systems in addition to their age-old religious practices. Ghetto dwellers shared a common fate and when necessary pulled together for mutual support. Freud himself was a beneficiary of one such practice in the form of financial loans and gifts, received when he was a poor and aspiring student, from older and more established friends such as his teacher Samuel Hammerschlag and later Josef Breuer.

Jewish religious life itself provided a means for distancing Jews from their worldly troubles. Within the traditional religious sphere, the Christian world was of little consequence, something to be tolerated and appeased but of no real importance in comparison to the spiritual mission set for the Jews by their God. They had been chosen to introduce the precepts of the Torah to the world, a task whose import easily transcended the vulgarities and miseries of everyday existence. It was into this mythos that the Jewish child was born. He[8] was expected to observe the rules and regulations of the covenant, to study, to prepare himself, to hone his intellectual abilities so that he might one day adequately fulfill the special role expected of all Jews. Jewish history was made to come alive, full of noble, valiant, and resourceful heroes and role models. He was made to feel an integral part of it and, as such, something special. All of these practices served to provide purpose and meaning to life as well as a sense of importance and dignity.

The traditional Jewish family in turn strongly reinforced this sense of specialness. Theories of self-concept formation suggest that minority children internalize society's negative views of them. To the extent that the family could intervene in this process and provide a different and more positive mirror for the child to gaze into, the negative impact of a demeaning and deprecating world could be overcome. In the home the child had to be made to feel special, to feel that alternatives existed, and that he or she could become an important and valued member of society. Within the tightly knit Jewish family, children were typically pampered, coddled, and made the center of attention, their needs put before those of their parents. They were after all the hope for the future. In return much was expected of them by way of achievement, performance, moral stature, and responsibility. The internalization of these values, which allowed them more than adequately to perform and compete in the secular world, the feelings of specialness they felt from parents and community, and the intellectual development that was demanded of them as Jews all provided valuable armament for dealing with an often hostile and unfriendly world.

But there could be a destructive and shadow side to the insulated Jewish family as well. Karl Menninger has suggested that in response to their own sensitivities and fears as Jews, parents often turned away from the world and compensated for this by overemphasizing the family bond and overprotecting and overestimating their children.[9] Such actions eventually took their emotional toll. They created, first of all, high aspirations and compulsive striving for superiority as well as unrealistic feelings of superiority and specialness. Such internalized specialness would eventually lead to discomfort in relations with others, social isolation, and a sense of disappointment and disillusionment when the child discovered that his parents, being human, were not entirely sincere in their adulation and affections. Totally centered on themselves, Jewish children from such homes could not help but experience indifference or even the least bit of inattention as tragic rejection. As a result, they learned the lesson that no one could be completely trusted, Jew or non-Jew alike. The consequence of such a psychic scenario was the wounded self-esteem and basic mistrust of the narcissistically scarred child. Some of these very aspects will become evident in Freud's make-up as his biography unfolds.

In the assimilated Jewish world, access to the ethnic mechanisms of psychological survival described above depended entirely upon how much tradition was valued and retained within the family. It did not matter whether the household retained an Orthodox approach to Judaism or adopted a more modernized and reinterpreted form. What mattered was the retention of the attitude of specialness. A positive ethnic identity depended not on how much assimilation had occurred but rather on how successful parents were in protecting the child from gentile hostility and at the same time providing an environment that could nurture the development of a healthy self-image. Rejecting one's Jewishness meant internalizing the values and assessments of the Christian majority, and this was not a strategy through which the Jew could win psychologically. Jewish parents who were themselves conflicted lacked the ability to protect their children in the manner described above and inevitably produced offspring who were themselves unsure of who they were and where to turn for succor. Parental conflicts in the

## The Dynamics of Jewish Identity

realm of ethnic identity were thus mirrored in and passed onto the child.

As will become apparent in chapter 4, the Freuds were typical heirs of this Jewish familial psychology and their ethnicity played a decisive role in their son's upbringing. Jacob Freud was born a Hasidic Jew in a small *shtetl* in Galicia and died a follower of the Reform movement in Vienna, personifying in his own biography the winds of religious change that were blowing through the Jewish world of his day. His wife, Amalie, remained more traditionally Orthodox in her outlook. Together, however, they created an atmosphere of protection and support for their Jewish children. From early on in fact there existed within the family a overshadowing myth and feeling that Sigmund was destined for something special, and throughout his formative years he was treated in a decidedly deferential manner. Precocious to a fault, he gloried in the excessive attention, overestimation, and overprotectedness of his very Jewish home, but he would in time (like so many other Jewish children) fall prey to the narcissistic wounds that the real world ultimately held in store. The insatiable narcisissm and the hypersensitivity to rejection that were the inevitable consequences of such an upbringing, well-intended though it may have been, would in fact come to define much of his subsequent personal psychology. It is nothing short of ironic however that Freud, so vehement in his attack on Jewish chosenness and specialness, should have grown up in an environment that so perfectly exemplified these very qualities.

These then are some of the dimensions of Jewish identity formation. With them as a cornerstone, we are now ready to move onto a detailed recounting of Freud's life as a Jew.

# 4
# Growing Up Jewish

Schlomo Sigismund Freud was born to Jacob and Amalia Freud on 6 May 1856 in Freiberg, Morovia. His two names— the Hebrew Schlomo in honor of Jacob's recently deceased father and the Germanic Sigismund probably after a particularly tolerant Polish monarch—would in time come to symbolize a life-long struggle within him between the very culture each represented. Similarly, the town of his birth—Freiberg—dominated by the steeple of its Catholic church and the anti-Semitic attitudes of its majority, would serve as a portent of his own Jewish life lived in the shadow of an all-encompassing Christian presence.

As was customary for male children in the Jewish tradition, Sigmund was circumcised on the eighth day of his life. The following Hebrew inscription, written by Jacob in the family Bible, described the traditional ceremony.

> My son Schlomo Sigismund, may he live, was born on Tuesday Rosh Hodesh Iyar [5]616, 6:30 P.M., on May 6, [1]856 and was circumcised on Tuesday, the 8th day of the month of Iyar, on May 13, [1]856. The Mohel [circumciser] was Reb Shimson Frankel of Ostrau, the godparents were Reb Lippe and his sister Mirel Hurwitz, children of the rabbi of Czernowitz. The sandek [the man who holds the infant during the circumcision] was Reb Shmuel Samueli.[1]

With this event Sigmund Freud was welcomed into the Jewish covenant and officially acknowledged as a Jew.

Freud's mother, Malke Amalie Nathansohn, came from Brody in northeast Galacia, not far from the Russian frontier. Descending from a famous Jewish scholar, Samuel ChaRMaZ (an acronym representing various scholarly attributes), the Nathansohn family probably took its name from their first identifiable ancestor, Nathan, when in 1787 all the Jews of Galacia were forced to adopt a family name. Amalie's parents moved to Odessa (then the residence of their two older sons) where Amalie spent part of her girlhood and then the family moved on to Vienna, where she was married to Jacob Freud at the tender age of nineteen.

Of his paternal Jewish ancestry, Sigmund wrote. "I have reason to believe that my father's family were settled for a long period in the Rhineland (at Cologne), that in the fourteenth or fifteenth century they fled to the east from an anti-Semitic persecution, and that in the course of the nineteenth century they retraced their steps from Lithuania through Galicia to German Austria."[2] According to family documents, Freuds had resided in Buczacz, Galicia, for at least four generations when Schlomo, Sigmund's grandfather, relocated to Tysmenitz, thirty-five miles to the west. The name Freud like that of the Nathansohns was probably adapted from Freide, Schlomo's grandmother's name.

Jacob Freud's early life is of particular interest because it entailed a radical departure from an Orthodox Jewish upbringing, the first evidence in fact of assimilation touching the Freud family. Jacob was born in Tysmenitz, Galicia, in 1815 into what was most likely a Hasidic family. According to Freud, however, his father remained in his "native environment,"[3] probably implying strict religious observance, only for the first twenty years of his life. Jacob's early adherence to traditional Judaism is evidence by the fact that he was married to Sally Kanner at the young age of sixteen, a practice common among Orthodox Jews wherein the son-in-law resides with his wife's family in order to complete his religious education.

By 1855, however, the year he married Amalie Nathansohn, the influences of the Haskalah were already quite evident.[4] Jacob had by that date traded the *Shtreymel* and *Kaftan*[5] for western garb, spoke and signed documents in German instead of Yiddish or Hebrew, and was married in a ceremony officiated over by Rabbi Isaac Mannheimer, an exponent of Reform Judaism. The Bible in which he would the following year record the details of Sigmund's circumcision was in fact a Philippson version, a German translation with illustrations widely used by Reformed and free-thinking Jews. In Orthodox circles the practice of illustrating and translating the Holy Scriptures into the venacular was tantamount to blasphemy. By the time the Freud family moved to Vienna, Jacob, although still celebrating the Jewish holidays, was no longer observing the dietary laws and was most likely a active follower of the Reform movement.

Jacob's break with tradition was hastened by the necessity of traveling on business to Moravia with his maternal grandfather, Siskind Hofmann. He began these regular journeys several years after his first marriage and the birth of two sons, Emanuel and Phillip, who would later become Sigmund's grown brothers. While the winds of assimilation had been adrift in Tysmenitz during Jacob's youth and adolescence, the distance from family and community influences that travel afforded, not to mention the more assimilated ways of the Moravia Jews, made it far easier to discard traditional ways. There is no way of knowing exactly what transpired during Jacob's long absences from home. What is evident during this period, however, was a slow stripping away of the vestiges of Orthodox life.

Wool merchants by trade, Jacob and his grandfather faced the same severe restrictions, such as the constant battle to have their passports and residency permits extended, that were placed on all Jews wishing to remain or trade in Moravia. For over a decade in fact he traveled between Freiberg and Tysmenitz. He persevered and slowly built up the family business in spite of the unending paperwork and the applications required of the "tolerated" Jews by local officials.

Some of these documents have recently been unearthed by J. Sajner and R. Gicklhorn from Czech archives. Not only do they provide more specific information about Jacob's travels and tribulations in Freiberg but also clearly attest to the close and oppressive scrutiny to which Jews were subjected in Moravia. Consider, for example, Susskind Hoffman and Jacob Freud's application for tolerated status in the City of Freiberg in 1844:

> Esteemed Magistrate
>
> Whereas I am known to trade in linen, wool, honey, tallow, etc. and have been resident partly in Freiberg and partly in its environs for several years for the purposes of business, it is now my intention to establish my domicile in Freiberg, because that town is most advantageous to my trade for more than one reason, firstly because it is on the main road, secondly because the whole populace is engaged chiefly in the manufacture of cloth, and thirdly because Freiberg lies in the midst of numerous villages devoted to the clothmaking trade and is therefore an extremely propitious trading center.
>
> Because I buy woolen cloth in Freiberg and its environs and have it dyed and finished in the locality and despatch it as merchandise to Galicia: and in return convey Galician products such as wool,

honey, hemp, and tallow for sale in Freiberg; and because Freiberg is visited by foreign merchants who buy this merchandise from me and also because I rent cellars in which this merchandise is deposited, the need arises for my permanent stay in Freiberg.

Because I, as an old man, now counting sixty-nine years, can no longer negotiate the difficulties of trade without assistance, I have engaged as a trading partner my grandson Kalman Freud, who will direct the outside trade, while I myself will be solely concerned with buying and selling in Freiberg itself. For the purpose of trade, I have also obtained from the respected Lemberg Regional Authorities the adjoining traveling passport issued for the duration of one year both to myself and also to my grandson Kalman Freud. I accordingly pray the Esteemed Magistrate to be gracious enough to intervene in our behalf in the appropriate high places that we may be granted certificates of toleration in Freiberg for the duration of the passport, namely, until 18 May [1]845. Freiberg, 24 June [1]844. Siskind Hoffman Kolomon Jacob Freud.[6]

This request was evidently granted but at a cost of ten guilders each in taxes. They subsequently but unsuccessfully protested this sum as oppressive, for it amounted to as much as 2 percent of their yearly turnover.

What emerges next is a real mystery in the Freud family history. Probably encouraged by a general easing of restrictions against Jews in Moravia,[7] Jacob evidently took the opportunity to relocate his family in Freiberg. The 1852 city registry,[8] which listed Jacob and his two grown sons,[9] made no mention however of Sally Kanner but instead listed a Rebekka, aged thirty-two as Jacob's wife. Two years later, the year before Jacob's marriage to Amalie, Rebekka just as mysteriously disappeared from the city registry, like Sally Kanner never to appear again. Although it is unclear whether Sigmund was aware of this bit of family history, he never mentioned it in his writings. One is thus left with unanswered questions as to what actually happened to Sally Kanner and the mysterious Rebekka. Conjecture among biographers has run rampant, however, and suggestions have ranged anywhere from Rebekka actually being a ficticious name used by Jacob to procure a travel permit for Sally to Rebekka having been Jacob's second wife whom he divorced because she had not produced a child for him.

Jacob was married to Amalie Nathansohn on 29 July 1855. Most significant about the match was the great disparity in their ages. Jacob was then forty; his bride was not yet twenty. During the previous year Jacob had left the family business in Emanuel's care and traveled to Vienna on several different occasions, probably to arrange a marriage for himself. The basis for the ensuing marriage was unclear, however. Amalie was young and attractive, and it would not have been typical for her to be "married off" to a man old enough to be her father unless the family was too poor to supply a respectable dowry or some special family connection had been sought (such as a business partnership). It has been suggested by Gicklhorn that Amalie was rather unhappy when she first saw the one-room dwelling in which Jacob and his family resided in Freiberg. Perhaps this indicates that Jacob may have misrepresented his true financial situation to her parents. Jacob for his part must have been delighted with the match and the opportunity once again to assert his manhood. In any case the family constellation into which Sigmund was born a year later was indeed a unusual one: an aging father and a young and attractive mother, stepbrothers who were the same age as his mother, and a nephew who was his own age. It is hard to overlook, even at first glance, the striking similarities that exist between elements of this family tableau and Freud's later notions of the oedipal drama and the primal horde, two concepts that figure prominently in his later theories.

Temperamentally, the Freuds were as disparate as were their ages. Jacob was now in the second half of life with one grown family already to his credit. He was in addition by all indications beginning to withdraw from the external demands of life. He was increasingly willing to leave the matter of earning a living to his sons and the running of the household to his young wife. With time he grew more and more content to just study, read, visit friends, and play with his small son. This emerging aloofness, not untypical of the traditional Jewish patriarch, is well captured by Judith Heller in her description of a visit to her grandparent's home in Vienna.

> Freud's father lived somewhat aloof from the others in the family, reading a great deal—German and Hebrew (not Yiddish)—and seeing his own friends away from home. He would come home for meals, but took no real part in the general talk of the others. . . . But what I think struck me most about my maternal grandfather was how, in the midst of this rather emotional household, with its three young women who sometimes did not get on well with one another, and their mother, who was usually troubled and anxious—probably with financial worries—he remained quiet and imperturb-

able, not indifferent, but not disturbed, never out of temper and never raising his voice.[10]

Personally, Jacob was of a gentle disposition and well loved by everyone in the family. He was bright, yet lighthearted in his approach to life. His grandson Martin remembers the small gifts he always brought and the stories he used to tell, "mostly with a little twinkle in his great brown eyes, as if he wanted to say, Isn't everything we are doing and saying here a great joke?"[11] Physically large and broad-shouldered, he carried himself with great dignity and grave demeanor. From his father Sigmund felt he had received his "sense of humor, his shrewd skepticism about the visissitudes of life, his custom of pointing a moral by quoting a Jewish anecdote, his liberalism and free thinking and perhaps his uxoriousness."[12] With age Jacob evidently grew more expansive and less practical, a fact that may have frustrated his son Sigmund, upon whom increasing amounts of responsibility for the family's welfare fell; this might have motivated the comment that his father was "always hopefully expecting something to turn up."[13]

Amalie, on the other hand, was young and vital, a unending source of energy in the household. Her astuteness and intelligence, even at twenty, increasingly filled the void left by her husband's withdrawl from the mundanities of life. Slim and quite attractive, she remained throughout life lively, sociable, and highly concerned with her appearance and the impression she made on others. Family lore in fact holds that at ninety she refused the gift of an expensive shawl because it "made her look too old" and at ninety-five was displeased with her photograph in the newspaper because it "made her look like a hundred."[14]

Family members were privy to a different and less attractive side of her personality, one that emerged with age. Judith Heller, who confessed fearing her grandmother and being less than partial to her because her grandmother had a decided preference for the "male members of her brood over the female ones"[15] writes: "She was charming and smiling when strangers were about, but I, at least, always felt that with familiars she was a tyrant, and a selfish one. Quite definitely, she had a strong personality and knew what she wanted."[16] Martin Freud in turn evinced a bit of prejudice of his own when he described her as typical of Galician Jews—"highly emotional and easily carried away by their feeling," moody and domineering—and went on to say: "These people are not easy to live with, and grandmother, a true representative of her race, was no exception. She had great vitality and much impatience; she had a hunger for life and an indomitable spirit. Nobody envied Aunt Dolfi, whose destiny it was to dedicate her life to the care of an old mother who was a tornado."[17] To this side of his mother Freud attributed his own "sentimentality,"[18] that is, the strong emotions of which he was clearly capable.

In spite of this less than flattering picture, her children were deeply devoted to her, especially her sons, and she remained, particularly after Jacob's death in 1896, the glue that held the family together. Of this devotion Judith Heller writes the following. "My grandmother's sitting room on Sunday mornings was the weekly meeting place for her busy sons, her daughters and daughter-in-law, her grandchildren and their children. Even when convalescing from operations and illness, Professor Freud would always find time on a Sunday morning to pay his mother a visit and give her the pleasure of petting and making a fuss over him. When he could not come, her younger son, Alexander, with his son would be there to listen to all her troubles."[19] Her two sons shared equally in her financial support as well as that of their sister Dolphi, who lived with and took care of Amalie. Sigmund more often than not offered the moral and emotional support she demanded; his brother took care of the practical details. The two were the apples of her eye, especially her oldest, Sigmund, and she made no attempts to hide her decided preferences for her sons.

Little is known about Amalie's Jewish background or preferences. Her father, also named Jacob and a trade agent by profession, was probably an observant Jew. She was clearly neither markedly religious nor observant and seemed willing to defer to her husband's desires regarding family practice. While Jacob was alive, the Freuds observed some religious holidays in the home, but after his death these too disappeared and were replaced at Amalie's initiative with festive family gatherings on Christmas Day and New Years Eve. On several occasions she is reported to have invoked God's help in some worldly matter, but it is unclear whether this reflected any real faith or belief on her part. All that she seemed to retain from the past was the Galician Yiddish that she spoke exclusively, even in Vienna. While Jacob's response to assimilation was trying to bring the past into the present, that is, retaining yet modifying his Jewishness, Amalie's seemed to be one of disengagement and turning away.

In all Jacob and Amalia Freud produced seven children within a period of ten years. (An eighth, Julius, had not survived.) Sigmund and Anna, the oldest and second oldest, were born in Freiberg; the rest—Rosa, Marie, Adolfine, Paula, and Alexander—in Vienna. A close-knit Jewish family, they lived in close proximity, visited together often, and shared family occasions and holidays throughout their time in Vienna. Unfortunately, and like so many other Jewish families of that place and time, their story ended in tragedy. Anna and her husband Eli Bernays[20] had fortunately emigrated to New York years earlier. Sigmund and Alexander with their families in tow barely escaped to England. Sadly, the four youngest daughters all perished in the Holocaust—Dolfi in Theresienstadt and the other three most likely in Auschwitz. The Freuds like most Jews of their time refused to acknowledge the danger until it was too late. Only poor Dolfi, the maiden aunt who had dedicated her life to caring for her mother, seemed to have any intuition of what was to come. Martin Freud tells of walking through the streets of Vienna with her one day and of her gripping his arm in terror at the passing of a seemingly ordinary gentile and whispering, "Did you hear what that man said? He called me a dirty stinking Jewess and said it was time we were all killed." Martin as well as the rest of the family laughed it off, attributing it either to a "pathological phobia" or the irrational ramblings of a "lovable but rather silly old maid."[21]

\* \* \*

The world into which Sigmund Freud was born bore a strong resemblence to the traditional Jewish ghetto from which both his parents had come. While Jacob and under his influence Amalie increasingly took on the trappings of assimilation, their inner tendencies were still very much traditionally Jewish, and the household they created was characteristic of what they themselves knew in childhood.[22] Crowded and physically close, emotionally volatile and intense, humble and materially limited—the Freiberg household served as a backdrop for the early events of Sigmund's life, which, according to psychoanalytic theory, would permanently and irrevocably shape and mold his personality. Most of what is known of these early years comes from Freud himself, through material dredged up during his self-analysis at the age of forty. Obviously, such personal data, produced as it was during a period of great emotional stress, must be held somewhat suspect.[23]

Jacob, Amalie, Sigmund, and later Anna Freud lived in a small, single room on the second floor of a house (at No. 117 Schlossergasse) rented from Johann Zajic, a locksmith whose family occupied the other second-floor room and whose workshop was located on ground level. The entire dwelling measured only thirty feet by thirty feet, so one can imagine the close quarters in which the family lived. Jacob's son Phillip rented a room across the street, and Emanuel and his family (his wife Maria and three children) lived within close walking distance. By all accounts the family was exceedingly close and most likely had frequent daily interactions. Jacob was in business with his two older sons, and Sigmund had his nephew John as an almost constant companion. Add to this scene several other Jewish families residing in Freiberg with whom the Freuds were friendly and periodic visits from relatives from Tysmenitz, Vienna, and elsewhere, and what emerges is an exceedingly rich interpersonal world in which Sigmund spent his first three years of life. Not only did it serve as a model for all future personal relations[24] but also as a buffer against the potentially hostile non-Jewish world that surrounded the small Jewish minority in Freiberg.

From the beginning Sigmund was afforded a special place in the family hierarchy. He was clearly his parents' favorite and, as the first-born son, was the regular recipient of both special favors and extremely high expectations. He was born in a caul,[25] a traditional sign of future good fortune and fame, and when Amalie was subsequently told by a shopkeeper that she had brought a great man into the world, she became firmly convinced that the prediction would come true. Freud, for his part, was more skeptical. "Such prophecies," he wrote, "must be made very often; there are so many happy and expectant mothers, and so many old peasant women and other old women who, since their mundane powers have deserted them, turn their eyes toward the future; and the prophetess is not likely to suffer for her prophecies."[26] Yet as a small boy, no doubt frequently reminded of the prediction, he could not help but be affected by it. Family lore also tells of another prophecy, this time by a wandering poet in a Viennese restaurant, when Sigmund was eleven or twelve, who predicted that he would become a minister in the Austrian legislature. Freud does acknowledge the sizable impact of that prophecy, especially in relation to his early interest in studying law.

There is little doubt that these prophecies and the expectations they engendered in his family contributed to the enormous ambition and unceasing drive to succeed that he felt throughout life. Freud's ambitions were clearly excessive and beyond the bounds of proving ordinary competence. Rather, his goals and dreams were grandiose and lofty and entailed nothing short of leaving his mark on the entire world. Falling short of these impossible demands would always leave him temporarily depressed and dejected, but it is a tribute to his enormous energy and staying power that he would always renew the battle and did in fact eventually gain the exposure and worldwide notoriety he so desperately sought.

A more immediate consequence of the prophecies however was an early sense of self-confidence. At two, for example, and after having wet his bed, family lore has it that Sigmund stood up to a disapproving and probably angry Jacob, even offering his father comfort: "Don't worry, Papa. I will buy you a beautiful new red bed in Neutitschein" (the largest town in the district).[27] And after a physical battle with a larger and stronger John, he justified his part in the fray by saying: "I hit him because he hit me,"[28] previewing a pugnacity that would emerge periodically throughout his life.

While both Jacob and Amalie shared equally in their hopes for "Sigi's" future, their motivations were quite different, as were their relationships with him. To Amalie he was throughout life *mein goldener Sigi* (Sigi, my gold), the veritable apple of her eye. Inexperienced as a parent, she tended to indulge her son's every whim and left the more difficult task of setting limits to others, including her husband and Sigmund's two surrogate mothers—Emanuel's wife Maria and a gentile nursemaid who will be introduced shortly. Anna tells of an incident in Vienna in which Amalie had the family piano removed from the apartment because Sigmund found it annoying and disturbing.[29] To him his mother gave unconditional positive regard, and he later attributed (in theory at least) his own self-confidence to this early unwavering devotion. "A man who has been the indisputable favorite of his mother keeps for life the feeling of a conqueror, that confidence of success that often induces real success."[30]

Sigi represented to Amalie an avenue through which she could vicariously satisfy and fulfill her own needs. Obviously a clever and competent woman, she must have found the patriarchal Jewish world with its limited opportunities for women to express their talents highly frustrating. In addition, it is unlikely that she found much personal satisfaction in her marital relationship to Jacob. He was after all a man twice her age, frequently absent from home for long periods of time, and in the process of his own withdrawl from the demands and intensities of life. Marianne Krull attributes to Amalie, in spite of her appearance, a strong masculine side and a desire "to have her unfulfilled ambitions achieved by her sons."[31] In support of her case she quotes Freud himself. "A mother can transfer to her son the ambition which she had been obliged to suppress in herself, and she can expect from him the satisfaction of all that has been left over in her of her masculinity complex."[32] Amalie would always take enormous pride in Sigmund's later accomplishments and she basked in their acknowledgment as if they were her own. Judith Heller tells of her grandmother's insistence on attending a *Jause* (coffee party) in celebration of Sigmund's seventieth birthday. "She had to be carried down the stairs from her own home and up the stairs to the Freuds', but she did not mind as long as she could be present to be honored and feted as the mother of her 'golden son'."[33]

Sigmund for his part was deeply devoted to his mother, but not without a healthy measure of ambivalence. Throughout his life and in spite of a very demanding schedule and in time a worsening illness, he always found time to visit her each week and to feed her excessive demands and need for attention. His attachment to her, according to both his own veiled suggestions and the analysis of most biographers, was probably more physical and erotic than traditionally maternal. She was after all young (especially in relation to her husband), quite attractive (and it is probable, given their limited living space, that he saw her on occasion without clothes or at least in varying stages of undress), and evidently more than willing to eschew the traditional motherly role. Such a relationship, as Freud pointed out so well in his later description of the Oedipal drama, was far from stress-free. It is thus not surprising, given the combination of his own forbidden feelings and his mother's demanding and highly intrusive nature, that he should develop some conflict in his feelings for her. In this regard Sigmund is reported to have regularly developed a case of indigestion every Sunday morning before his visits with her and was evidently, according to his son Martin, terrified by the possibility that she might outlive him and have to be told of his death.

Unlike Amalie, Jacob was an old hand at parenting and had already raised two adult sons. It is thus likely that he would have been able and willing to make demands and to set clear limits for his son. Ernest Jones has suggested that while Amalie represented to young Sigmund the pleasure principle, his father played the role of its nemesis, the reality principle.[34] Jacob's limit-setting was no doubt particularly evident in relation to toilet training and later masturbation, which is strongly discouraged among young, traditional Jewish men. Freud's later suggestion of a relationship between masturbation and castration anxiety could well have had its roots in Jacob's own directives on the subject. For the Jewish boy in particular, for whom castration in the form of ritual circumcision is not a very distant reality, such fear can be easily imagined or engendered.

Although not a harsh Jewish patriarch, Jacob demanded respect from his son and evidently got it. Viennese pianist Moritz Rosenthal tells of Jacob's intervention in an argument he was having with his father in the street. According to Rosenthal, Jacob laughingly reproached him by saying: "What, are you contradicting your father? My Sigmund's little toe is cleverer than my head, but he would never dare to contradict me."[35]

Like Amalie, Jacob favored his son and held great hope for his future. Sigmund, for example, was the only child whose birth Jacob saw fit to inscribe in the family Bible, the same Bible that would be presented to his son on the occasion of his thirty-fifth birthday, "as a token of love from your old father."[36] As we shall see, he took great pains in personally educating Sigmund, and as the boy grew older his father increasingly sought his advice on family matters.

Sigmund's reactions to his father were mixed. Jacob, large in stature and with a full beard and an intense gaze, was no doubt an awe-inspiring figure to the young boy. That this looming figure paid him such special attention and took such pride in his clever utterances and daily accomplishments could not help but inflate his emerging self-esteem. At the same time he must have feared his father's displeasure, especially around the issues of masturbation and competition for Amalie's attention and affection. Finally, one must add to this complex of emotions a growing sense of burden in regard to the family. Jacob's retreat from the world was paralleled by an increase in Sigmund's responsibility for the family's welfare. From various remarks it is probably safe to conclude the he was highly frustrated by his father's growing passivity and blamed Jacob for his own ineptitude with finances and his slow career advancement. No doubt on numerous occasions he wished that Jacob had been more like some of the surrogate fathers and benefactors he would find later in life.

That Sigmund's enormous ambition and striving was tied to his father's early expectations is evident in his reaction to a reprimand by Jacob at the age of seven or eight. After having urinated in his parents' bedroom, evidently deliberately, his father angrily reacted with a very out-of-character statement: "That boy will never amount to anything." Freud recalls his own reaction to the event. "This must have been a terrible affront to my ambition, for allusions to this scene occur again and again in my dreams, and are constantly coupled with enumerations of my accomplishments and successes, as if I wanted to say: 'You see, I have amounted to something after all.'"[37]

It is against this web of family interrelationships that one must begin an exploration of the forces that shaped Freud's identity as a Jew. While young Sigmund's special status in the family gave him sufficient self-confidence and personal assurity to withstand the anti-Semitism that he as a Jew would inevitably face, certain events occurred within this insulated world that would disrupt his inner development and in turn his attachment to the Jewishness of his home and family.

The first involved his nursemaid, Resi Wittek. She came into the Freud household early in 1858, when Sigmund was less than two years old. The occasion for her being hired was probably the illness of Amalie's second child, Julius, who subsequently died at six months of age. A month prior to Julius's birth, Amalie's brother, also named Julius, died of tuberculosis at the age of twenty. This loss, coupled with her newborn's illness, and subsequent death, probably rendered Amalie incapable of watching over Sigmund and Resi Wittek was brought in to fill the gap. For much of the ensuing nine months during which Amalie became pregnant with Anna, the nursemaid was probably solely responsible for Sigmund's care.

Old and ugly by description, she was a Czech and a Catholic, and evidently Sigmund grew quite attached to her. She conversed with him in her native language and unbeknownst to the family took him to church services with her. Devoutly religious, she would preach to him incessantly about the church and heaven and hell. So impressed was he by this unknown and unfamiliar world that he would, according to his mother, stand before the rest of the family and give little speeches about "how God conducted His affairs."[38] Freud also gives some indication that she was his first "instructress in sexual matters," and "primary originator,"[39] although what exactly he meant by this remains rather vague. In any case Resi Wittek was caught stealing coins by Philipp, was sent to prison, and suddenly disappeared from Sigmund's life when he was but two-and-a-half years old.

The loss of such an important caregiver coupled with the general inaccessibility of Amalie during the period of development Margaret Mahler called separation-individuation could not help but have a lasting impact upon him. He would always remain hypersensitive to the loss and perceived loss of those near to him and would respond characteristically with agitation and depression. Also as a result of this disruption in normal development, Sigmund developed a tendency toward "splitting," that is, experiencing the world in extremes as good or bad but seldom as both.

Of great significance for our purposes here is the fact that Resi Wittek had introduced him to the world of the non-Jew and because of its lure and the intensity of his attachment to her and its sudden loss, it would always hold a strong attraction for him. In his lifelong interest in classical antiquities, his less sustained romance with German culture, his commitment to the scientific process, and his attraction to Carl Jung and his Swiss contingent of psychiatrists, there would always be the lure of the unfamiliar that created tension with his Jewishness, making it difficult, perhaps impossible, ever to make total peace with it. We see here also the beginnings of his ambivalence, a connection to the non-Jewish world that would always stand in counterdistinction to his equally strong and positive ties to the Jewish world. Much of Freud's ethnic biography will in fact entail various attempts, some symbolic, others actual, to integrate emotionally these two discrepant and discordant sides of his personality.

The second event that served merely to exacerbate the effects of the first was also a loss: the family's departure from Freiberg and eventual relocation in Vienna (with a short residence in Leipzig in between). What young Sigmund lost in this case was the safe and familiar world of his first two-and-a-half years and what replaced it was by all accounts quite different and far less satisfying. Jacob's motivation for leaving Freiberg remains unclear. While it was originally thought that rising anti-Semitism and a worsening economic climate for Jacob's business were responsible, recent research by Sajner and Gicklhorn have shown neither of these to be the case. More likely however are other possibilities, specifically that: Jacob sought to protect his older sons from conscription into the Austrian army;[40] the family was involved in some illegal activities centered around forgery; the family business was lost and a more populated locale was need for survival; or Jacob wished to separate Amalie from his son Phillip, with the implication that some romantic attachment had developed between the two.

In any case the departure was a hasty and emotional one that caused young Sigmund enormous anxiety and panic. He later described the episode, including and perhaps especially the train ride, as a "catastrophe."[41] Of it he wrote: "Breslau plays a part in my childhood memories. At the age of three I passed through the station when we moved from Freiberg to Leipzig, and the gas jets (gas lamps), which were the first I had seen, reminded me of souls burning in Hell,"[42] no doubt a reference to the frightening lessons his nursemaid had taught him while under her tutelage.

Beyond the actual journey, the move represented a radical change in circumstances for Sigmund. Gone was the secure and insulated world of Freiberg and along with it many of the family members who had been so important to him: Philipp, Emanuel and his family, including his beloved companion John, his nursemaid Resi Wittek, and the other Jews of Freiberg. Those who remained with him, most notably his parents, would also exhibit significant changes. His father would grow increasingly passive and distant, incapable of or uninterested in earning a living. His mother, now back in a more familiar environment, would become more assertive and demanding. It was furthermore a time of poverty and hardship for the family. They would share space with others, change residences frequently, and require financial help from relatives.

Finally, Vienna was a very different Jewish world from the one Sigmund was familiar with. His son Martin suggested that this early transition from an idyllic small town environment surrounded by rural countryside to the dirty and overcrowded Jewish quarter of Vienna, the Leopoldstadt, must have been quite a shock for the young boy. What he encountered in short was a ghetto, teeming and overcrowded with Jewish refugees from Eastern Europe. Here Freud could be exposed, probably for the first time, to anti-Semitism, to the realities of Jewish intergroup squabbling and bickering, and to a very different kind of Jew, what Martin called "not of the best type." According to Martin: "A popular song in Vienna which contained the passage 'When the Jews were crossing the Red Sea, all the coffee-houses in the Leopoldstadt were empty,' suggests where they spent much of their time."[43] Freud's notion of what it meant to be Jewish could not help but be colored by these new circumstances and the negative feelings about his new home.

* * *

Little is known of the Freud family's first years in Vienna, but they seem to have been difficult ones and fraught with financial troubles and problems in adjusting to a radically different lifestyle. Obviously not wishing to delve too deeply into this transitional period, Freud summarily dismissed it as follows: "They were hard times and not worth remembering."[44] Ernest Jones, however, chose to offer the following portrait of the developing youngster during this time. "One gets a picture of him as having been a 'good' boy, not an unruly one, and one much given to reading study. His mother's favorite, he possessed the self-confidence that told him he would achieve something worth while in life, and the ambition to do so, though for long the direction this would take remained uncertain."[45]

Sigmund's formal education began at home. From a recollection of an early interaction with his mother one gets a sense of his early precociousness, tinged as it was even then with skepticism. At six years old, Freud's mother tried to convey to him the belief that all people are made of earth and will therefore return to earth. When he expressed doubt and disbelief, she rubbed her palms together in a manner similar to that used in making dumplings and showed him the "blackish scales of epidermis produced by the friction." Freud's astonishment knew no bounds, and he "acquiesced in the belief which I was later to hear expressed in the words 'Thou owest Nature a death.'"[46]

The task of dealing with such a demanding pupil may well have taxed Amalie's patience and in short order may have been turned over to her husband. Much of Sigmund and Jacob's time together was spent reading from the Scripture, and a later inscription in the family Bible suggested that this activity began when Sigmund was seven.[47] Both father and son seemed to derive great pleasure from it. For Jacob this time spent with his son must have brought back fond memories of studying with his own father. It may however have simultaneously stimulated vague feelings of guilt, especially when he realized just how far he had wandered from his Orthodox roots. Were they not now reading the Bible in German rather than in the traditional Hebrew? In any case Jacob must have been heartened by his son's quick and voracious mind and encouraged that his enormous hopes for Sigmund's future might in fact be realized. Sigmund in turn could not miss the great store his father put in scholarly pursuits, or how easily he could satisfy him in this regard.

The Bible stories themselves seem to have touched Freud deeply. In his autobiography he wrote: "My deep engrossment in the Bible story (almost as soon as I had learned the art of reading) had, as I recognized much later, an enduring effect upon the direction of my interest."[48] By this he was probably referring to what he later called a lifelong need to unravel the "riddles of the world"[49] and somehow to satisfy his early "longing for philosophical knowledge."[50] During the course of his life he would have occasion to identify strongly with several biblical figures, in particular Joseph and Moses, and he would continuously draw upon biblical scenes and metaphors for self-understanding, especially when stressful times presented themselves.

Sigmund probably attended a private *Volksschule* (elementary school) for a year or two before passing the examination that enabled him to enroll in the local *Sperlgymnasium* (high school). He was nine at the time, a year earlier than was typical. Not surprisingly, he showed himself to be an excellent student. He stood at the head of his class for the last six of his eight years there, was awarded "preferential pupil" status, and graduated summa cum laude. As a reward for these accomplishments, Jacob offered him a trip to England to visit his older brothers.

During his *Sperlgymnasium* days, he approached his studies with the same intensity and near obsessive quality that would come to pervade his every endeavor. He read voraciously and incessantly during adolescence and thoroughly familiarized himself with the classics of German, Latin, Greek, and English literature. His family for its part accommodated itself to his routine. He was usually closeted in the long narrow chamber that served as a combination bedroom and study carrel. This small space would be his residence until his mid-twenties when he took a medical residency at a local hospital. His sister Anna remembers that "the only thing that changed in this room was the increasing number of crowded bookcases added to the writing desk, bed, chairs and shelf which furnished it." While everyone else had candles in their bedrooms, Sigmund required and got an oil lamp. It was at this time in the family history that Amalie had the family piano removed because its music interrupted his studies. Freud frequently did not join the family for evening meals but chose rather to take them alone in his "cabinet." Even his friendships revolved around his studies, for as Anna described later, he brought home studymates rather than playmates.[51] The following description of his friendship with Eduard Silberstein contained in a letter to his fiancée Martha bears out her point.

> We became friends at a time when one doesn't look upon friendship as a sport or asset, but when one needs a friend with whom to share things. We used to be together literally every hour of the day that was not spent on the school bench. We learned Spanish together, had our own mythology and secret names, which we took from some dialogue of the great Cervantes. . . . Together we founded a strange scholarly society, the "Academic Castellana" (AC), compiled a great mass of humorous work which must still exist somewhere among my old papers; we shared our frugal suppers and were never bored in each other's company.[52]

These school years also witnessed the emergence of two inner traits that would come to dominate his more mature personality. The first was a willingness to oppose injustice, even it it meant standing alone, a trait he later attributed to his Jewishness.[53] The second was a seemingly insatiable ambition to succeed and fulfill his destiny. Of the former he wrote, again to Martha. "One would hardly guess from looking at me, and yet even at school I was always the bold oppositionist, always on hand when an extreme had to be defended, and usually ready to atone for it."[54] What he was referring to here was an organized effort by students with himself as a ringleader to remove a particularly objectionale gymnasium teacher. In the same year he was also involved in several protests against unfair punishment of classmates. His early ambitions in turn found their first real expression in relation to the *Matura*, the exiting gymnasium exam. Of it he wrote. "I seem to remember that throughout the whole of this time (of preparation) there ran a premonition of a task ahead, till it found open expression in my school-leaving essay as a wish that I might during the course of my life contribute something to our human knowledge."⁵⁵ And he soared even higher upon receipt of a very positive evaluation of his work. To a friend he boasted:

> My professor told me—and he is the first person who has dared to tell me this—that I possess what Herder so nicely calls an idiotic style—i.e., a style at once correct and characteristic. I was, suitably impressed by this amazing fact and do not hesitate to disseminate the happy event, the first of its kind, as widely as possible—to you, for instance, who until now have probably remained unaware that you have been exchanging letters with a German stylist. And now I advise you as a friend, not as an interested party, to preserve them—have them bound—take good care of them—one never knows.⁵⁶

Of Freud's Jewish education beyond the Bible study with Jacob there exists a fairly clear picture,⁵⁷ for religious education was compulsory in all Austrian schools during his youth. To meet the state's requirement one could either study religion as part of the public school curriculum or privately. In both cases teachers of Jewish religion had to be certified by the *Kultusgemeinde*, a local board of Jewish educators that also provided tutors and private classes. It was felt that students should develop "piety" as well as academic talents and to ensure this grades were assigned as in any other subject. The standardized Jewish curriculum for both the *Volksschule* and *Gymnasium* included the teaching of the Hebrew Bible, supplemented by lessons in Jewish history and liturgy. A textbook was added to provide instruction in religious doctrine. The study of Hebrew itself, although in practice quite limited, was an essential part of the curriculum. According to the staff of the *Kultusgemeinde*, the goal of such instruction was to promote a "personal encounter" with the "spirit of Judaism,"⁵⁸ a sentiment that no doubt would have appealed to Jacob Freud in his Reformed leanings.⁵⁹

Ironically, the textbook employed by Samuel Hammerschlag with whom Freud most likely studied religion for this entire period and to which he was thus no doubt exposed was written by Leopold Breuer, the father of his future mentor and collaborator Josef Breuer. In it Breuer stressed a Mendelssohnian approach to "natural religion," the universality of "moral law, Judaism as "a religious confession,"⁶⁰ and the importance of good citizenship, all concepts squarely in line with an Enlightenment highly assimilated interpretation of Judaism.

Evidently, Sigmund and his religious teacher Hammerschlag

developed a mutually warm and deep attachment for each other and this fact could not help but positively color his attitude toward the subject matter. Of their relationship Freud later wrote. "He has been touchingly fond of me for years; there is such a secret sympathy between us that we can talk intimately together. He always regards me as his son."[61] Add to this the following description provided by Reuben Rainey, and one begins to sense the depth of the relationship.

> Freud remained a lifelong friend of his teacher and was often a visitor in his home. In a letter to his financée, Freud confessed that he was feeling disgruntled with his work, but a visit with Hammerschlag would cheer him up. When Freud was a young medical student in financial need, it was Hammerschlag who provided him with a sum of money on several occasions. Freud also held Hammerschlag's family in high esteem: "I do not know any better or more humane people, or so free from any ignoble motives." He named his youngest daughter after a daughter of Hammerschlag and another after a niece. Later on in his life, Freud advised Hammerschlag's grandson about his studies.[62]

Hammerschlag would become one of several older men, the first being his brother Emanuel then in England, whom Freud would seek out during his young adulthood as father-substitutes for Jacob, who increasingly was losing favor in his son's eyes.

This information provides interesting insights into aspects of Freud's Jewish identity. It is clear, first of all, especially given his exemplary grades in religion, that he was far from ignorant of Jewish tradition, as he on several occasions implied. Thus protestations such as the following must beheld somewhat suspect. "In the time of my youth our liberal religious instructors set no store by their pupils acquiring a knowledge of the Hebrew language and literature. My education in this field was therefore extremely behind hand, as I have since often regretted."[63] It will later be argued that this professed ignorance actually represented an unconscious effort to distance himself from Jewish ritual and observance, a key ingredient in his ambivalent feelings about his ethnic identity. Unlike many of his contemporaries whose experience in religious education was at best tortuous,[64] his was a very positive one and thus not likely to be a source of his inner conflicts. It is also important to realize that the kind of Judaism to which he was exposed, first by his father and later by his esteemed teacher, allowed for the existence of agnosticism and the rejection of traditional Jewish ritual and observance, two positions toward which he would shortly gravitate. Finally, its central concepts of universalism and messianic idealism were important enough to Freud eventually to find expression as core values in psychoanalysis itself.

A more likely culprit in the evolution of his Jewish ambivalence, which had the effect of compounding the already existing tension caused by the loss of his nursemaid and the departure from Freiberg, was an experience he described in *The Interpretation of Dreams*. Between the ages of ten and twelve, Freud's father began taking him on walks and sharing with his son his views on life. On one such occasion Jacob told the following story to show how much better things were for Jews currently than they had been during his own youth. "When I was a young man," he said, "I went for a walk one Saturday in the streets of your birthplace; I was well dressed, and had a new fur cap on my head. A Christian came up to me and with a single blow knocked off my cap into the mud and shouted: 'Jew! get off the pavement.'" "And what did you do?" young Freud asked anxiously. "I went into the roadway and picked up my cap," his father answered calmly. This struck Sigmund as "unheroic conduct on the part of the big, strong man who was holding the little boy by the hand." Freud remembered contrasting this behavior with a scene from the history of Hannibal in which his father, Hamilcar Barcas, "made him swear he would take vengeance on the Romans." Since that time, Freud remembered, Hannibal had played a prominent part in his "phantasies."[65]

In addition to the enormous disillusionment about his father and related deflation of self this experience must have engendered in Sigmund, it introduced a real conflict into his conception of Jews and Judaism. He was himself a Jew but did not wish to identify with such cowardice. Instead he choose to model himself after a very different kind of Jew, the Semite Hannibal, who, unlike his father, had vowed to take revenge on the enemies of his people.

At about this time, and no doubt in response to the above experience, Sigmund entered what Ernest Jones called his "unmistakable militaristic phase." According to Jones, Freud remembered "how he pasted onto the backs of his wooden soldiers little labels bearing the names of Napoleon's marshals. His favorite one was Masséna, usually believed to be a Jew; he was aided in his hero worship by his mistaken belief that they were both born on the same date, a hundred years apart."[66] The Franco-Prussian War broke out during this period and he followed it with great interest, keeping careful track of developments on a large map with small flags and lecturing to his sisters on the intricacies of war. While this phase diminished with the passing of youth, he always retained a sensitivity to even the slightest hint of anti-Semitism and was more than willing to defend himself when confronted physically.

On several occasions later in fact he would find himself, like his father, confronted by hostile anti-Semites. His response however was always quite different. His "first great adventure" in this realm took place on a train in Saxony when he was twenty-six. Someone called him a "dirty Jew," and he stood his ground, although he was alone and his assailant was surrounded by friends. "I was not in the least frightened of that mob . . . I was quite prepared to kill him." While "jeers, abuses and threats broke out,"[67] Freud would not give an inch, and finally the situation calmed down and returned to normal. Martin Freud reports a similar incident that he actually witnessed as a boy. On holiday at Reichenhall in Bavaria, Freud's way was blocked by an anti-Semitic mob that would not let him pass. In response he charged into their midst, swinging a walking stick, and they dispersed. One cannot help but be aware of the parallels between this situation and the one Jacob described many years earlier and wonder about the impact of such different responses upon the young observers. The incident must have made a deep impression on Martin, for he claimed to still vividly remember both his father's bravery and "the faces of these crusaders in racial hatred"[68] more than fifty years later. Martin obviously took the lesson to heart, for as a student he like his father felt no compunction about taking on "those who thought it excellent sport to humiliate and insult Jewish students."[69] While at the same university attended by his father, he participated in two duels and received a knife wound in an anti-Semitic "brawl." Freud's overt response to such incidents was always sympathy, but one could easily imagine the great delight and pride that existed below the surface.

In identifying with Hannibal, young Sigmund may have unconsciously "split" the Jewish world into two camps. For traditional, Orthodox Jews such as his father, who refused to defend themselves, he felt contempt. This inner rage may have in turn generalized itself into his later rejection of organized religion, Jewish and non-Jewish alike. One can also discern the possible inner consequences of Freud's painful experience with his father in his eventual embracing of agnosticism, his antipathy toward

Orthodox Jews and his disdain for Jewish ritual and observance. While none of these attitudes was out of character for turn-of-the-century Vienna's assimilated Jews, Freud's obsessive commitment to each suggested the existence of a deep and unresolved conflict. Each represented an inner compromise unconsciously adopted by Freud in order to accommodate his ambivalent feelings about Jacob and about being Jewish. While he could not attack and reject his father directly, he could symbolically reject his father's God, those Jews who most reminded him of his father's cowardly behavior, and the religious rites that set them and his father apart from other Jews. But to turn one's back on even a portion of one's people, let alone one's father and the tradition he represents, is a heavy burden indeed, not to mention a source of great potential guilt. Thus, with this event and its various potential psychic accommodations, Freud's Jewish ambivalence may have become rigidified.

Each of these attitudes emerged and took form as part of Sigmund's adolescent development. By his last year in the Gymnasium, for instance, he had become an avowed agnostic. A voracious reader, he had by then plowed through most of the Enlightenment thinkers, not to mention Shakespeare and the Greek and Roman classics. There was clearly in this array ample material for nurturing and sustaining his growing disbelief. His agnosticism is plainly evident in several letters written during this period. To a Freiberg friend, for example, he wrote of accidently meeting a girl as follows: "truly any more such strokes of Providence could convince me of the inscrutable workings of divine power."[70] And a bit later to the same young man: "The next time you feel a 'burning' desire for something, pray to God, 'Grant me this or that,' and add, 'But not too soon.'"[71] Or consider another piece of correspondence in which he thanks a friend for a loan. "I thank you for the friendly way in which you helped me out of my embarrassment. If there is a God he will take note of your deed and repay you a thousandfold, and if there is not, then there exists at least one man who will remember it and consider it one more reason for remaining fond of you."[72] In spite of the intended humor, his mockery of God and religious belief is quite clear and is worlds apart from his parents. There is no evidence however that any conflict existed around this issue at home. In all likelihood he was probably rather judicious about its expression. His commitment to agnosticism would in time deepen with his attendance at the university, where he was introduced first to radical materialist and then to scientific positivist views under the influence of his beloved teacher Ernest Brucke.

Freud's early resentment of provincial Jews was particularly extreme but would recede with age as more and more of his energies were directed toward attacking religion per se. His intensity however comes through quite clearly in a letter written in 1872 describing Orthodox traveling companions on a train journey from Freiberg to Vienna.

> This being my unlucky day, I ended up in the company of a most venerable old Jew and his correspondingly old wife with their melancholy languorous darling daughter and cheeky young "hopeful" son. Their company was even more unpalatable. A casual remark I made, red with rage, could not sweeten my boredom. . . . Now, this Jew talked in the same way as I had heard thousands of others talk before, even in Freiberg. His very face seemed familiar—he was typical. So was the boy, with whom he discussed religion. He was cut from the cloth from which fate makes swindlers when the time is ripe: cunning, mendacious, kept by his adoring relatives in the belief that he is a great talent, but unprincipled and without character. . . . In the course of the conversation I learned that Madame Jewess and family hailed from Meseritsch [a Moravian town]: a proper compost heap for this sort of weed.[73]

Such an attitude was not uncommon among Vienna's assimilated Jews, who blamed the "backward' and "unwashed" Galacian immigrants for the rising anti-Semitism. For many, these newcomers were an uncomfortable reminder of their own past and a convenient target for their frustrations. In Freud's case the antipathy was exacerbated by the additional factor of his distasteful experience with Jacob.

Sigmund's attitude toward religious ritual grew less tolerant with age. Although his approaching marriage to Martha would signal a dramatic increase in its intensity, as an adolescent he seemed willing to submit grudgingly to the few practices, primarily observances of Jewish festivals, that still existed in the Freud home. Of these he offered a sarcastic but humorous rendering. In March of 1873, for instance, he wrote the following to a friend about a family Purim party.

> I want to tell you that we had a little theatre performance on the occasion of Purim (which, moreover, fell on the 13th day of March, so sacred to us all; the day, too, when Caesar was murdered). A lady from the neighbourhood with time hanging heavy on her

hands, drilled my sisters, my little brother and a few other children into actors and actresses, thus forcing us to earn our Purim dinner (well known to be not among the worse) the hard way by an artistic treat of the strangest kind. May you never find yourself in the dilemma of being the brother of such ambitious actresses![74]

And in a similar spirit he wrote a year later that "religion is often unjustly accused" of being "too metaphysical," but he went on to suggest that in his mind anyway it "is intimately related to the senses," especially the stomach. He then proceeds to enumerate how different holidays affected digestion. Passover "causes constipation." Yom Kippur is a "dreary day," not because of "God's wrath," but because of the "plum preserves" that are traditionally served at its conclusion. And he always confused Purim and New Years because nothing special was served on either day. In any case, "our festivals have outlived our dogma, like the funeral meal has outlived the dead." When "we children of the world" partake of food, "we no longer think, like the pious, that we have done a good deed, rather we are simply conscious of having eaten a good dish."[75]

In the fall of 1873 Sigmund Freud entered the University of Vienna. He did not really know what career to pursue and in typical fashion his father had left the matter totally in his hands. As an aspiring Jew, however, he had basically only three options open to him: business, law, or medicine. He had much too far-ranging a mind for the first, and because of his father's past difficulties, his associations with the world of commerce may not have been good ones. His interest in the law in turn had faded with his dream of being a minister of state and with the changing political climate. That left medicine, a prospect that did not truly excite him then or after more than forty years of medical practice. Freud would actually confess late in life that he had never felt truly at home as a physician and secretly yearned to quit his practice in favor of speculative science. He had evidently never gotten over his boyhood fantasy of unraveling the great "riddles of the world," a dream first stimulated by the many questions that the biblical tales he read with Jacob had left unanswered in his young and fertile mind. His choice of medicine was finally made on the basis of Goethe's essay on nature that he heard read aloud shortly before graduation as well as a growing excitement over the then-topical theories of Darwin. For two years however he would flounder about academically, bouncing from one department

## Growing Up Jewish 79

of natural science to another, never finding a comfortable niche.

Part of his alienation no doubt was the widespread anti-Semitism he encountered at the university. This was probably his first direct experience with a decidedly anti-Jewish environment. Of it he later wrote:

> When, in 1873, I first joined the university, I experienced some appreciable disappointment. Above all, I found that I was expected to feel myself inferior and an alien because I was a Jew. I refused absolutely to do the first of these things. I have never been able to see why I should feel ashamed of my descent or, as people were beginning to say, of my "race." I put up, without much regret, with my non-acceptance into the community; for it seemed to me that in spite of this exclusion an active fellow-worker could not fail to find some nook or cranny in the framework of humanity.[76]

Always a barometer of Austrian politics, the University of Vienna had during Freud's tenure there it the 1870s and 1880s became a hotbed of nationalistic and anti-Semitic activity. Its liberal leanings of the previous decades had been quickly and summarily forgotten. Since almost 30 percent of Freud's class was Jewish and the medical faculty even more disproportionate in its numbers, the atmosphere on campus must have been a tense one indeed. In keeping with the emerging ethos, the national German fraternities in 1878 expelled their Jewish members and shortly thereafter the Landsmannschaften, made up of students from the same home regions, followed suit. Jewish students could defend their honor through dueling until even that right was removed by the Waldenhofen Manifesto of 1882, issued by the German-Austrian student body of the university, which stated unequivocally, as follows, that Jews were not even worthy as opponents:

> Every son of a Jewish mother, every human being in whose veins flows Jewish blood, is from the day of his birth, without honor and void of all the more refined emotions. He cannot differentiate between what is dirty and what is clean. He is ethnically subhuman. Friendly intercourse with a Jew is therefore is dishonorable; any association with him has to be avoided. It is impossible to insult a Jew; a Jew cannot therefore demand satisfaction for any suffered insult.

Nor would the situation change appreciably for a long time, for Sigmund's son Martin would face an equally repulsive scene during his student days forty years later. It is not known how young Sigmund fared on a daily basis with the anti-Semitism. While he did not report any specific incidents or speak of his own participation in dueling, he did acknowledge excitement over his friend Carl Koller's success in a duel with a fellow physician who had called him a "Jewish swine." Freud wrote: "We all would have reacted just as Koller did."[77] It could be surmised perhaps that he would not have backed down if confronted, but would have chosen to avoid trouble when possible, preferring to gain satisfaction through academic and scientific achievement and in that manner show them of what Jews were made.

* * *

After two years of study at the university, Sigmund was provided a no doubt welcomed respite from his tense university existence. The occasion was a long-anticipated trip to England to visit his half-brothers, a delayed graduation present from Jacob. His seven-week stay with Emanuel's family in Manchester evidently had a profound impact upon him, for after his return to Vienna he frequently spoke of going back, perhaps on a permanent basis. In one letter to a friend he confessed:

> As for England itself, I . . . can say straight out that I would sooner live there than here, rain, fog, drunkenness and conservatism notwithstanding. Many peculiarities of the English character and country that other continentals might find intolerable agree very well with my own nature. Who knows dear friend, but that after I have completed my studies a friendly wind might not blow me across to England and allow me to practice my hand there.[78]

Two things seemed to have motivated his enthusiasm. The first was his brothers' material circumstances. Both had in a relatively short period risen from a state of immigrant poverty to one of respect and financial comfort. Jacob, who left Freiberg at the same time, had not done nearly as well in Vienna, a sore point with Sigmund. Both of his brothers were shopkeepers, Emanuel selling cloth and his younger brother, jewelry. They lived in one of the city's better neighborhoods and were founding members of the South Manchester synagogue. Emanuel, to whom Freud was especially drawn, "had," according to Martin who met him a number of years later, "become in every possible detail a dignified English gentleman."[79] Emanuel, equally taken with Sigmund, had evidently spoken to him at length about their father's circumstances. No doubt he sensed his younger brother's bitterness and was able to alleviate it somewhat.

The second attraction of England for Sigmund was the experience of being a Jew in a much more hospitable environment. He had never before left the confines of the Austrian Empire, and given recent events at the university vis-à-vis anti-Semitism, the sense of opportunity, freedom, and mobility England afforded its Jews must have been striking. It is likely that he was making such comparisons with Vienna when he wrote the following. "The thought of England surges up before me with its sober industriousness, its generous devotion to the public weal, the stubbornness and sensitive feeling for justice in its inhabitants."[80] His half-brothers had not been noticeably hampered by anti-Semitism, and at the time of his visit, Benjamin Disraeli, a Jew, was prime minister of England. So strong were his feelings for England that he would name his second son after Oliver Cromwell, the first English leader to welcome Jews back after their earlier expulsion. Why Freud never chose to emigrate to England prior to his escape in 1938, especially given a lifelong and frequently vocalized antipathy for Vienna, will always remain a mystery.

Shortly after his return to the university, he found at long last a compatible place for himself in the physiological laboratory of Ernst Brucke. He would remain there for six years, not including one spent in compulsory military service. During this period he carried out several major research projects for Brucke. In each he sensed the possiblity of a revolutionary discovery and instant fame and fortune. Unfortunately, something would go awry and rob him of the acknowledgment and recognition he so desperately craved. He finally completed the requirements and examinations for his medical degree in 1881. His time in the laboratory was brought to an end however by a kindly Brucke, who was obviously aware of Sigmund's propensity for overlooking the necessity of earning a living, and felt honor-bound to remind his young student of the bleak prospects that awaited him should he choose to remain in the laboratory. Two assistants, both rather young, were already in line ahead of Sigmund to succeed Brucke. Besides, an assistant's pay was shockingly low, and Freud, himself perpetually on the edge of bankruptcy, had no way of making up the difference and thus of supporting himself over time. Small honoraria from his publications and an occasional university grant were the only income he could earn himself. His father could barely support the family, let alone continue to provide for his son's education, and he was already borrowing regularly from friends. His chief benefactor had become Josef Breuer, with whom he had already run up a considerable debt. It was clearly time for a professional change.

Freud evidently appreciated Brucke's gesture. "The turning point came in 1882," he wrote in his autobiography, "when my teacher, for whom I had the highest possible esteem, corrected my father's generous improvidence by strongly advising me, in view of my bad financial position, to abandon my theoretical career. I followed his advise, left the physiology laboratory and enter the General Hospital,"[81] finally to pursue the clinical work necessary for qualifing as a physician. Brucke would retain a warm interest in Sigmund's career and later sponsor his application for promotion to the rank of *Privatdocent* and help him procure a traveling grant to Paris where he would study under Charcot.

His decision was punctuated by a final and unexpected turn. In April of that year he met and fell in love with Martha Bernays. When on 17 June they became engaged to be married, he was faced with the added question of how he would support a wife and family. His fate was sealed, and on 31 July 1882 he took up residency at the General Hospital of Vienna, where he would remain for three years rotating through the various specialities, including five months in Theodor Meynert's psychiatric clinic.

Sigmund and Martha's engagement lasted for over four years. The long delay resulted primarily from their limited financial circumstances and Freud's self-imposed restriction that they wait until enough money had been saved to carry them through their first year of marriage. Clearly, his own family's continual monetary difficulties while growing up had left their mark upon him in the form of an unusually strong need for future security. During this time, Freud wrote over nine hundred letters to his fiancée, and all have survived, thanks to the intercession of Martha's daughters, when she had considered burning them after the death of her husband. The correspondence provides an uncanny glimpse into Freud's inner thoughts and ideas as well as into the external events that took place during the period of 1882–86. Included are lengthy descriptions of Sigmund's immersion in medical practice at the hospital, his promotion to *Privatdocent*, the frustration and embarrassment surrounding his cocaine research, his time in Paris with Charcot, and the many trials and tribulations that surrounded their route to the altar. A critical issue that would emerge almost immediately and remain a major stumbling block during their courtship was Martha's Orthodox background.

Martha Bernays, born on 26 July 1861 and thus five years Freud's junior, came from an old and distinguished Jewish family. Her grandfather Isaac Bernays had served as chief rabbi of Hamburg and was an outspoken opponent of the Jewish Reform movement in Germany. A relative of Heinrich Heine, his name frequently and fondly appeared in the poet's correspondence. One of his sons, Michael, became professor of German at the University of Munich, a position open to him only because of his willingness to convert. A second brother, Jacob, who in keeping with Jewish tradition went into mourning for his wayward brother, taught the classics at the University of Heidelberg but remained a Jew and thereby forfeited any chance of promotion. Martha's father Berman was a merchant and a deeply observant Jew. He and his wife Emmeline, also Orthodox, moved to Vienna from Hamburg when Martha was eight. He unexpectedly died ten years later, and their son Eli became the head of the family.

Vienna's Jewish middle class in Freud's day was a tight and insular community, and it is perhaps not at all surprising that there were so many social connections between him and Martha. Eli Bernays, Martha's brother and a friend of Sigmund's, was engaged to Anna Freud, and Martha's younger sister, Minna, was engaged to Sigmund's best friend, Ignaz Schonberg. The couple in fact met in the Freud living room. Martha and Minna were visiting the family when Sigmund returned home from work. Although he characteristically rushed right to his room to resume his studies, irrespective of visitors, something had caught his attention about one of the young women and to the amazement of the entire family, he remained and joined the conversation. He was immediately smitten with Martha, and with his usual intensity undertook a whirlwind courtship that resulted in their engagement two months later. Their engagement was at first kept a secret because Martha feared her mother's reaction—Sigmund was both without means or prospects and unsympathetic to the family's traditional religious views—and perhaps she wanted time to prepare the way. When they finally made their announcement six months later, Mamma was still far less than enthusiastic about her daughter's choice.

Normally reserved and highly controlled in his manner, the demands of love brought out a very different and surprisingly passionate side of Freud. In relation to Martha his emotions grew intense and mercurial—one moment at the height of bliss, the next in the depths of despair. The epitome of the spoiled, insecure, and narcissistic child, his need for love seemed nearly insatiable. Although Martha gave him no reason to doubt her devotion, he was plagued by perpetual uncertainty and demanded constant reassurances. He would in fact settle for nothing less than possessing her totally. Such total commitment could only be proven through a complete identification with him and his opinions, feelings, and actions. And her commitment had to be tested constantly. Jealous and possessive to a fault, he could tolerate no competitors for her affection or attention and, as will become obvious shortly, this would include not only rival suitors but also her beloved Mamma and her brother.

Where this complex of intense emotions and need came from is uncertain. Freud was clearly unschooled in the ways of love. His only previous relationship had been a predominantly fantasied one with Gisela Fluss during a visit to his birthplace at the age of sixteen. Perhaps part of his need was merely inexperience. Or more likely, as several authors have suggested, it reflected a flaw or blind spot in his emotional development. Paul Roazen, for example, attributed this need to dominate to a fear of women,[82] while Erich Fromm saw it as a manifestation of his "dependence on his mother," which would be repeated in his subsequent relationships with "men, older ones, contemporaries and disciples, upon whom he transferred the same need for unconditional love, affirmation, admiration and protection."[83] And we have already considered Menninger's notion of the overindulgent and overestimating Jewish family and its ability to create a narcissistic child whose symptoms are not unlike those described above. In any case it made for an emotional rollercoaster that took all of Martha's considerable maturity and tact to keep under control and out of the realm of disaster. Interestingly enough, once he was married Sigmund's passions for his new bride would wane considerably. It was as if, finally assured of her love and devotion and having properly ensconced her in what would be her lifetime role as *hausfrau*, he could return to a more balanced and well-controlled existence. Shortly, however, a new passion in the form of his budding ideas for a new science of the mind would come completely to overshadow her presence.

Most problematic for Martha were Sigmund's demands that she bow to his wishes rather than to those of her mother or brother. Even the slightest hint of concern or consideration for her family could invoke a hurt reaction in him such as the following. "If that is so, you are my enemy: if we don't get over this obstacle we shall founder. You have only an Either-Or. If you can't be fond enough of me to renounce your family, then you must lose me, wreck my life, and not get much yourself out of your family."[84] He intensely disliked her mother and brother and would go out of his way to find fault with them and to come between them and Martha. Eli, once a close friend, would become "unbearable" to him, "his most dangerous rival"[85] for her affection. On several occasions in fact Sigmund became so angry with him that he stopped speaking, and Eli followed suit.[86] Eli's wedding to Freud's sister Anna came during one of their falling-outs and Sigmund did not attend. It is unclear however how much of this was motivated by his dislike for formal rituals. Of his future mother-in-law, Freud wrote early on:

> She is fascinating, but alien, and will always remain so to me. I seek for similarities with you, but find hardly any. Her very warm-heartedness has an air of condescension, and she exacts admiration. I can foresee more than one opportunity of making myself disagreeable to her and I don't intend to avoid them. One is that she is beginning to treat your brother, of whom I am very fond, badly; another is my determination that my Martha's health shall not suffer by yielding to a crazy piety and fasting.[8]

His last reference is to Emmeline Bernays's strict adherence to Jewish religious observance, and we are already familiar with the direction his feelings on that topic were taking during his adolescence. In the interim or perhaps because of his dislike for his future mother-in-law, they had intensified and grown decidedly negative.

Early on in their relationship Freud undertook to wean Martha of her "religious prejudices" and "foolish superstitions" and thought her "weak" for not standing up to her mother and denouncing them. Out of consideration for her mother's observance of the Sabbath, for example, she would at first not write to him at all on the Sabbath and then use only a pencil instead of pen and ink and only out of her mother's sight. Such concessions infuriated him and only reinforced his resolve. He once remarked to her: "They would have preferred you to marry an old Rabbi or *Schochet* [ritual slaughterer]," and on another occcasion he boasted: "Eli little knows what a heathen I am going to make of you."[88]

To a large extent this prophecy would come true, for their home would remain free of any signs of traditional Judaism. As if to underline this point, Martin described how his Grandmother Emmeline's Orthodox ways seemed so foreign in the household. She was a practicing, Orthodox Jew who strictly observed Jewish law including the custom of wearing a *scheitel*, a wig worn by pious religious women from the time of marriage in place of their own hair. Martin recalled his grandmother's occasional visits and her chanting of Jewish prayers on Saturdays "in a small but firm and melodious voice." Such practices, he continued, "seemed alien to us children who had been brought up without any instruction in Jewish ritual."[89] Elsewhere he would describe the family festivals as: "Christmas, with presents under a candle-lit tree, and Easter with gaily painted Easter eggs."[90] One can be sure, however, given Sigmund's prejudices, that such activities were totally secular and devoid of any religious significance. Such activities, as will become evident below, were most likely undertaken so that the children would not feel different or excluded because of their Jewishness.

But all of this did not mean that Martha had totally submitted or been won over. Ernest Jones described her as "very tough and spirited in her personality and when forced to an issue, an art in which Freud was accomplished, she could stand up for herself with even greater tenacity than he could maintain."[91] She was instead a pragmatist and a peacemeaker and chose to strike an unspoken bargain in her relationship with her husband. She would forfeit certain externals, such as Orthodox observances, in order to ensure domestic tranquility, but she would never compromise her inner spirit or values. Thus she would always think of herself as a traditional Jew and retain the personal and emotional connections that followed from such a position. Her children ware aware of this and at her funeral in 1951 arranged to have a rabbi speak. This is something they did not do for their father.

While Martha was clearly accommodating and sensitive to

her husband's foibles in this area, there is some indication she may have derived some pleasure from baiting him a bit. Isaiah Berlin, for instance, reported that even in 1938 the Freuds were still carrying on a longstanding argument, which he described as humorous yet serious, over lighting candles on Friday night.[92] Martha would point to the enormous stubbornness of this *Unmensch*[93] who would not allow her to perform the ritual. Sigmund in turn would maintain that it was still idle foolishness. Ralph Steadman, in his book of caricatures of Freud's life, recreated a humorous account of this scene, worth reproducing here. Freud speaks first:

> "What the blazes is this?"
> "You know perfectly well, dear. It's the Sabbath."
> "But I thought we settled this years ago."
> "We did, dear. But the children are fascinated and they want us to celebrate it."
> "But haven't you explained?—its merely the survival of some tribal neurosis!"
> "Yes, dear."
> "One of the many outward signs of a collective superego!"
> "I'm sure, dear."
> "Obsessional neurosis! Defending the tribe against incestuous wishes and the death wish against the father!"
> "We know all that, dear. Now will you recite the blessings or shall I? The children can't wait to see you castr—er—uh—cut the challah. Collectively, that is."[94]

Freud, even with all of his bluster around the subject of religion, may well have felt some respect for his wife's inner faith. A. A. Brill, for example, reported that during Freud's trip to America in 1909 he wired Jewish New Years greetings to his family. To reiterate a basic tenet of this work, Freud's rejection of Jewish ritual did not mean a rejection of his Jewishness. The latter, as shall become evident, is a step he would never take. He made this very distinction in a letter to Martha during their engagement. "And as for us, this is what I believe: even if the form wherein the old Jews were happy no longer offers us any shelter, something of the core, of the essence of this meaningful and life-affirming Judaism will not be absent from our home."[95]

The problem of what to do about the wedding ceremony had still not been resolved when Sigmund and Martha finally felt that they had saved enough to proceed with the marriage.

Mamma, of course, wanted an Orthodox service. Freud for his part had in his mind something quiet, secret, and clearly nonreligious. He was by this time in fact nearly phobic about the idea of participating in a traditional Jewish rite. He had once attended the Jewish wedding of his friend Josef Paneth and was so horrified by the scene that he had gone home and written sixteen pages describing it, in abject mockery. He had even given passing thought to conversion as a means of escape, but he was easily dissuaded from this by Josef Breuer's succinct advise: "Too complicated!" His final escape plan rested on the fact that in Germany, where they were to be married, a civil ceremony was all that was required. Martha however pointed out that although Germany did not require a religious ceremony, Austria did, and without it they would not be considered wed when they moved to Vienna. He had no choice but to submit. Martha in characteristic fashion made it as easy as possible for him. It was scheduled for a weekday when few friends could attend. It would take place at her mother's house. And formal evening dress would not be required. Sigmund spent the two nights preceding the ceremony at the home of Martha's uncle, Elias Philipp, supposedly being coached in the required Hebrew blessings. It is also rumored that he experienced what might be considered a panic attack as the event drew near but that he recovered in time. As Ernest Jones would put it: "He probably bit his lip when he stepped under the *chuppe* [the wedding canope], but everything went off well. Only eight relatives were present besides the immediate family, and the couple then departed for Lubeck."[96]

The couple returned to Vienna where Sigmund had begun a small and struggling medical practice five months earlier. The date he chose to open his office was Easter Sunday, a strange choice since everything would be shut down in religious Vienna. But perhaps he was unconciously asserting himself, thumbing his nose at the anti-Semitic world that had caused him and those he loved so much pain. Things steadily improved with his practice, and in 1892 the Freud's moved to Berggasse 19, several apartments over a butcher shop, where they would live and raise six children. This would be their home and his office for the next forty-six years, until, as Jews, they would be driven out of Vienna by the Nazi invasion.

Martha fell easily into the role of *hausfrau*. She was a good manager, had plenty of help, and ran a tight and predictable ship. She did everything for her husband including choosing his clothes, laying them out for him, and even, it is rumored, putting toothpaste on his toothbrush. Most importantly, however, she saw to it that Sigmund was not disturbed during the day and that the family's life revolved around his work schedule. A terrible creature of habit, he would have been continually unhinged by any less precision or structure. Thoroughly Victorian in his attitude toward women, he felt most comfortable with her in the externally subordinate role she had so easily taken on. She would soon begin a process of receding into the background of his life as his revolutionary ideas took form and precedence over all else. She would in time also have to content herself with sharing him first with her sister Minna, then her daughter Anna, and finally with a string of female disciples who would in later life vie with her for his attention. For the present, however, he was all hers. Freud's work with Breuer, which would herald the beginning of psychoanalysis, was still years off. Just making a living and getting by occupied their full attention. Often they would sit together and wait for patients to arrive. He continued to sense the enormous potential that existed within him, but he could give it no form or direction as of yet. The way he put it was: "I still have something wild in me which has not yet found any proper expression."[97]

# 5
# Freud's Jewish Identity

The previous chapter traced Freud's development from birth through young adulthood with a particular focus on those experiences that colored his perception of Jews and Judaism and in turn shaped his ethnic identity. With this chronology in place, it is now possible to inquire into the impact of these early experiences on his adult life as a Jew. Ethnic identity formation is far from a static process. In order to truly appreciate its ever-changing and developmental character, one must trace the ebb and flow of feelings about being Jewish across an entire lifetime and in addition correlate these variations with specific inner and outer events. This is the task that will be the focus of the next two chapters. In chapter 5 the specific content of Freud's Jewish identity will be delineated, including his work on religion. In chapter 6 I will focus in turn on the ethnic dimension of his relationships within the psychoanalytic movement. Between the two a full chronology of Freud's life will unfold.

Freud's Jewish identity, like that of most Jews of his day, could best be characterized as ambivalent. Ambivalence implies the concurrent existence of two very contradictory tendencies, with neither predominating. One side of Freud's personality drew him to his Jewishness. Having its ultimate roots in early positive experiences with ethnicity, this aspect of self allowed, even encouraged, him to value and draw pride and strength from it. Another side, however—growing out of the residue of painful negative Jewish experiences—pushed him away from and caused him unconsciously to reject his Jewish past. To this aspect of self the fact of his ethnicity was nothing more than a source of embarrassment and a continual hindrance to the lofty hopes and dreams he had set for himself. As will become apparent, both tendencies existed side by side within Freud's psyche. They were in almost perpetual conflict and often created within him contradictory thoughts, feelings, and behaviors in relation to his Jewishness.

Three crucial events in Freud's early life have been identified. There may well indeed have been others, but they never reached consciousness or the attention of his biographers and so are lost forever. The first—the experience with his nursemaid at two-and-a-half—created within him both a strong attraction for the non-Jewish world and a deep fear of religion and religious ritual. The second—the sudden departure from Freiberg at four—introduced him to a very different and less attractive Jewish world and attached to it a sense of personal loss. And the third—the story Jacob told Sigmund of an anti-Semitic incident—caused the twelve-year-old boy disappointment and embarrassment and then anger at his father's cowardice. These feelings, which had to be repressed because they flew in the face of other inner impulses that instructed him to the "Honor thy father," generalized in time to color various other aspects of his Jewishness. Together these experiences coalesced into an emerging core of Jewish negativity, which, as we have seen, found its first expression during adolescence in his agnosticism and antipathy for Orthodox Jews and Jewish ritual. These same tendencies would continue with some modifications in their expression into adulthood and combine with later experiences, especially those revolving around anti-Semitism, to form the content of his adult Jewish identity. With age Freud would experience a lessening in the intensity of his Jewish ambivalence. As a result first of his self-analysis at age forty and later in relation to his break with Jung and the increasing anti-Semitism that was being directed toward his work, he was able unconsciously to integrate some of the disparate elements of his Jewish identity and thus find a modicum of inner peace. As will become apparent, a significant amount of this inner processing took place in relation to his psychological theorizing and found ultimate expression in the theories of psychoanalysis.

\* \* \*

Freud's rejection of Jewish ritual and tradition continued throughout his life but in a more contained and less emotional manner. Much of the energy that earlier had sustained it would in time be redirected and sublimated through his writings and theorizing about religion. What had begun as a mocking of Jewish observances during adolescence and had grown into an intense hatred and near-phobic reaction to it during his courtship of Martha, eventually settled into a pattern of low-key resistence, which most often found expression in the adoption of decidedly non-Jewish practices and tastes.

Freud had made it quite clear from the start that their home would be free of the "foolish superstitions" with which Martha had been raised, and by all accounts he succeeded in this effort. One of the first acts he undertook in this regard was to change from the Jewish to the Gregorian calendar in the reckoning of personal dates. For his birthday Freud chose 1 April, although it is not known if this day held any special significance.[1] Throughout his correspondence, also, he defined dates in relation to the Christian holidays of Christmas and Easter with few if any references to their Jewish counterparts. The Freuds, at Sigmund's insistence, named their children after living rather than deceased friends and relatives, as was customary among traditional Jews, and to make matters even worse chose to name their sons after non-Jews. Finally, they took to keeping dogs as family pets. The family, especially Sigmund, according to Martin, had "unconsciously become dog-lovers." Neither of his parents had grown up with dogs, in Martha's case because Jewish tradition considered the dog an unclean animal and therefore not appropriate as a household pet. "In father's case, it was a matter of poverty," Martin wrote, poking fun at his father's rigidity in this area, "he never permitted himself to be affected by religious considerations."[2]

Perhaps most exemplary of Freud's unconscious contempt for Jewish tradition was his passion for collecting Greek, Roman, and Egyptian statuary. He surrounded himself in his office with these pieces of art, spent more than he could actually afford on them, according to his own assessment, and took enormous delight in each new acquisition. A practice that was common among assimilated Jews wishing to show their urbanity, it both demonstrated their knowledge of antiquities and showed their willingness to mock Jewish tradition through a flaunting of is most sacred tenet—the First Commandment and its ban on idolatry. Freud's collection may have in addition stimulated unconscious memories of the strange and mysterious world to which his nursemaid had introduced him, or even evoked images of illustrations from the Philippson Bible he had studied with Jacob as a boy. Marianne Krull has pointed out an uncanny resemblence between some of Freud's statuary and these illustrations. In any case the collection was so important to him that his wife and their maid Paula used painstaking care to place them in their precise order on his desk in their new residence in London. Freud would die a year later and requested that the ashes from his cremation, a final affront to Jewish tradition, be placed in one of these statues, a favorite Grecian urn that had been a gift from Marie Bonaparte.

\* \* \*

Another manifestation of Freud's discomfort with his Jewishness can be found in relation to his role as a parent and the concerns he felt for the future of his children as Jews. Freud was both an affectionate and highly indulgent Jewish parent. In regard to the latter, Ernest Jones told the following story of his response to a near-fatal illness in his first-born.

> When his eldest daughter was five or six years old she nearly died of diphtheria. At the crisis the distracted father asked her what she would like best in the world and she answered "a strawberry." They were out of season, but a renowned shop produced some. The first attempt to swallow one induced a fit of coughing that completely removed the obstructive membrane and the next day the child was well on the way to recovery, her life saved by a strawberry—and a loving father.[3]

His children were the only things that took precedence over his work. He rarely got angry with them, would always make himself available if they needed comforting or support, and took great pride in them and their accomplishments. On several different occasions he described them to colleagues as his "pride" and "riches."

His pampering and leniency did not have the negative effect that one might expect, however, for much was demanded of the children as well. His and Martha's submissiveness was paralleled by an equal amount of firmness that expected of them punctuality, order, self-discipline, a respect for each other, candor, and honesty. Martin reported the experience of his father looking him straight in the eye and seeming to be able to read his thoughts. In short, the Freuds treated their sons and daughters like adults and expected them to respond in kind. The result of this child-rearing strategy unusual for its time was an amazingly harmonious family atmosphere. The children were encouraged to share with each other; selfishness was frowned upon; and none of them as adults could recall a quarrel among themselves, let alone with either parent.

Much of the credit had to be given to Martha, for she was almost wholly responsible for their education. Freud in fact seemed to back away from the role of educator, especially in matters related to sexuality. Although he believed that children should be informed about sex before the age of eleven, he was not willing or able to perform the function himself, and instead, he sent his sons to the family doctor for instruction. One sees here one of the ironic truths about the founder of psychanalysis, with its legendary enlightened views on sexual mores: that he was an extremely shy and puritanical man, who found it difficult, if not impossible, personally to practice what he suggested in theory. It is interesting to note here that "Martha would not allow," as Paul Roazen put it, "psychoanalytic ideas to invade the nursery."[4] Theodor Reik in fact reported the following regarding Martha's reaction to her husband's work. "From conversations on walks on the Semmering, near Vienna, I got the decided impression that she not only had no idea of the significance and importance of psychoanalysis, but had intensive emotional resistances against the character of analytic work."[5]

Freud set a grueling work schedule for himself, and although he was always available when needed—his office was only several rooms away from the living quarters—he was seldom present for the daily interactions of the family. This psychological distance was not uncharacteristic of his own father or for that matter of traditional fathers within Jewish culture in general, where the woman would take charge of the family and all its worldly interactions in order to allow the man to pursue his scholarly activities without distraction. The following exerpt from Ernest Jones's biography provides an excellent flavor of his presence in the family.

> The family lunch was at one o'clock. This was the only time when the whole family would usually be together, the evening meal was often so late that the younger members had already retired to bed. It was the chief meal of the day, and was a substantial one of soup, meat, cheese, etc., and a sweet. Freud enjoyed his food and would concentrate on it. He was very taciturn during meals, which would sometimes be a source of embarrassment to visitors who had to carry on a conversation alone with the family. Freud, however, never missed a word of the family intercourse and daily news. If a child should be missing from a meal, Freud would point mutely at the vacant chair with his knife or fork and look inquiringly to his wife at the other end of the table. She would explain that the child was not coming in to dinner or that something or

other had detained him, whereupon Freud, his curiosity satisfied, would nod and silently proceed with his meal. All he wanted was to be kept in touch with the family doings.[6]

The only exception to Freud's highly regimented routine was during family holidays, which often lasted the entire summer. During these periods the family would go off en masse into the countryside to take up residence at some resort or spa or out-of-the-way village. At these times, and when he was not traveling on his own or with a colleague, the children would have his undivided attention and he became for them a playmate as much as a father. In this regard one is again reminded of Martin's description of his grandfather Jacob.

Beneath the often playful exterior Freud experienced significant anxiety over his childrens' future. Unlike his own mother, however, he kept these feelings to himself, not wishing to burden his family with personal concerns or worries. His role as father was to protect not to burden those around him. His greatest hope and concurrently his most significant fear was that his children be spared the hardships he had experienced earlier in life. His concerns resided in two areas: poverty and anti-Semitism.

He had, first of all, spent much of his life worrying about finances. His family had lived in poverty for their first several years in Vienna and he had become largely responsible for its welfare at a relatively early age. The Freuds had regularly borrowed money from relatives during this period, and on several occasions Sigmund had felt the need to contact his stepbrothers in England with an urgent plea for help. Throughout the unversity years he continued on a limited budget and in medical school found it necessary to borrow extensively. Such dependence on others, even when it was necessary for survival, was not something that sat well with Freud, however.[7] Monitary woes had also intruded themselves into his life in regard to the four years of engagement he and Martha had tolerated and the decision to forsake a research career for medical practice in the hope of better future earnings. He was currently responsible for supporting not only a wife and six children but also his mother, his maiden sister, and Martha's sister Minna. And even with growing fame, money never ceased being a matter of concern. According to Jones, for instance, in 1913 the Austrian tax department wrote to him expressing their astonishment that his income was not larger, "since everyone knows that his reputation extends far beyond the frontier of Austria." To this he replied: "Prof. Freud is very honored at receiving communication from the Government. It is the first time the Government has taken any notice of him and he acknowledges it. There is one point in which He cannot agree with the communication: that his reputation extends far beyond the frontier of Austria. It begins at the frontier."[8] In sum, the lack of money had caused him great pain in his life and he vowed to spare his children such indignities.

To this end he was determined to give his children everything they desired both for their pleasure and education and to do so until they were able to earn their own livings. He somehow always managed to do this even when times were bad, as for example after World War I when inflation had eroded away most of the family's savings. It was equally important to him that his children be kept in the dark about family financial problems, for again the point was to allow them to grow up anxiety-free. He was generous to a fault and refused absolutely to skimp on his children in matters of health, education, or travel. He also believed strongly that being well-dressed was important to a child's self-respect.

Freud was equally if not more concerned about his children's, especially his sons', futures as Jews. Because he himself felt so little control over the outside world and its anti-Semitism, he unconsciously sought to protect them in a variety of ways. His sons he named after eminent non-Jews—Martin for Charcot, Oliver for Cromwell, and Ernst for his teacher Brucke—as if by sympathetic magic he could imbue them with the stature and freedom from persecution that each of their namesakes enjoyed. His daughters, obviously of less concern in this regard, were named after Jews and after family friends at that: Mathilde for Josef Breuer's wife, Sophie for Professor Hammerschlag's niece, and Anna for the professor's daughter. He also strongly discouraged his sons from pursuing careers in medicine. He hoped no doubt to spare them the anti-Semitism and special obstacles to career advancement that he as a Jewish physician had continually encountered since leaving medical school.

An unspoken strategy the Freuds adopted to insulate their Jewish children from a hostile world was to make them as indistinguishable from gentiles as possible. There is a picture of Freud's three sons as children[9] that showed them dressed to the teeth in traditional German garb, sporting wooden rifles at their side. One could not possibly tell from the picture that these were Jewish youngsters. In various subtle ways—clothing, manners, habits, and activities—he also sought unconsciously to instill in his children the bearing and demeanor of non-Jews. Martha, thoroughly German in her manner and highly cultured in her ways, was a useful model and teacher in this regard. Freud for his part had done all he could to remove a Jewish consciousness from their home and even consented, or perhaps suggested, the introduction of a Christmas tree and Easter eggs so that the children might not feel different, that is, Jewish. What becomes apparent in Freud in relation to these various efforts is a discomfort and even embarrassment at obvious signs of Jewishness. In this regard one is reminded of his adolescent antipathy for traditional Jews, who like his traveling companions on the train from Freiberg were so conspicuous in their stereotyped Jewish traits and behaviors.

Martin Freud tells the story of an incident that occurred in the Biergarten at St. Bartholmae while the family was on vacation that dramatically portrays this discomfort in Freud. The incident was particularly memorable to young Martin because of the enormous impact it had on his father. Seated next to the Freuds was a typical middle-class, Jewish Berlin family with a son about the same age as the Freud children. The boy was sent to fetch some water from a well and managed in the process to drench himself as well as spill water on an irate guest. Freud himself was not in the least amused by the scene, but rather remarked coldly and in a voice loud enough for the boy's parents to overhear that he hoped his own children would never give "so shocking a display" if sent on a similar task. Freud's anger was uncharacteristic, and Martin later interpreted it as related to the boy's ethnicity. "The boy who had disgraced himself so much in his father's eyes was plainly Jewish in an unmistakable and not attractive way . . . and this was quickly seen by the Gentiles of the Biergarten who watched the performance with amused disdain." Martin further suggested that perhaps his father feared that his own Jewish children might someday meet a similar fate because of "bad upbringing" and like the boy "in effect let our side down." Evidently, Freud was successful in shaping the demeanor of his children, for Martin and his siblings were not conscious of any racial discrimination against them during childhood. "Although we were not easily recognized as Jewish, we could not be mistaken for Bavarian or Austrian Gentiles. 'Your children, Frau Professor,' a polite German lady once remarked to mother, 'look so Italian.'"

Also related to Freud's concern for his children was a dream he described in *The Interpretation of Dreams*. In this classic work, believed by many to be the seminal text of psychoanalysis, he offered his ideas on the relationship between dreaming and the unconscious and used analyses of his own dreams as illustrations. Dreams, Freud believed, were "the royal road to the unconscious," for during sleep the inner censor relaxes and emotions and conflicts too threatening to be acknowledged in waking consciousness emerge in disguised form. The data reported by Freud in *The Interpretation of Dreams* was so intimate and revealing—coming as it did from his own self-analysis—that he postponed its publication for several months and later in his *Autobiography* regretted the inclusion of material "in which I had to surrender so much of my initimate nature."[11] A number of the dreams recorded therein deal quite explicitly in fact with Freud's Jewishness and in particular his desire to leave it behind.

The dream in question, called within the literature "My Son the Myops," focuses specifically on his anxiety over his sons' destiny as Jews. In it, because of certain unusual events that have taken place in Rome, "it had become necessary to remove the children to safety." Freud was seated on the edge of a fountain near the Porta Romana at Siena, "greatly depressed and almost in tears." A female attendant or nun escorted two boys out of the double doors of the gate and returned them to their father who was not Freud. The older of the two is Freud's eldest son. The face of the second boy is not visible. The woman asked the boy to kiss her farewell. At this point in the dream Freud is aware of her having a "red nose." The boy would not kiss her but rather held out his hand in parting and said *"Auf Geseres"* to her and then *"Auf Ungeseres"* to the others. "I had a notion that this last phrase denoted a preference."[12]

According to Freud, this dream was "constructed on a tangle of thoughts" encouraged by his viewing of a play *The New Ghetto*, written by Theodor Herzl. The play dealt with an assimilated Jewish family's painful and desperate desire to transcend their origins and gain entry into mainstream culture. It ended with the hero's dying plea: "I want to get out; Out! Out of the Ghetto!"[13] Since Freud was not a regular theater-goer, the play itself must have held some special meaning or attraction for him. He interpreted its general significance as follows: "The Jewish problem, concern about the future of one's children to whom one cannot give a country of their own, concern over educating them in such a way that they can move freely across frontiers—all of this was easily recognizable among the relevant dream thoughts."[14]

Less transparent yet equally accessible throught the dream's symbolism were Freud's own conflicted feelings about getting out of the ghetto at any cost, that is, religious conversion. The dream is set in Rome, which for Freud served as a symbol of Christianity and the non-Jewish world. Traveling to Rome in turn came unconsciously to represent a rejection of his Jewishness. It will be remembered that at Jacob's disclosure of what his son experienced as cowardice in the face of an anti-Semitic affront, Sigmund transferred his allegiance and identification to Hannibal, who had sworn "to take vengeance on the Romans."[15] Porta Romana in Siena, the actual scene of the dream, also held strong associations of anti-Semitism for Freud, for he had recently heard that a Jewish doctor working at the insane asylum there had been forced to resign because of discrimination. The fountain and his weeping at it Freud associated with the opening lines of the 137th Psalm. "By the rivers of Babylon there we sat down, yea, we wept, when we remembered Zion." This psalm deals with the destruction of the Temple and the Jewish people's subsequent exile and suffering as "strangers in a strange land" and ends with a warning of the dire consequences that should befall "If I forget thee, O Jerusalem," perhaps a reference to the enormous personal price a Jew must pay in order to convert.

The nun who represented the church and bore a strong resemblance to Freud's nursemaid, the very person who had first introduced him to the world of the gentile, was turning his sons over to a new father and thus severing the ties to him and his heritage. Freud's eldest son, however, refused to kiss her good-bye, perhaps indicating his displeasure with what was taking place. Instead, he said to her *"Auf Geseres,"* a play on words with the traditional German goodbye (*Auf Wiedersehn*), and to the others *"Auf Ungeseres,"* which Freud felt implied some kind of preference. *"Geseres"* is Yiddish and means "imposed suffering and doom," again possibly an allusion to the consequences of conversion for the Jew. Freud further associated the word pair *Geseres-Ungeseres* with the unleavened bread that Jews eat at Passover as a symbol of their exile. He however referred to it as Easter, a not uncommon habit for him, but in this context likely a reflection of his ambivalence.

Through this dream in which Freud revealed his own uncertainty over the ultimate wisdom of conversion, the character of his son emerged on the side of remaining Jewish. Buried in the symbolism is the implication that the cure, in this case conversion, might well prove more hazardous than the disease, that is, retaining one's identity. This thought brings us to the opening lines of the dream. According to Freud, "myops" was a term constructed by joining "myopia" and "Cyclops" and it implied shortsightedness or limited vision. This in turn could refer either to a child cut off from his or her heritage and thus unable to look back or an impulsive decision, as in the act of conversion, to further one's career or social position, made without full consideration of its ultimate implications. With this dream Freud made the unconscious decision to remain a Jew. As will become apparent in our fuller discussion of Freud's inner struggle around the problem of conversion, this choice marked a significant turning point in the evolution of his Jewish identity and helped partially to resolve his longstanding ambivalence.

\* \* \*

Freud's feelings about Zionism offer yet another aspect of his ambivalence. While he was fully aware of the movement and its evolution in his home city of Vienna and was in many ways personally connected to it, he could never quite bring himself to endorse it fully or become a militant Zionist like so many of his Jewish contemporaries. This did not mean, however, that he did not support it in a variety of ways.

His sons Martin and Ernest were both Zionists and belonged to Kadimah and the Kartell Judischer Verbindungen[16] respectively while they were students at the University of Vienna. Freud fully approved of their participation and was in fact himself made an honorary member of Kadimah in 1936. In the 1920s he made several "substantial" contributions to Hechalutz, another Zionist organization, and for a number of years he followed quite closely the happenings in the Middle East. In 1917, for example, in the midst of a deep depression over the dismal events of World War I, he wrote: "The only cheerful news is the capture of Jerusalem by the English and the experiment they propose about a home for the Jews."[17] When the

Hebrew University was founded, he willingly agreed to serve on its board and even dreamed, for a short while anyway, of establishing there a chair in psychoanalysis for Max Eitingon, who had settled in Palestine in 1933. Lastly, Freud was an admirer of Chaim Weizmann, Israel's first president, who had informed him through Ernest Jones "that immigrants from Galicia arrived there with no clothes, but with copies of *Das Kapital* and *Die Traumdeutung (The Interpretation of Dreams)* under their arms."

In his statements on Zionism, however, there was always a sense of reservation and a lack of willingness to commit himself fully. In a 1926 letter to Professor Friedrich Thieberger, for example, he wrote. "Towards Zionism I have only sympathy, but I make no judgment on it, on its chances of success and on the possible dangers facing it."[18] In 1935 he told Joseph Wortis that he was not as ardent a Zionist as Einstein and in the Preface to the Hebrew edition of *Totem and Taboo* he claimed a lack of "nationalistic ideals"[19] in his connection to Judaism. Only once did he seem to wholeheartedly support the cause, and this in relation to a non-Jewish Italian journalist who, after offering substantial critism of psychoanalysis, was exceedingly more generous in his assessment of Zionism. In this instance Freud seemed more interested in playing the role of defender of the faith than in offering his honest feelings. On several occasions he even spoke of Palestine in romantic and mystical terms. He called it a "strange and fantastic country"[20] in a letter to Arnold Zweig, and elsewhere he wrote "Strange secret yearnings rise up in me—perhaps from my ancestral heritage—for the East and the Mediterranean and for a life of quite another time."[21] But once something like that was stated, something within him would resist and require a negative or at least distancing rejoinder.

Three possible reasons for Freud's hesitancy vis-à-vis Zionism suggest themselves. The first was his longstanding suspicion of nationalistic movements. This attitude is well-captured in his reply to Arnold Zweig, who had found Palestine a restrictive environment in which to live and work.[22] "Your letter moved me very much. It is not the first time that I have heard of difficulties the cultured man finds in adapting to Palestine. History has never given the Jewish people cause to develop their faculty for creating a state or a society. And of course they take with them all the shortcomings and vices in the culture of the country they leave behind them into their new abode."[23]

As an enlightened thinker, Freud would have by intellectual inclination tended to mistrust national movements, much in the same way that such a worldview would have sensitized him to the evils of religion and religious institutions. But, as was evident from our analysis of the latter, personal as well as intellectual concerns fueled Freud's attacks on religion. A similar dynamic might be suspected in relation to his hesitancy about Zionism as a national movement. In his youth Freud had in fact identified strongly with Germany and German culture. As a student, for instance, he had belonged to the Leseverein der deutschen Studenten, a student fraternity that advocated the annexation of German Austria by Germany proper.

His fascination with all things German faded quickly however when he realized the intimate connection between German nationalism and anti-Semitism. One can almost sense in the following 1926 quotation an underlying anger and possibly even embarrassment at his previous naivete. "My language is German. My culture, my attainments are German. I considered myself German intellectually, until I noticed the growth of anti-Semitic prejudice in Germany and German Austria. Since that time I consider myself no longer German. I prefer to call myself a Jew."[24] Freud first expressed his reservations in this regard many years earlier in a letter to his then fiancée Martha in which he described an evening at Charcot's home in Paris. "Toward the end I embarked on a political conversation with Giles de la Tourette (a prominent neurologist), during which he of course predicted the most furious war with Germany. I promptly explained that I am a Jew, adhering neither to Germany nor Austria. But such conversations are always very embarrassing to me, for I feel stirring within me something German which I long ago decided to suppress."[25] Given this bit of biographical background, it would not seem surprising for Freud to feel some reserve or hesitation when the topic of nationalism arose, even Jewish nationalism, or for him to suppress any surges of Zionistic excitement, were they to well up inside of him.

A second possible cause of Freud's hesitancy may have been related to his antipathy toward the Jewish religion and the fear that once established, a Jewish homeland might stimulate a rebirth of interest in Orthodoxy. Freud made this very point in a conversation with Joseph Wortis about a Jewish homeland. "I was afraid for a while . . . that Zionism would become the occasion for a revival of the old religion, but I have been assured by people who have been there that all the young Jews are irreligious, which a good thing."[26] A similar sentiment emerged in a letter to Arnold Zweig. "How strange this tragically mad land you have visited must seem to you. Just think, this strip of our mother earth is connected with no other progress, no discovery or invention . . . . Palestine has never produced anything but religions, sacred frenzies, presumptuous attempts to overcome the outer world of appearance by means of the inner world of wishful thinking."[27]

Finally, there is the possibility that Freud's ambivalence toward Zionism was related to his feelings about its founder, Theodor Herzl. It is strange, first of all, that the two never met, at least according to Freud. They lived on the same block in Vienna, almost across the street from each other. Their daughters were friends. And being approximately the same age, both Jewish and aspiring middle-class professionals, they must have at various times in their lives moved in similar social circles.

Also puzzling was Freud's seeming disregard for Herzl's accomplishments. Herzl's name, a veritable household word in Vienna, was never once mentioned in Freud's voluminous correspondence. This is in spite of the fact that he regularly commented on current news and happenings of the day, especially when they involved his fellow Jews. He particularly focused, for example, on Emile Zola in his letters to Wilhelm Fliess during the period of the Dreyfus trial in Paris, but he made no mention of Herzl, who covered the trial for his favorite newspaper *Die Freie Presse* and gained substantial renown because of it. Freud in addition omitted Herzl's name as author of *The New Ghetto* in his discussion of the "My Son the Myops" dream, as well as a dream episode involving the founder of Zionism that eventually found its way into *Introductory Lectures on Psycho-Analysis*. Such omissions were especially unusual for Freud, who was always meticulous in his scholarship and the citing of references. And in his only formal contact with Herzl, a written request that the journalist review *The Interpretation of Dreams* for *Die Neue Freie Presse,* Freud is courteous but clearly cautious in his remarks. "But at all events, may I ask you to keep the book as a token of the high esteem in which I—like so many others—have held since many years the poet and the fighter for the human rights of our People."[28]

Freud's avoidance of Herzl may have had dual sources. The

first was related to the "My Son the Myops" dream. It may well have been that Freud unconsciously associated religious conversion with Herzl, and since he was himself conflicted over the issue, he may have avoided reference to Herzl as a way of distancing himself from his own inner struggles. Two pieces of evidence are relevant here. In a second dream in which Herzl actually appeared to Freud, a message similar to that of "My Son the Myops" emerged again. Dr. Josef Freud, a relative of Sigmund's who attended the lecture in which Freud described it, remembered Freud's description as follows: "An appearance filled with glory, with a dark yet pale countenance, adorned with an attractive black beard, and with eyes which expressed infinite grief. The apparition attempted to persuade Freud of the need of immediate action, if the Jewish people was to be saved. These words astonished him by their logic and their pent up emotion."[29] Freud added that he had never previously seen Herzl, but had once subsequently encountered him on a bus and was astonished by the similarity between his real appearance and that of the apparition. Freud reported several other instances of personal experiences with the "uncanny" such as this one, and each involved the potential breakthrough of highly emotional and repressed inner material. Freud may have also associated Herzl with conversion because prior to commiting himself to the establishment of a homeland as a solution to the Jewish problem, Herzl had briefly toyed with the idea (until the editors of his paper blatantly refused to support him) of a mass conversion of Jewish children.

It is also possible that Freud harbored secret jealousies of Herzl and of his eminence. Freud was an exceptionally ambitious man. He desperately craved success and fame, but such rewards were slow in coming because of the enormous resistance his ideas evoked. He did not in fact really live long enough to see the full impact of his work. In addition he experienced grave doubts about his own abilities and these would always color his assessment of his work and rob him of the true magnitude of his greatness. Ernest Jones for instance suggested that Freud did not really feel himself to be a "great man,"[30] in spite of all the early prophecies. He saw promise in his ideas but not in himself and in fact believed, according to Jones, that he had poor intellectual capacities. His own estimate of what he had accomplished in life was rather guarded. "Looking back, then, over the patchwork of my life's labors, I can say that I have made many beginnings and thrown out many suggestions.

Something will come of them in the future, though I cannot myself tell whether it will be much or little."[31] Given also the traumas of the final years of life—the illness and suffering, the necessity of leaving much of his life behind in Vienna, the Nazi's almost total destruction of psychoanalysis on the European continent, and the substantial criticism that even his last work received—he might well have felt himself a failure in the end.

Herzl's success, on the other hand, was more immediate, and unlike Freud, he was much more the extrovert: self-assured, somewhat of a dandy and showman, comfortable and highly effective in the political arena, and more than willing to bask in the glory of his fame. Freud for his part was rather inept at wielding power. One need only witness the many intrigues and defections that filled the history of psychoanalysis. Several biographers have in fact described him as politically naive and, surprisingly enough, a rather poor judge of character. Freud himself may have been well aware of these inadequacies. A bit of self-awareness in this realm may unconsciously have fueled his usual reluctance to enter the political arena and his pessimism about political solutions to problems. His reply of July 1923 to a young friend in Germany who asked his advice about fighting Nazism was typical: "I would advise you against wasting your energies in the fruitless struggle against the current political movement. Mass psychoses are proof against arguments. It is just the Germans who had occasion to learn this in the world war, but they seem unable to do so. Let them alone. Devote yourself to the thing that can raise the Jews above all this foolishness."[32] Freud was clearly more interested in the politics of the inner life and made it the object of his life's work.

In his emergence as a international political figure, Herzl was living out Freud's early fantasy of becoming a great statesman. "It was the days of the 'bourgeois Ministry' . . . There were even Jews among them so that every diligent Jewish schoolboy carried a ministerial portfolio in his satchel."[33] Like Freud, Herzl identified with the figure of Moses and in fact became a contemporary leader of his people, leading them out of a modern exile. Unconsciously, Freud shared a similar vision for himself, as we shall see in the discussion *Moses and Monotheism*.

Freud's own early life had been spent forsaking fantasies, one after the next—cabinet minister, great writer, eminent research scientist, England. His youthful dreams were repeatedly overshadowed by the realities of just surviving in the world, and it would not be surprising in the least for him to harbor envy for someone, perhaps not very different from himself, who like Herzl was living out those very fantasies of greatness. To single out a public figure such as Herzl and to develop an emotional attachment to him, as is being suggested here, was not out of character for Freud. He had done the same in fact with Arthur Schnitzler, the famous Viennese novelist and playwright. On the occasion of Schnitzler's sixtieth birthday Freud wrote the following to him. "I shall make you a confession ... which you will kindly, in consideration of me, keep to yourself and not share with either friend or stranger. I have been struggling with the question of why I have never, in all these years, made any effort to meet you and to talk with you.... I think I have avoided you out of a kind of a fear of finding my own double *(Doppelgänger)*.... When I read one of your beautiful works I seem to encounter again and again, behind the poetic fiction, the presumptions, interests, and conclusions of my own thoughts."[34]

\* \* \*

The years from 1894 to 1901 were particularly critical and difficult ones for Freud. The period began with his break with Josef Breuer, was followed two years later by the death of his father, which in large measure stimulated his self-analysis, and ended with the completion of that analysis as symbolized by his delayed yet successful visit to Rome. In the interim he would experience severe personal and professional isolation, a seemingly unending series of painful discoveries about himself, a full-blown bout of anxiety neurosis, and the repeated rejection of his application for promotion to the rank of professor extraordinarius. He would emerge from it, however, a revitalized man: largely free of neurotic symptons, in possession of the basic seed-notions of psychoanalysis, and emotionally prepared to return to the world and begin his forging of the psychoanalytic movement. This outcome, perhaps more than any other evidence he could offer over the years, stood as clear testimony to the value of his therapeutic method.

Jacob's death at eighty-one was an unexpected trauma for the then-forty-year-old Sigmund. He wrote the following to Fliess a week after his father's passing. "By one of the obscure routes behind the official consciousness the old man's death affected me deeply. I valued him highly and understood him very well indeed, and with his peculiar mixture of deep wisdom and imaginative light-heartedness he meant a great deal in my life. By the time he died his life had long been over, but at a death the whole past stirs within one. I feel now as if I had been torn up by the roots."[35] In the preface to *The Interpretation of Dreams*, which along with his letters to Fliess served as the primary sources of knowledge about his self-analysis, he called a father's death "the most important event, the most poignant loss, of a man's life."[36] By this he was referring not only to the physical passing of his father, but also to the heightened awareness and loss of innocence that the self-analysis brought about. Through it he discovered the presence of unsettling, even shocking, feelings toward himself and those he loved, in particular his father for whom he consciously had never been aware of anything but deep love and respect. These previously unknown and unacknowledged feelings—passion, ambition, hostilities, resentment, and guilt lurked beneath the surface, yet were still a very integral part of his personality. From these painful insights he would in time fashion his theory of the unconscious.

Otto Rank has suggested that part of the potency of Freud's reaction may have stemmed from his recent rejection of Breuer[37], who in many ways had served as a substitute father by giving him many of the things Jacob could not: money, personal advice, professional guidance and support. As will become clear in the next chapter, Freud could tolerate neither his personal debt to the older doctor nor what he experienced as Breuer's cowardice at not being willingly to pursue the sexual etiology of hysteria, a clear reverberation from the past. Unable to directly grieve or acknowledge his sense of loss at the rejection of Breuer, he unconsciously channeled his feelings through the death of his father. The break with Breuer would mark the beginning of what he called his "splendid isolation,"[38] almost ten years of intellectual isolation, with Fliess his only audience and outlet. He had by then almost totally alienated Vienna's medical establishment with his ideas on sexuality.

During the 1890s, especially the latter half, Freud suffered from what he himself diagnosed as an anxiety neurosis. It consisted of exteme changes of mood as well as more localized symptons, including occasional attacks of dread of death, anxiety over rail travel, and a fear of traveling to Rome. Jones described the mood shifts as follows: "The alteration of mood were between periods of elation, excitement, and self-confidence on the one hand and periods of severe depression, doubt, and inhibition on the other. In the depressed moods he could neither read nor concentrate his thoughts . . . unable to continue at anything for long. . . . Sometimes there were spells where consciousness would be greatly narrowed: states, difficult to describe, with a veil that produced almost a twilight condition of mind."[39] Freud also took to complaining incessantly about his health, as witnessed in his letters to Fliess. This was particularly uncharacteristic behavior, for he would spend the last twenty years of his life in progressively increasing pain due to cancer of the jaw, but with little complaint about his condition. So severe were the neurotic repercussions of his father's death that by the middle of 1897 he undertook a formal self-analysis. This he did by systematically applying the methods he had developed for his patients to himself. As is often the case with such analyses, his symptons grew worse before they improved, but by the end of the century he was experiencing significant relief.

A contributing source of anxiety for Freud was his lackluster medical career. His practice was erratic at best and clearly feeling the effects of diminishing professional referrals because of his shocking views on sexuality. Most of his patients were in fact coming from outside Vienna, sent by more sympathetic colleagues elsewhere. He was in particular frustrated by the fact that he had been a *Privatdocent* for almost twelve years. In addition to being a blow to his ego, the exceptionally long delay in promotion was a financial matter, for to attain the rank of professor in status-conscious Vienna was an almost certain guarantee of patients and substantially increased fees. The reality, however, was that his colleagues on the Faculty Council were far from enamored with his work, and the Minister of Education, Wilhem von Hartel, was an anti-Semite who always saw to it that Jewish candidates were somehow passed over. After a few early attempts to rally support and gain the promotion, Freud gave in to the seeming futility of it and subsequently did little to further his own cause.

In January of 1897, however, he was approached by his former teacher Professor Carl Nothnagel, who was outraged by the fact that Freud had been passed over for a colleague who was his junior in his specialty, with an offer to intercede on his behalf along with Professors Kraft-Ebbing and Frankl-Hochwart. But he warned Freud: "You know the further difficulties; perhaps we should achieve nothing more than 'putting you on the carpet.'"[40] Freud was touched by their efforts and submitted halfheartedly the required materials as they requested, but he was once again passed over. This would continue until 1901.

Soon after Freud's contact with Nothnagel, he met two Jewish colleague's from the university who had also been passed over for promotion: one because of a criminal accusation leveled against him, the other merely because he was a Jew. The latter had in fact confronted the ministry and had been told the reason in no uncertain terms. That night Freud had a dream, "The Uncle with the Yellow Beard,"[41] in which he transformed the second colleague into his Uncle Josef, a simpleton brother of Jacob who had gotten in trouble with the law during Sigmund's youth. Freud submitted the dream to a detailed analysis and was shocked by the naked feelings and associations that emerged. He discovered: that to be Jewish was to be somehow tainted; that to satisfy his enormous ambition for promotion he would disavow his identity as a Jew, and that, harkening back to his youthful fantasy of becoming a minister of state, he secretly identified with the power of the anti-Semitic minister of education.

The discovery of such feelings must have truly unsettled Freud, for consciously he saw himself as a loyal, although godless, Jew. Repeatedly throughout life, he affirmed his Jewish identity. "My parents were Jews and I have remained a Jew myself."[42] "My service to the Jewish cause is confined to the single point that I have never denied my Jewishness."[43] "I have never lost the feeling of solidarity with my people."[44] And "The present writer a Jew who has never sought to disguise the fact that he is a Jew."[45] There is in fact little evidence that Freud ever gave serious conscious contemplation to the idea of converting to Christianity. The only possible exception was the fleeting idea to change his "confession" as a means of avoiding a religious wedding ceremony. He was so quick to abandon the idea at Breuer's suggestion, however, that it was more an act of posturing than anything seriously considered.

Conversion as a means of solving one's problems as a Jew was not an unfamiliar notion to Freud, however. His favorite poet Heinrich Heine had called baptism an "entrance ticket" to European society and had himself taken that decisive step, as had Freud's other intellectual hero, Ludwig Borne.[46] So influential were these two literary figures that he sought out their graves during his time in Paris with Charcot. Borne, a highly principled man whose works Freud received as a present on his thirteenth birthday, chose to convert in order more fully to participate in mainstream culture. His intention at the time was to change it. Heine converted to ensure a livelihood for himself, that is, to gain more alternatives in employment. Always sarcastic and biting, he summarized his motivations as follows: "If one could lawfully steal silver spoons I would not have been christened."[47]

Both men had changed their names on the occasions of their baptisms: Heine from Harry to Heinrich and Borne from his original name, Lob Baruch. One must wonder if Freud was at all influenced by either when he decided to call himself the more Germanic-sounding Sigmund, as opposed to Sigismund, which was a frequently used name in anti-Semitic jokes of the day. Both Heine and Borne had however retained their old initials, a not uncommon unconscious practice among Jews who changed their names for social purposes. It is not known how Borne fared as a convert, although it is clear that he remained connected to Judaism. Heine, for his part, was far from happy with the consequences. "I am very sorry I was christened; I do not see that things have gone any better with me since; on the contrary, I have had nothing but ill luck from that time. Is it not fooling? No sooner have I been christened than I am cried down as a Jew."[48] More than likely Freud also knew other Jewish converts personally, for the decision was a very common one among Viennese Jews. In the year 1900, for example, 559 of his fellow Jews took the fateful step.

After his analysis of the "The Uncle with the Yellow Beard" dream in *The Interpretation of Dreams*, Freud introduced "a series of dreams that are based upon a longing to visit Rome."[49] These four dreams are of great importance because they lead to the roots of his desire to disavow his ties with Judaism and also they uncover inner material that helps to explain some of his career difficulties. Between 1895 and 1898 Freud had vacationed in Italy on five different occasions without once reaching Rome, though he desperately desired to do so. He had even gotten to within fifty miles, but as always, he found a reason to turn back. Travel, like cards and cigars, was a passion for Freud, but one associated with much anxiety. He would later as part of his self-analysis trace the roots of his train phobia back to the unhappy journey at the age of four when he left Freiberg with his parents. Rome, for its part, was associated with such inner discomfort that to travel there was for a long time impossible.

In each Rome dream the city somehow eluded Freud, or more correctly, he found a means of hiding it and its true meaning from himself. In the first dream he dreamt he was viewing the River Tiber at the Pont Sant' Angelo from a train carriage window. As the train pulled away, he realized he had not "so much as set foot in the city." In the second dream he was led to the top of a hill to view Rome "half-shrouded in mist." He was struck by the fact that he could see so clearly in spite of the great distance. There was further content in it that Freud chose not to share, but its theme, he acknowledged, was "the promised land seen from afar." In the third dream Freud found himself in Rome but was disappointed to find that its scenery was rural: a narrow stream of dark water with black cliffs on one side and meadows full of large white flowers on the other. Freud then saw a Herr Zucker with whom he was slightly acquainted and was "determined to ask him the way to the city." In a fourth dream, which took place soon after the third, he found himself once again in Rome. He saw a streetcorner and "was surprised to find so many posters in German stuck up there."[50]

In his associations to the first dream, Freud was reminded of a sentence he had read long ago. "Which of the two, it may be debated, walked up and down his study with the greater impatience after he had formed his plan of going to Rome— Winckelmann . . . or Hannibal"[51] Winckelmann had converted from Protestantism to Catholicism in order to take a Vatican position there; Hannibal had vowed to destroy it. The sentence in turn reminded him of his boyhood attachment to the latter. During his later school days Hannibal had been a favorite hero to Freud. While studying the Punic Wars, for instance, he identified not with the Romans, but rather with the Carthaginians. "When in the higher classes I began to understand for the first time what it meant to belong to an alien race, the anti-Semitic feelings among the other boys warned me that I must take up a definite position, the figure of the Semitic general rose still higher in my esteem." In his mind Hannibal and Rome came to symbolize the struggle between the tenacity of the Jews and the structure of the church. "Thus the wish to go to Rome had become in my dream-life a cloak and symbol for a number of other passionate wishes."[52]

That one of these "passionate wishes" was in fact an unconscious desire to reject his father and by association the heritage he represented became clear at this point in the analysis, for it was here that he recalled and told the story of Jacob, the anti-Semitic insult, and his determination to follow in Hannibal's rather than his father's footsteps. The association of Freud's father with the Rome series of dreams provides insight into the intensity of the effects of Jacob's death for his son. On the night of Jacob's funeral Freud had had another dream in which he was reproached by his family for his late arrival at the ceremony. The day residue for this one, which is referred to in the literature as "You Are Requested to Close The Eyes" because of a sign to that effect that appeared in the dream, was an actual disagreement among family members over Jacob's ceremony and involved Freud's desire to reduce its religiosity to a minimum. The dominant emotional theme was guilt and self-reproach. If one juxtaposes this dream, the day residue that stimulated it, and insights gained through the Rome series, what emerges is the realization that what Freud wanted his father to close his eyes to was his son's desire to disavow his Jewishness. This unconscious wish had stimulated feelings of guilt and shame in Freud, which in turn blocked his entry into Christian Rome.

In the second Rome dream, much of which Freud refused to report, he offered the first hint of his identification with Moses as well as an attraction to Rome, not Israel, as the promised land. In the third dream, an association was established between Rome and the act of baptism, which Freud unconsciously viewed as a cure for the constitutional disease of Jewishness. The theme of Jewishness as a disease surfaced in yet another dream of this period[53] in which great anger is directed toward Jacob for his role as the transmitter of the social humiliation, poverty, and taintedness of being Jewish. In the final dream of the series, Freud relocated the scene of the drama and his Jewish problems to their actual setting in waking consciousness, German Austria. Through this custer of dreams, Freud's inner psychology concerning Rome and his reluctance to travel to it emerged and thus set the stage for its resolution.

Because of the distasteful story Jacob had shared with Sigmund, the young boy came to believe that there were only two ways a Jew could relate to the Christian world: to conquer it outright, as Hannibal had intended to do, or to succumb to it, as he felt his father had done. Within Freud's personal mythology, in addition, succumbing had come to mean conversion. Rome both attracted and repelled him, for it simultaneously represented the world of antiquities that he admired and to which he was powerfully drawn and the Catholic church, which he regarded as his enemy. To enter Rome as anything but its conqueror however was tantamount to defeat and submission, for in spite of his underlying negative feelings about his father and his Jewishness, he could not bring himself consciously to renounce either. These then were some of the complex forces fueling Freud's inability to enter Rome. To make matters even worse he developed the magical belief that if he could only somehow reach Rome all of his worsening career problems would be resolved.

The curative value of his self-analysis and its positive role in resolving some of these inner conflicts revolving around his Jewishness is attested to by the fact that in September of 1901 he finally entered Rome. Some progress to this end was evident in the "My Son the Myops" dream, which appeared at a later stage in the self-analysis. In it Freud had already entered Rome and in the process of the dream's drama made the decision to remain Jewish and not to convert. This unconscious working through no doubt robbed Rome of some of its mythical power and thus paved the way for his actual visit. His actions at home upon returning from Rome also demonstrated the resolution of his dicotomized thinking about being Jewish, that is, one either conquered the gentile world or is conquered by it. Such thinking explained Freud's general reticence in the matter of gaining support for his promotion; if he could not claim a total victory over the anti-Semitic minister and Faculty Council, then the only alternative was to give in and succumb completely.

Freud returned from Rome revitalized and able for the first time since the death of his father to function adequately and with some pleasure in his mundane role as a physician. No longer obsessed with magical solutions to his identity as a Jew, he was willing to do what was necessary to survive. He wrote the following to Fliess:

> When I got back from Rome, my zest for life and work had somewhat grown and my zest for martyrdom had somewhat diminished. I found that my practice had melted away. . . . I reflected that waiting for recognition might take up a good portion of the remainder of my life, and that in the meantime none of my fellow-men were likely to trouble about me. And I wanted to see Rome again and look after my patients and keep my children happy. So I made up my mind to break with my strict scruples and take appropriate steps, as others do after all. One must look somewhere for one's salvation, and the salvation I chose was the title of professor."[54]

Freud diligently pursued his goal of promotion. He reenlisted the support of Nothnagel and Kraft-Ebbing and in addition sought help from certain well-placed former patients in an effort to overcome the negative influence of von Hartel. As irony would have it, Freud won his position as the result of the intercession of a patient who upon hearing of her therapist's dilemma befriended the education minister and finally traded an expensive painting to be donated to a new university gallery in exchange for Freud's professorship. He could even joke about the whole matter to Fliess. "The population is participating extensively. Congratulation and bouquets are just now raining on me as if His Majesty had officially recognized the role of sexuality, the Council of Ministers had confirmed the importance of dreams, and the necessity of a psychoanalytic treatment of hysteria had been passed in Parliament with a two-thirds majority."[55]

But Rome had clearly taught him a valuable lesson in regard to the reality principle, at least as far as work was concerned. He would finally confess to Fliess. "In the whole affair there is one person with very long ears . . . and that is myself. If I had taken those few steps three years ago I should have been appointed three years earlier, and should have spared myself much. Others are just as clever, without having to go to Rome first."[56]

Freud's self-analysis, although it did not result in any major changes in character structure,[57] did manage to relieve much of the inner pressure that had built up over the preceeding years. Thwarted ambition—in the form of two barely missed opportunities for scientific fame (involving discoveries in neuron structure and cocaine), not to mention growing rejection by the Viennese medical community of his ideas about hysteria and sexuality—had been a major contributor to his anxiety neurosis. He emerged from the self-analysis with both a new resolve to continue his work and a specific vehicle upon which he could pin his hopes for fame and fortune success, the rudiments of psychoanalytic theory. In the process of exploring his own inner life he had stumbled upon what would become the cornerstones of his future system: infantile sexuality and the Oedipal complex. Interestingly enough, Freud chose to censor much of the sexual material that emerged during his self-analysis, and fortunately for the present purposes, what he presented in *The Interpretation of Dreams* was largely a study of the childhood roots of his enormous ambition in which his Jewishness played a major role. The principles that he gleaned from the sexual material would appear in later works and in a less personal form.

As an aside, it is interesting to note here that two theories explaining Freud's rejection of the seduction theory, the precursor to the Oedipal complex, have been recently put forth. Both relate to personal issues that emerged during the period of Freud's self-analysis. Jeffrey Masson, excommunicated by the analytic establishment for his recent heresy, has suggested that Freud gave up the seduction theory and the idea that hysterical patients actually were seduced as children to protect his friend Wilhelm Fliess, who had botched an operation on one of Freud's patients, and thus help to salvage what remained of his medical career, in what Masson portrayed as a failure of courage. Marianne Krull, on the other hand, believes Freud rejected the seduction theory and introduced the Oedipal complex in its place in order to distance himself sufficiently from the personal discoveries he was making about his parents. This manuever allowed Freud to continue with his self-analysis. According to Krull, the shift in concepts served to transfer blame from the father to the son and thereby removed any guilt he might have experienced at suggesting actual seduction and provided the son (in this case Freud) with his own justification—it was a universal process.

The emerging theory of psychoanalysis also served as a useful tool in mitigating some of Freud's hostility toward his father. In his unconscious he had been for years constructing a list of grievances against "the old man"—cowardice, a lack of German refinement, a passing on of defective Jewish genes, a poor provider, a failure, the source of all of Sigmund's problems, especially his Jewishness. The purpose of these accusations was to justify a rejection of Jacob so that he might in turn reject his Jewish heritage. Jacob's only crime in fact had been that he was what Marthe Robert has called a "vague" Jewish father,"[58] caught between the ghetto and the assimilated world, with little of substance from the past other than his perpetual insecurity to pass on to his son.

Beyond the cathartic release of hostility his self-analysis offered, Freud was able to displace additional anger onto the universal father of his theories by killing him off in the mind of the young boy child and in the actual deed of the prehistoric primal horde. As Krull has suggested, as the Oedipal father, Jacob could not be held accountable. These various strategies obviously had their desired effect, for from this point on in time Freud began to identify himself with the father as opposed to the son. He would no longer seek out father-substitutes such as Breuer and Fliess, but would instead become the father, as in the next significant relationship of his life, that with Carl Jung.

Psychoanalytic theory in turn offered Freud an avenue out of the dilemma of being either the conquering or conquered Jew. Hints of an emerging solution first appeared in a dream called "Count Thun,"[59] after the imaginary character created by Freud within it, which presented itself toward the end of the self-analysis. Freud once again found himself on a train, this time confronted by hostile gentiles who make him feel inferior. Rather than reacting with his characteristic anger and bravado, however, he was seized by a hatred for society and an image of himself as a revolutionary. This psychic solution was as pragmatic as it was cathartic. By declaring war on society he could simultaneously remain a Jew, demonstrate his outrage at the unjust treatment of his people, and leave his mark on the world, yet do so without isolating or incapacitating himself with an impossible dream like conquering Rome. His vehicle would become the science of psychoanalysis. But unlike the dilemma he had cornered himself with in relation to his promotion, he was now free to avail himself of whatever resources could be mustered, even including the use of gentiles in the development and transmission of his ideas.[60] That Freud felt such a solution would be acceptable to his father and within the bounds of his filial duties was clear from the final portion of the dream in which he was transformed from the revolutionary-savior to a lowly physician tending to a sick and elderly gentleman, his father.

The conquest of Rome was for Freud a first step toward a partial integration of some of the disowned aspects of his identity as a Jew. Because of it, he was able increasingly to accept and thereby to defuse both the attraction he felt for the non-Jewish world and the desire to reject his Jewishness. Given the situation of Jews in turn-of-the-century Vienna, his responses were not at all unusual. But he had unconsciously equated both with the necessity to convert and thus felt enormous guilt over them. The violation of so sacred a fatherly trust had caused him to turn them into ghosts by investing them with enormous amounts of psychic energy. By confronting these ghosts in his dreams, however, he was able to disarm them somewhat and thereby bring them under normal conscious control. This he accomplished in much the same way that he had managed to transform his mythical Rome into an earthly city and himself into an ordinary tourist.

Freud returned to Rome on a number of subsequent occasions. With each new visit he found himself a bit more comfortable there, perhaps a sign of increased self-acceptance as a Jew. In 1913, for instance, he sent a postcard to Karl Abraham from Rome. It contained a picture of the Arch of Titus, erected in honor of the Roman Inquisition of the Jews, and on the back he wrote: "The Jew survives it."[61] Although he would never be totally free of his Jewish ambivalence, his self-analysis had made him aware of previously unsuspected inner conflicts and helped to move him a step or two closer to a more mature and less self-destructive relationship to his past. He would always feel a certain amount of guilt and unworthiness when confronting the forbidden world of the gentiles, but these feelings were no longer overwhelming, and he would continue to find unconscious mechanisms for mediating them.

He would always retain, for example, a strong dislike for Jewish converts as well as self-hating Jews. These tendencies probably stemmed from a combination of reaction formation, the need periodically to shore up his own inner doubts, and from remnants of his Hannibal complex. An anecdote in this regard has it that in the 1930s a fictitious story circulated that the Jews of Berlin had paraded through the street carrying signs reading: "Throw us out!" Believing this to be the truth, Freud grew highly indignant and wrote to Arnold Zweig suggesting that such undignified behavior was typical of the Jewish character and that his only salvation was that these people were half German.[62] Or on the occasion of discovering that the author of a letter condemning psychoanalysis as an "abortion" of the Jewish spirit, Theodor Lessing, was himself a Jew, Freud, after recovering from the shock, commented: "Don't you think that self-hatred like Th. L.'s is an exquisite Jewish phenomenon."[63]

He would in addition frequently advise others against conversion, for he saw it at varying times as "undignified," "outright foolish," and "essentially dishonest"[64] To Max Graf's question as to whether it was better to bring up his son, the famous Little Hans, in the Christian faith, Freud replied. "If you do not let your son grow up a Jew, you will deprive him of those sources of energy which cannot be replaced by anything else. He will have to struggle as a Jew, and ought to develop in him energy that he will need for that struggle."⁶⁵ Finally, Freud, whether intentionally or unintentionally, placed the convert's behavior within the realm of the psychopathological when, during his discussion of unconscious slips of the tongue in *The Psychopathology of Everyday Life*, he presented an anecdote about a Jew who had become a Christian convert but who betrayed himself, while visiting a Christian family, by telling his children to go into the garden, calling them *Juden* (Jews) instead of *Jungen* (young ones.)⁶⁶

\* \* \*

Freud also found some relief from the daily frustrations of being a Jew through his passion for Jewish humor. He frequently punctuated his conversation and writings with Jewish jokes, and at an even a deeper level, according to Elliot Oring, he identified personally with the joke characters and found within them seeds for his later psychoanalytic discoveries. During his analysis of the Rome series, for instance, his dream associations led him on several occasions to Jewish anecdotes that proved especially revealing when analyzed. Jones even described this "fondness for relating Jewish jokes and anecdotes" as his most prominent external Jewish feature.⁶⁷

According to psychoanalytic theory, the telling of such jokes by Jews served a psychological as well as a social purpose. Freud himself made a strong distinction between these jokes and anti-Semitic ones, which he described as brutal farces. Heavily saturated with self-criticism, Jewish humor offered a socially acceptable means of expressing anti-Jewish feelings without directly acknowledging them. It served in other words as an excellent release valve for the frustrations that were part and parcel of being a minority in a majority world. It is not in the least surprising then that such humor was so popular in Freud's day among the highly ambivalent Jews of Vienna. Witness, for example, the enormous popularity of Karl Kraus's journal *Die Fackel*, which depended so heavily on its unending criticism of Jewish ways and mores. It found its biggest audience among the literate Jews of turn-of-the-century Vienna. It is interesting in this regard that Freud, a year after his father's death and at about the time he undertook his self-analysis, admitted to Fliess a strong interest in Jewish jokes. "Let me confess that I have recently made a collection of deeply significant Jewish stories."⁶⁸ Perhaps the significance to which he here referred was their revelance to his own Jewish ambivalence, which would shortly come to consciousness during his self-analysis. This collection did not in fact survive, and it is likely that he destroyed it himself in 1908 along with many other papers because they were too personally revealing.

Jewish humor also served to soften the blow of anti-Semitism. By inuring oneself through humor to the hurt of the anti-Jewish sentiment before it actually took place, it was possible to deflect its impact and thereby defuse it a bit. After his self-analysis Freud was increasingly able to joke about anti-Semitism. Where he could now use humor as a defense, his only response had once been belligerent confrontation. One cannot help but be struck in particular by the way in which he later in life resorted to humor in the face of Nazi insults. In a letter to Wilhelm Reich, for instance, he remarked about Hitler that many people have wondered how in *A Midsummer Nights Dream* Shakespeare could make a lady fall in love with a donkey. "And now, think of it" he added, "that a nation of sixty-five million have...."[69] And in May of 1933, when his books were being burned in Berlin, he wrote, not realizing the ultimate irony of his words: "What progress we are making. In the Middle Ages they would have burnt me; now they are content with burning books."[70]

\* \* \*

This chapter has so far focused only on the rejecting aspects of Freud's Jewish ambivalence. But what of his positive attachments to Judaism? In May of 1926 the B'nai B'rith Lodge, the only social organization to which he ever belonged, held a special celebration in his honor on the occasion of his seventieth birthday. Although his family attended, he was too embarrassed to join them. "When I am attacked I can defend myself; but when praised I am helpless"[71] His written reply of thanks to the membership represented the most comprehensive statement of the meaning of his Jewishness.

> What tied me to Jewry was—I have to admit—not the faith, not even national pride, for I was always an unbeliever, have been brought up without religions, but not without respect for the so-called "ethical" demands of human civilization. Whenever I have experienced feelings of national exaltation I have tried to suppress them as disastrous and unfair, frightened by the warning example of those nations among which we Jews live. But there remained enough to make the attraction of Judaism and the Jews irresistible,

many dark emotional powers all the stronger the less they could be expressed in words, as well as the clear consciousness of an inner identity, the familiarity of the same psychological structure. And before long there followed the realization that it was only to my Jewish nature that I owed the two qualities that have become indispensable to me throughout my difficult life. Because I was a Jew I found myself free of many prejudices which restrict others in the use of the intellect; as a Jew I was prepared to be in the opposition and to renounce agreement with the "compact majority."[72]

Freud began by stating quite explicitly what his Jewish identity was not based on. If was, first of all, not derived from any attachment to Judaism as a religion. His antipathy for Jewish ritual and observance has been well documented, and it was not out of character for him to speak of himself as he did on various occasions as "an infidel Jew"[73] or as "a completely Godless Jew."[74] His reference to the "so-called ethical demands of human civilization" alluded to his background, gained under his father and Hammerschlag's guidance, in Reformed Judaism with its emphasis on the universal morality that underlies traditional Judaism. Reformed Jewish ideology suggested that as long as this essence remained, traditional outward trappings could be discarded. Nor was Freud's allegiance based on any kind of nationalistic feelings. His strong reservations about Zionism were described earlier in this chapter.

Freud's attachments to Judaism were centered on the experience of being a Jew and his feelings of connection to other Jews. He once wrote to a stranger in Italy: "Although I have been alienated from the religion of my forebears for a long time, I have never lost the feeling of solidarity with my people."[75] And remembering how his early ideas had made him a pariah in the medical circles of Vienna, he wrote the following to his brothers in the B'nai B'rith Lodge, who had more than thirty years before welcomed him. "I felt as though outlawed, shunned by all. This isolation aroused in me the longing for a circle of excellent men with high ideals who would accept me in friendship despite my temerity. Your Lodge was described to me as a place where I might find such men. That you are Jews could only be welcome to me, for I was myself a Jew."[76]

Socially, Freud lived and worked in a totally Jewish environment. The vast majority of his friends and social acquaintances were Jews, as were those who were attracted to psychoanalysis and in time became his followers. Ernest Jones, the first prominent non-Jew to become an integral part of Freud's world, commented on several different occasions on the decidedly Jewish character that pervaded the movement. His specific phrase was a "Jewish outlook."[77] The few organizations to which Freud belonged—specifically, the Israelitische Kultusgemeinde (the Jewish educational body in Vienna), the B'nai B'rith and later in life the board of the Hebrew University—were also exclusively Jewish in their missions and membership. We have already spoken of his connections to Zionism and Zionists, and it is interesting to note that he would never accept royalties from the translation of his books into Hebrew. Finally, none of his siblings or children ever intermarried or converted.

For Freud a central aspect of his connection to other Jews was the shared experience of anti-Semitism. He expressed this sentiment particularly well when he spoke of physicist Josep Popper-Lynkeus,[78] who also had experienced "the bitterness of the life of the Jew." Freud respected Popper-Lynkeus as a Jew who had not succumbed to prejudice but had risen above it. "A special feeling of sympathy drew me to him, since he too had clearly had experience of the painful life of a Jew and the hollowness of the ideals of present-day civilization."[79] Always keenly aware of anti-Semitism, Freud grew particularly bitter in spite of his ability to joke about it after World War I, when he wrote: "I belong to a race which in the Middle Ages was held responsible for all epidemics and which today is blamed for the disintegration of the Austrian Empire and the German defeat. Such experiences have a sobering effect and are not conducive to make one believe in illusions."[80] As will emerge in the next chapter, Freud always sought out other Jews, albeit very selectively, with whom he could share his feelings and frustrations about being Jewish. While he probably did not speak of such matters with his father, his teacher Samuel Hammerschlag, with whom he spent much time, was a likely candidate. We know he consulted with Josef Breuer about his desires to avoid a religious marriage ceremony, and his letters to Fliess and later Karl Abraham and Arnold Zweig were full of references to anti-Semitic incidents and the plight of Jews in Vienna and elsewhere.

To his Jewishness Freud attributed the two qualities that he felt most prepared him for the development of psychoanalysis: his independence of thought and the courage to hold ideas in spite of opposition. What Freud was referring to in terms of the former was the ability to see clearly, that is, to look beyond the distortions that self-interest can breed and see a thing for what it was. As perpetual outsiders and mere guests, and unattached as they were to the status quo, Jews were in a better position than their majority counterparts to criticize the ways of society. They had much less to lose. Freud would later suggest that for similar reasons Jews took more readily to the science of psychoanalysis. Psychoanalysis, he felt, required the ability to transcend self-delusion. This form of truth was perhaps similar in conception, although Freud might well have disagreed to the religious Jew's concern over idolatry and the worship of graven images in place of the true God. Freud believed that compared to the Greeks the Jews had overdeveloped their use of the intellect but he did admit his own preference in this direction. Finally, he attributed the very survival of his people to their obsession with ideas. To the representatives of the Hebrew community of London, who greeted him upon his arrival in 1938, he stated: "We Jews have always known how to respect spiritual values. We preserved our unity through ideas, and because of them we have survived to this day."[81]

Freud first referred to the development of intellectual courage in relation to his days at the university "I was made familiar with the fate of being in the Opposition and being put under the ban of the 'compact majority.' The foundations were thus laid for a certain degree of independent judgment."[82] It was to this very same quality that he attributed a central role in the founding of psychoanalysis. "Nor is it perhaps entirely a matter of chance that the first advocate of psychoanalysis was a Jew. To profess belief in a new theory called for a certain degree of readiness to accept a position of solitary opposition . . . a position with which no one is more familiar than a Jew."[83] Freud was here possibly speaking from the experience of his own isolation from 1894 to 1903. From such negative experiences, however, he would always find a benefit, a way in which he had grown strong from the ordeal. In a similar spirit he advised Karl Abraham "the fact that things will be more difficult for you as a Jew will have the effect, as it has with all of us, of bringing out the best of which you are capable."[84]

Later in life and no doubt piqued by a worsening anti-Semitism everywhere he turned, Freud became increasingly chauvinistic about Jews and Judaism. The following excerpt from his conversations with Joseph Wortis,[85] dated between 1934 and 1935, is worth reproducing.

[Wortis:] "I wish I could clear up the problem for myself. I have no strong Jewish feelings, and up to recently was satisfied to think of myself mainly as an American. How far ought I to let my allegiances to Jews bring me?"

"That is not a problem for Jews," said Freud, "because the Gentiles make it unnecessary to decide; as long as Jews are not admitted into Gentile circles, they have no choice but to band together."

"But how about the program for the future? I would like to see the Jews become assimilated and disappear, and Einstein talks as if they ought to be preserved forever."

"The future will show how far that is possible," said Freud. "I personally do not see anything wrong in mixed marriages, if both parties are suited to each other, though I must say that the chances for success seem greater in a Jewish marriage: family life is closer and warmer, and devotion is much more common. My married children have all married Jews, though it may be that they would have married Christians if they had found the right ones. It simply happens that the Gentiles who courted them or with whom they came in contact were not up to standard, and the Jews of their circle seemed superior. It may well be however that they simply did not have access to the best Christian circles. There is no reason why Jews ought not to be perfectly friendly with Gentiles; there is no real clash of interests. . . . Jews ought to meet on the common ground of irreligion and humanity. Jews who are ashamed of their Jewishness have simply reacted to the mass suggestion of their society."

"But I don't know what the Jews stand for," I said. "I can pledge allegiance to a scientific group, or a political or cultural group because they represent certain ideals, but what does Judaism stand for; in what ways to its ideals differ from other group ideals?"

"Ruthless egotism is much more common among Gentiles than among Jews," said Freud, "and Jewish family life and intellectual life are on a higher plane."

"You seem to think the Jews are a superior people then," I said.

"I think nowadays they are," said Freud. "When one thinks that ten or twelve percent of the Nobel Prize winners are Jews and when one thinks of their great achievements in sciences and in the arts, one has every reason to think them superior."

"Jews have bad manners," I said, "especially in New York."

"That is true," said Freud; "they are not always adapted to social life. Before they enjoyed emancipation in 1818 they were not a social problem, they kept to themselves—with a low standard of life it is true—but they did not go out in mixed society. Since then they have had much to learn. In countries where they have enjoyed real freedom, however, as in Italy, they are indistinguishable in this respect from Italians. The old saying is true: 'Every country has the Jews that it deserves.' America certainly hasn't encouraged the best kind of social conduct."

"It is also said that Jews are physically inferior," I said.

"That is no longer true either," Said Freud, "now that the Jews have access to outdoor life and the sports, you find them the equal of the Gentiles in every respect, and we have plenty of champions in all fields."

"And finally," I said, "the Jews are over-intellectualized; it was Jung who said, for example, that psychoanalysis bears the mark of this Jewish over-intellectualization."

"So much the better for psychonanlysis then!" said Freud. "Certainly Jews have a strong tendency to rationalize—that is a good thing. What Jung contributed to psychoanalysis was mysticism, which we can well dispense with . . . But I do not want to go too much in the direction of nationalism either." Freud continued. "I am not much of a Zionist—at least not the way Einstein is, even though I am one of the curators of the Hebrew University in Palestine. I recognized the great emotional force, though, of a Jewish center in the world, and thought it would be a rallying point for Jewish ideals. If it had been in the Uganda, it would not have been anything near so good. The sentimental value of Palestine was very great. Jews pictured their old compatriots wailing and praying as in the olden days at the old wall—which by the way was built by Herod, not by Solomon—and felt a revival of their old spirit. I was afraid for a while though that Zionism would become the occasion for a revival of the old religion, but I have been assured by people who have been there that all the young Jews are irreligious, which is a good thing . . .[86]

When pressed to define the essence or core of his Jewishness, however, Freud was always at a loss for words. In his B'nai Brith statement he referred to "dark emotional powers all the stronger the less they could be expressed in words."[87] In a letter to Barbara Low on 19 April 1936 he used a similar idea in describing his relationship to David Eder, a close friend who had recently died in London. "We were both Jews and knew of each other that we carried that miracuous thing in common, which—inaccessible to any analysis so far—makes the Jew."[88] To Karl Abraham he spoke of a "racial kinship" existing between them, a similarity of "intellectual constitution"[89] and in another letter he spoke of consanguineous Jewish traits."[90] And to Arnold Zweig in describing Palestine he wrote that it was "impossible to say what heritage from this land we have taken into our blood and nerves."[91] It is nothing short of surprising that Freud, always so precise, meticulous, and empirical in his thinking, could tolerate such imprecision as this. But as we shall see shortly, he would, stimulated by the crisis of Carl Jung's defection, undertake in 1912 a series of works, beginning with *Totem and Taboo*, on the origins of religion in which he would make that mysterious essence of what the Jew was "accessible to the scientific mind."[92] Again, in *Moses and Monotheism*, the last of his works on religion, he would take up the quest for those irresistible bonds that tied all Jews to their heritage.

\* \* \*

The period between 1902 and 1912 was an exceedingly productive one for Freud. He had received his professorship and had emerged from the isolation of his self-analysis with the ghosts of the past laid to rest, temporarily anyway, and ready to embark on a new mission. He stood on the brink of the development and dissemination of psychoanalytic theory. In the years that followed he produced a number of his most influential works: *The Psychopathology of Everyday Life, Jokes and Their Relation to the Unconscious*, and *Three Essays on the Theory of Sexuality*, to name but a few. This period also witnessed the creation of an international network of followers commited to him and his ideas. By 1911, for instance, the International Psychoanalytic Association had met in Congress for the third time with fifty-five in attendance and 106 members in all; both the American Psychoanalytic Society and the New York Psychoanalytic Society had been formed; and two psychoanalytic journals, the *Jahrbuch* and *Imago*, were being published. There had also already been two major defections from the ranks in the persons of Alfred Adler and Wilhelm Steckel, and a third, that of Carl Jung and his Swiss compatriots, was looming on the horizon.

It was at this point that Freud undertook a whole new direction in his work in the form of a series of papers and books that focused on religion and religious experience. Ostensibly, the series represented an application of the basic concepts of psychoanalysis to an understanding of religion, society, and the history of civilization. At a deeper level, however, like his efforts in *The Interpretation of Dreams*, these works masked a highly personal drama. This was the reawakening of his Jewish ambivalence and his hostility toward his father, and his unconscious attempts to once again resolve them. These efforts would last to the very end of his life.

Numerous authors have commented on how these works, which included *Totem and Taboo, The Future of an Illusion, The Moses of Michelangelo,* and *Moses and Monotheism,* diverged so significantly from Freud's usual style of careful scholarship and impeccable logic. The case studies and clinical analyses that preceeded them were masterpieces of painstaking detail and accuracy: well-thought-out, well-documented, and masterfully conceived and argued. The works in his religion series, on the other hand, were poorly constructed, often erroneous in their facts, and frequently premature and unsubstantiated in their conclusions. David Bakan, for instance, called Freud's *Moses and Monotheism* "incredibly bad" and has suggested that it would have received no attention whatsoever if Freud had not been the author.[93] This diminution in quality cannot be blamed on Freud's age or a lessening of his intellectual prowess, however, for his 1940 manuscript of the *Outline of Psychoanalysis* bore the stamp of his earlier clinical efforts. Most critics have agreed that Freud's religion series was stimulated primarily by personal rather than scientific motives. Freud's inner state during their creation provides an additional clue. His moods ranged from euphoria to deep depression and were highly reminiscent of his earlier bout with psychoneurosis. He was plagued by incessant doubts about the validity and quality of these works and in fact repeatedly hesitated and postponed their publication, as if they were just too transparent and self-revealing for disclosure.

The religion series was clearly overdetermined, that is, it served a number of different personal motives for Freud. It gave concrete expression, first of all, to his lifelong antipathy for religion, which had up to that point found expression primarily through atheism and an abhorrence for Jewish ritual and observance. The reemergence at this time of anti-Semitism as a central theme in his life clearly reinforced the new direction in his work. Stimulated simultaneously by the defection of his Swiss gentile followers, the Catholic church's sustained attack on psychoanalysis, and the emergence of Nazism, it was easy for him to bring forth and ignite the revolutionary within him to do battle with a longtime foe in order to vent his growing frustrations.

His work on religion would also offer him an opportunity

to discover once and for all the essence or core of his Jewishness, which had to that point remained "inaccessible to analysis." This was in fact the very goal he set for himself in the Preface to the Hebrew translation of *Totem and Taboo*, his maiden effort in the new series. "No reader of . . . this book will find it easy to put himself in the emotional position of an author who . . . is completely estranged from the religion of his fathers . . . but . . . who feels that he is in his essential nature a Jew. . . . If the question were put to him . . . 'what is there left to you that is Jewish?' He would reply: 'A very great deal, and probably its very essence.' He could not now express that essence clearly in words; but some day, no doubt, it will become accessible to the scientific mind."[94] The need to make this essence concrete was also stimulated by Freud's desire to disassociate himself from Jung and his tendency toward "the mystical element."[95] He was no doubt uncomfortable with this intellectual vagueness in himself, but with Jung's rejection of psychoanalysis he grew particularly determined to put as much distance as possible between the latter's "Aryan religiousness" and the "Jewish objectivity" and "unflinching adherence to the actual facts"[96] that he saw in himself and his Jewish followers. Thus he saw in *Totem and Taboo* a powerful opportunity to reply to the defecting Swiss, which, as he wrote to Abraham, "would serve to make a sharp division between us and all Aryan religiosity."[97]

Finally, the series would serve as an arena for once again confronting the ghosts of his Jewish ambivalence that had been set free by the departure of Jung. Freud's self-analysis, over ten years earlier, had given him a new freedom of movement as a Jew. Fearful that the psychoanalytic movement would be incapacitated by anti-Semitism, he actively courted Carl Jung and other Swiss psychiatrists for the movement. This is something of which he would not have been capable prior to his visit to Rome. The relationship had turned sour, however. This left Freud deeply hurt and disappointed and Jung on the verge of a nervous breakdown. Freud for his part had lost not only a successor to the psychoanalytic crown but also a surrogate son, for he had actively dissuaded his own sons from medical careers and thus from participation in psychoanalysis. The break with Jung left the movement in exclusively Jewish hands once again and could not help but reawaken old hurts and frustrations of Freud, both as a Jew and a son. Ernest Jones has even suggested that after the break with Jung, Freud never trusted another non-Jew. Freud did have a propensity for rethinking a relationship after a defection and for doing so in the darkest possible terms. In Jung's case this involved retrospective accusations of hidden anti-Semitism. While the psychoanalytic movement would always have a number of loyal and valued gentiles, Jones included, the break clearly reminded Freud of who he was and left a lingering suspicion of the non-Jewish world. Witness, for example, Freud's surprised reaction to Thomas Mann's extreme kindness on the occasion of his eightieth birthday. "A noble *Goy* [non-Jew]! It's nice to know that these, too, exist. One is apt to doubt it sometimes."[98] In any case Jung's defection was the initial stimulus for undertaking *Totem and Taboo*, and, after it, the various works about Moses, with whom Freud increasingly identified. It was through Moses that he attempted a final and desperate integration of his reawakened ambivalent feelings about being a Jew.

The religion series represented a progression in Freud's thinking. In *Totem and Taboo* he defined the origins of religion. In *The Future of an Illusion* he explored the nature of religion's appeal and its future role in civilization, and finally in *Moses and Monotheism* he applied the concepts derived in the two earlier works to Judaism.

*Totem and Taboo* was written at a time of growing tension between Freud and Jung. The latter had recently begun to delve deeply into the fields of mythology and comparative religion, and the conclusions he was drawing and subsequently applying to his clinical work made Freud increasingly nervous. Most unsettling was the fact that they represented a clear departure from orthodox Freudian theory and from the primacy of sexuality. In response, Freud undertook *Totem and Taboo*, an undisguised effort to apply the Oedipal concept to an understanding of religious experience. It was as if he wished to show Jung that it was not necessary to break with orthodox thinking in order to gain clarity in this field, which seemed to stimulate Jung's mystical tendencies. There is little doubt that Freud saw *Totem and Taboo* as an extension of his earlier efforts in *The Interpretation of Dreams*, during which he discovered the Oedipal complex. In concluding the former he wrote: "The beginnings of religion, ethics, society and art meet in the Oedipal complex. . . . This is in entire accord with the findings of psychoanalysis, namely, that the nucleus of all neuroses, as far as our present knowledge goes, is the Oedipal complex."[99] His response to Jones's inquiry about the doubts he was having about *Totem and Taboo* also made the relationship clear. Referring to his earlier work he wrote: "Then I described the wish to kill one's father, and now I have been describing the actual killing."[100]

Freud's emotional state during the writing of *Totem and Taboo* was similar to the upheavals he had experienced during his work on *The Interpretation of Dreams*. He ranged from elation and certainty about the ultimate value of his efforts and the acknowledgement that I "have not written anything with such conviction since the *Interpretation of Dreams*"[101] to doubts, misgivings, and great inner turmoil. Of the down side he wrote. "I am in that mental and bodily state to which I am accustomed during inner intensive work—or rather, the preparation for such. It is a kind of misery"[102] Both groundbreaking works were written during periods of great stress stimulated by personal losses, and they involved unconscious efforts to resolve the same inner conflicts that revolved around Freud's father and Jewish tradition. That Freud was motivated and effected in the creation of *Totem and Taboo* by issues beyond mere scientific inquiry is clear from his less-than-enthusiastic attitude toward the ncessary background reading. "I am reading thick books without being really interested in them since I already know the results; my instinct tells me that."[103] And both works were received with great skepticism, doubt, and anger, as Freud correctly had anticipated. Giovanni Costigan is quite right when he asserted that because of *The Interpretation of Dreams*, Freud "had been charged with indecency; now he was accused of sacrilege as well."[104]

*Totem and Taboo* is divided into four essays, and in each Freud drew a parallel between the religious rites of primitive societies and the obsessive behavior of neurotic patients. In the first he dealt with the taboo against incest and emphasized the fact that primitive societies more fully enforced such restrictions that do modern ones. His implication here was that the primitive psyche did not possess sufficient inner restraints to guarantee the prohibition against incest. In the second essay he more fully explored the parallels between the external taboo and internal conscience and argued that the former was an early manifestation of the latter. He went on to describe the great ambivalence experienced by primitives toward taboos and its parallel in modern man's feelings toward death and toward his rulers. Finally, he suggested that the study of neuroses might provide useful insights into the origins of society. "The neuroses on the one hand display striking and far-reaching resemblances with the great social productions of art, religion and philosophy, but on the other hand they have the appearance of being caricatures of them. One might venture the statement that hysteria is a caricature of an artistic creation, the obsessional neurosis a caricature of religion, and paranoiac delusions a caricature of a philosophical system."[105]

In the third essay Freud explored animism and magic as humanity's first system of thought and method of structuring reality. He argued that this primitive belief in the power of one's thoughts and wishes was in time replaced by religious thinking with its projection of omnipotence onto the gods and the individual's attempts to influence these deities through ritual. Freud predicted a third stage of development, that of scientific thinking, which would one day predominate over the others. He also saw a parallel between these stages of cultural development and the development of the individual: the first stage corresponding to the narcissism of the infant, the second to the child's dependence on the parents and the third to the maturity of a life lived exclusively in relation to the reality principle.

The fourth essay was by far the most important and controversial, for in it Freud connected the previous themes to a historical parallel of the Oedipal complex. He saw a similarity, first of all, between the taboos that surrounded totemism and those related to the Oedipal sitituation. The totem animal, he argued, was in fact a substitute for the primal father, who had been killed long ago and eaten by the sons of the tribe when humankind first lived in small hordes or family groups. The sons' love for the father had emerged after the feast, however, and was transformed into guilt, which was the basis for the establishment of the taboos. These taboos marked the beginnings of religion (the taboo on patricide) and society (the taboo on incest). Manifestations of this ambivalence toward the father can still be identified in modern times in human responses to heavenly dieties and earthly rulers. At this point in his analysis Freud set off his first volley against contemporary religion by applying this logic to Christianity. Original sin, he suggested, was equated with the primal murder of the father, and the sacrifice of Christ the son served to expiate the resulting guilt. The son's ambivalence in turn found expression in his ascendance as a deity and through the introduction of the communion (totem) meal.

Freud was well aware of the reaction that his bold suppositions would elicit from the church and he backed off a bit in his concluding remarks by suggesting the uncertainties of his assumptions and the difficulties of his conclusions.[106] He was probably less aware however of the unmistakable relationship that existed between his theory of patricide and the tensions that were worsening within the psychoanalytic movement itself. He was by 1914 the father of an emerging school of thought, and it would have been a very short and simple step unconsciously to identify Jung and his Swiss compatriots with the envious sons wishing to overthrow the father.

Although more will be said about it in the next chapter, it is sufficient to point out here that Freud's relationships with his more creative disciples were always frought with the ambivalence of the Oedipal drama. The attachment between Freud and Jung as surrogate father and son was particularly deep and compelling. If Freud was in fact unconsciously thinking of Jung, and probably Adler and Steckel as well, when he posited the theory of the murdered patriarch and the rebellious sons, then the very creation of the theory would have provided him with some psychological distance from and an explanation for the very painful break that was about to occur. In much the same way that the rejection of the seduction theory had allowed him to continue with his self-analysis, so the positing of the primal Oedipal murder of the father allowed him to continue his work on psychoanalysis in spite of the repeated defections. It is also possible that Freud unconsciously used the same mechanism to vent further hostility toward Jacob, his own father. Throughout the remainder of his years, in fact, he would vacillate back and forth between identifications with the father and with the son.

Also related to Jung's break with him was Freud's paper on Michelangelo's statue of Moses, published in 1914. Since his first visit to Rome, Freud felt an especially strong attraction to the statue of Moses in the Church of St. Peter in Vincoli. He would visit it at least once daily when he was in Rome and spend hours transfixed in its presence. "No piece of statuary has ever made stronger impression on me than this. How often have I . . . essayed to support the angry scorn of the hero's glance! Sometimes I have crept cautiously out of the half-gloom of the interior as though I myself belonged to the mob upon whom his eye is turned."[107] This was a powerful and significant confession coming from a man who surrounded himself with an extensive collection of antiquities, and it attested to the statue's psychological import. Freud's analysis of the statue was also of interest because it so basically contradicted the opinion of experts in the field of art history. Instead of portraying Moses in a fit of rage prior to smashing the tablets, as was common among most experts, Freud saw him in control of his anger in order to save the tablets from destruction. In so doing, he drastically altered the traditional conception of Moses with which he was so familiar from his early biblical training.

> Michelangelo has placed a different Moses on the tomb ... one superior to the historical or traditional Moses. He has modified the theme of the broken Tables, he does not let Moses break them in his wrath, but makes him be influenced by the danger that they will be broken and makes him calm that wrath, or at any rate prevent it from becoming an act. In this way he has added something new and more than human to the figure of Moses; so that the giant frame with its tremendous physical power becomes only a concrete expression of the highest mental achievement that is possible in a man, that of struggling successfully against an inward passion for the sake of a cause to which he had devoted himself.[108]

It seems almost self-evident that Freud was speaking of himself here and projecting his own inner feelings upon the statue. He must control his own anger against Jung and the Swiss for the sake of psychoanalysis. He must sublimate his own passions for the sake of his work and remember the lesson of his self-analysis—that it is necessary and possible to control his rage against the gentiles. So transparent were Freud's intentions here that he would only allow the paper to be published anonymously, in spite of the pleas of his close and trusted associates. The following note prefaced the essay, which first appeared in *Imago*. Its true authorship would not become known for another ten years, until the publication of Freud's collected works. "Although this paper does not, strictly speaking conform to the conditions under which contributions are accepted for publication in this Journal, the editors have decided to print it, since the author, who is personally known to them, moves in psycho-analytic circles, and since his mode of thought has in point of fact a certain resemblance to the methodology of psychoanalysis."[109]

Freud's fascination with the Moses statue went beyond the conflict with Jung however and drew some of its energy from remnants of his Jewish ambivalence. He first gazed upon it at the time of his initial visit to Rome, five years before his first meeting with Jung. By this point his Jewish ambivalence had been slightly tamed, that is, brought under conscious control to the extent that it no longer haunted him or interfered with his work. A significant result of his self-analysis had in fact been a weakening of his identification with Hannibal. This bond had played a central role both in his inability to reach Rome and in his paralysis in pursuing promotion to professor. It seems likely that at this time in his psychic life Freud began to develop a strong attachment to the figure of Moses. This he did both as a replacement for Hannibal and as a screen upon which he could project his Jewish ambivalance and through which he might hopefully in time resolve it. During his self-analysis Freud had begun to speak of Rome as the promised land and later he would refer to himself as Moses and Jung as his Joshua.

One could almost see Freud's inner conflict and ambivalence graphically portrayed as he sat in a church in Rome, a powerful symbol of the Christian world and of conversion, at the tomb of Pope Julius II, as he stared at a graven image of Judaism's most important leader. A part of him no doubt felt pride and a surge of positive energy at the thought of his own connection to the tradition the lawgiver represented. Perhaps he even experienced a bit of defiance at having gained entry into the very core of his enemies' lair. But he must have also felt guilt and shame and connection with the Jews who had rejected Moses and worshipped the golden calf and thereby elicited his wrath. "How often have I mounted the steps of the unlovely Corso Cavour to the lonely place where the deserted church stands, and have essayed to support the angry scorn of the Lawgiver's glance. Sometimes I crept cautiously out of the half-gloom of the interior as though I myself belonged to the mob upon whom his eye is turned—the mob which can hold fast to no conviction, which has neither faith more patience and which rejoices when it has gained illusory idols."[110]

Freud's surprising interpretation of the statue's inner state and intentions represented a beginning step in his effort to transform Moses into a more acceptable figure, "someone superior to the historical or traditional Moses"[111] with whom he could identify unambivalently. This psychic processing around the figure of Moses that would continue to the end of his days would also provide an arena for the possible integration of his divided Jewish identity and hopefully some lasting relief from it. This inner work would ultimately find its fullest expression in *Moses and Monotheism*, to be discussed below. Freud would concurrently come increasingly to see himself in the image of the transformed biblical figure and to give unconscious expression to a fantasy of becoming the new Moses and of leading the Jewish people out of their contemporary wilderness. At the time of his paper on the *Moses of Michelangelo*, however, he was evidently experiencing substantial guilt over the liberties he was taking with the Jewish patriarch and so left the authorship anonymous, because he "did not want to disgrace the name of Moses by putting (his) name on it."[112]

The *Future of an Illusion* was the next in the religion series and appeared in print for the first time in 1928. It was a sequel to *Totem and Taboo* and in it Freud applied the logic of his earlier work to the questions of the inner motivation for religion and of its future. He reemphasized his contention that religion was "the universal obsessional neurosis of humanity" and that religious belief often spared believers the need to develop their own individual neuroses. Freud pointed to certain historical contributions that religion had made to civilization. In his list he included: overcoming helplessness in the face of nature's ominous forces, a beginning of ethical behavior, and a palliative against the fear of death. Its danger however clearly outweighed its merits. Her went on to argue that one could lead a good life without the help of a religion and he was no doubt mindful of his own life as an example of that. As to the future of religion, he again asserted it as a transitional stage in humanity's development, someday to be replaced by the "primacy of the intellect."

As with his other works on religion, Freud experienced substantial anxiety and concern over the publication of the *Future of an Illusion*. He criticized it as "weak analytically and inadequate as a self-revelation"[113] and he hesitated in its release because of concern for offending his close friend, the Swiss pastor Oskar Pfister. His worries in this regard anyway proved quite unfounded, for Pfister welcomed the work in typically gracious fashion. "Imagine that a public profession of what you believe could be painful to me. . . . Your marvelous life's work and your goodness and gentleness lead me to the deepest springs of life."[114]

A true source of Freud's uneasiness was more likely the growing criticism of psychoanalysis among clerics, conservative and liberal alike. This trend of church censure had been gaining momentum for several years and would in fact continue to worsen with time. In 1934, for instance, the Vatican would suppress the publication of an Italian psychoanalytic journal, and in his own Vienna a Father Schmidt would launch such an intense campaign against psychoanalysis that Freud feared that continued work on *Moses and Monotheism* might run "the risk of Catholic authorities officially forbidding the practice of analysis."[115]

*Moses and Monotheism*, Freud's last effort in the religion series, was by far the most interesting and self-revealing. It was, first of all, his only work that dealt directly with Judaism. While he had used other works, such as *The Interpretation of Dreams*, to struggle unconsciously with certain issues involving his ethnic identity, it was not until *Moses and Monotheism* that he directly and openly confronted the essence of Jewishness and the reasons for the continuing hatred and persecution of Jews. But even below the surface of this text there raged an unconscious drama within Freud—a last desperate attempt once and for all to come to grips with and resolve his Jewish ambivalence. It would be the final internal surge of a process of self-restoration that had begun over twenty years earlier with his paper on Michelangelo's Moses. Perhaps it was stimulated by his advanced age of 78 or by the fact that he was dying of cancer and thus it was time for a final reckoning of earthly accounts. Or maybe it was a need he felt to acknowledge the enormity of the anti-Jewish hatred that had come to pass or somehow to respond to the unspoken awareness of what was about to befall the Jewish people. By 1935 the existence of concentration camps was already a widely known fact. In any case the manuscript both haunted and comforted him for the last six years of his life. It provided an unsettling window into his own tormented Jewish psyche and at the same time an escape from his progressively painful medical condition and the darkening shadow of Nazism that was falling ever closer to Freud's own little world. Its final completion and publication offered a reason to continue his life.

Even more than the other works in the series, Freud was extremely hesitant about publishing *Moses and Monotheism*. Although he finished an initial draft in 1934, the first two essays did not appear in print until 1937, and the third was not published until after he had left Vienna and found a safe haven in England. There were of course his usual doubts about the veracity of what he was suggesting and the quality of his arguments. In this particular case the concerns happened to be well deserved. To Arnold Zweig he confessed that "this historical novel won't stand up to my own criticism,"[116] and in the preface to the third essay he wrote. "To my critical sense this book . . . appears like a dancer balancing on the tip of one toe."[117] But his doubts were not about the ideas he had originally presented in *Totem and Taboo*. Of these he had only grown firmer in the twenty-five years since they had first appeared in print. Rather, his uneasiness rested on their application to the Jews and in particular, on the introduction of the idea of primal patricide into Jewish history.

Freud was most distressed however over the potential reaction of his fellow Jews, for he knew full well that many would be deeply hurt and offended by his analysis. To the noted historian Charles Singer he wrote. "Needless to say, I don't like offending my own people. . . . But what can I do about it? I have spent my whole life standing up for what I have considered to be the scientific truth, even when it was uncomfortable and unpleasant for my fellow men. I cannot end up with an act of disavowal."[118] And he began the book itself with the similar rejoinder. "To deprive a people of the man whom they take pride in as the greatest of their sons is not a thing to be gladly or carelessly undertaken, least of all by someone who is himself one of them. But one cannot allow any such reflection to induce us to put the truth aside in favour of what are supposed to be national interests; and, moreover, the clarification of a set of facts may be expected to bring us a gain in knowledge."[119] Yet in spite of this scientific bravado he did hesitate and vacillate back and forth, clearly in emotional pain over the prospect of what he was about to do.

As he contemplated publishing the third essay he grasped at yet another and perhaps final reason for delay—the reaction of the Catholic church, which at that point was all that protected Austria from invasion by the Nazis. He confided the following to Zweig. "Any publication of mine will be sure to attract a certain amount of attention, which will not escape the notice of this inimical priest [Father Schmidt]." Thus, we might be risking a ban on psychoanalysis in Vienna and the suspension of all our publications here. If this danger involved me alone, I would be but little concerned, but to deprive all our members in Vienna of their livelihood is too great a responsibility."[120]

Balancing the doubts however was the great emotional upheaval *Moses and Monotheism* was causing within him and the enormous relief that publication would finally bring. To Zweig he wrote. "As to the Moses, leave me in peace. That this, probably final, attempt to create something has failed depresses me sufficiently. Not that I have broken away from it. The man, and what I wanted to make of him, haunts me incessantly."[121] And elsewhere he wrote: "Moses will not let go of my imagination."[122] There was even some evidence of the return of the symptoms of Freud's earlier psychoneurosis. Again to Zweig. "My mood is bad; very little is to my liking; my self-criticism has become much more severe. In someone else my diagnosis would be senile depression. I see a cloud of disaster closing in on the world, even on my own small one."[123]

An analysis of the major contentions in *Moses and Monotheism* makes it quite clear that what Freud was struggling with under the surface of this "historical novel" was none other than the old ghosts of Jewish identity, its rejection, and his guilt over it. The rewriting of Jewish history that was the work's ostensible purpose was in fact merely a cover for the more important task of rewriting his own personal history, projected for safety's sake onto the figure of Moses. Freud had undertaken a similar endeavor, although on a far less grandiose in scale, twenty years earlier in relation to Michelangelo's statue. But in that case he had had the artist to blame for the transformations he had rendered in the historic Moses. In *Moses and Monotheism*, however, he was solely responsible for the new identity in which he clothed the hero of the Jewish history, and he could find safety only in the assertion that the real facts had been suppressed long ago in Jewish tradition and that he, as a scientist, was only bringing them to light.

His great hesitancy and agitation over the work, his return to biblical themes of his childhood, his resurrection of the Oedipal drama and instinct theory[124] and the fact that although he was gravely ill, near death, and deeply disturbed by the outside world, he could still harness the energy to write such a book—all point to *Moses and Monotheism* as a last and final reckoning for him, a parting opportunity to find emotional peace and quietude, especially in relation to his Jewish identity. In December of 1938 he wrote Zweig: "I am just waiting for the *Moses* which is supposed to come out in March, and then I no longer need to be interested in any book of mine until my next incarnation."[25] And with Hanns Sachs he shared the feeling that: "The *Moses* is not an unworthy leave-taking."[126]

Freud would remain somewhat ambivalent about this creation to the very end. Nine months before his death he told Marie Bonaparte that it alternately impressed and displeased him. Although the unconscious processing that lay at its core did not once and for all resolve his ambivalence or finally lay to rest basic discomforts with his Jewishness,[127] it did bring sufficient emotional relief to allow him to die in peace and with integrity as a Jew. By spending his last days in England he had finally fulfilled the dreams of his youth and the fantasies that lay beneath them: to have been born his stepbrother Emmanuel's son and to have been able to bring up his children in an environment more hospitable to Jews.

Freud began *Moses and Monotheism* with the assertion that Moses was not a Jew, but an Egyptian, the son of a royal princess. He had been a follower of the Aten religion, which was a monotheistic cult introduced into Egypt by the pharaoh Akhenaten (Amenophis IV). After the pharaoh's death, Egypt had reverted back to polytheism, and Moses had chosen the Israelites, then residing in Egypt, to carry on the monotheistic tradition. The burdens and demands of the new religion (with its instinctual renunciation, prohibition against worshipping graven images, and circumcision) had proven too much for the Israelites, and they rose up and murdered Moses. Several generations later a new leader emerged, a Midianite shepherd also called Moses. He both introduced them to the worship of Yahweh, a demonic volcano God, and led them in the conquest of the land of Canaan. With time the two religions and images of Moses, extreme though their differences were, merged within the consciousness of the Jewish people. After a period of latency of many years, however, the monotheistic side triumphed and dominated the religion of the Jews. This account takes us through the first two essays, and at this point Freud added the idea of the murder of the primal father. Drawing a parallel between the history of the individual and that of the Jews, Freud suggested that after the latency period, the repressed memory of the killing of Moses returned, fueled doubly by the memory of the murder of the primal father. The result, according to Freud, was a longing for the murdered father, which in Judaism took the form of waiting for the Messiah, compounded by an enormous sense of guilt. The guilt in turn drew its power from two sources: remorse over the original act, combined with a need to expiate current feelings of hostility toward the father whose expression was strictly forbidden by Mosaic Law.

At this point in the narrative Freud turned his attention to Christianity and its comparative success in handling the problem of guilt. Christianity, according to Freud, had escaped the cycle of guilt by admitting the original sin, that is, the murder of the primal father, and by expiating it through the sacrifice of Christ. The lingering hostility toward the father found expression in the elevation of the son to the level of the father, that is, by Christianity becoming a "son-religion."[128] After the creation of Christianity and the redemption it provided by abandoning the concept of chosenness, "the Jewish religion was to some extent a fossil."[129]

But Freud felt that Christianity, especially Catholicism, had paid a price of its own, that of returning to a thinly veiled polytheism. It was free from the guilt of the primal patricide but in the process had sacrificed its intellectual integrity, falling once again susceptible to superstition and mysticism. This in turn would "prove a severe inhibition on the intellectual development of the next two thousand years."[130] The Jews for their part had retained both the guilt and their intellectual integrity, but had paid the price of anti-Semitism for their continued refusal to admit the original crime. Freud described this as follows:

> The poor Jewish people, who with their habitual stubbornness continued to disavow the father's murder, atoned heavily for it in the course of time. They were constantly met with the reproach "You killed our God!" And this reproach is true, if it is correctly translated. If it is brought into relation with the history of religion, it runs: "You will not admit that you murdered God (the primal picture of God, the primal father, and his later reincarnation)." There should be an addition declaring: "We did the same thing, to be sure, but we have admitted it and since then we have been absolved."[131]

What then were the unconscious consequences of Freud's "historical novel" of Moses and the Jews? He had, first of all, dealt Jewish theology a fatal death blow. In one fell swoop he had robbed the Jewish people of their central hero, attributed their greatest cultural achievement, monotheism, not to mention circumcision, to their ancient foes, and, as if all of this were not enough, he had charged them with the murder of Moses. The historic role Freud assigned to the Jews was certainly far less than compelling. "It is honour enough to the Jewish people," he wrote, "that they could preserve such a tradition and produce men who gave it a voice—even though the initiative to it came from the outside, from a great foreigner."[132] And he would finally call the Jewish religion a "fossil." Christianity, initially anyway, fared far better under Freud's pen. He portrayed it as a clear advance over Judaism, a forward step that had made Judaism obsolete. He had even boasted to a colleague prior to the book's publication that Christianity had nothing to fear from his "Moses." By acknowledging the ancient crime, Christianity had rid itself of the things Freud found most objectionable in Judaism: its chosenness and the mark of its special favor, circumcision.

But just when the rejecting side of his ambivalence seemed to have at last triumphed, he reversed himself and became a champion of the Jewish people. He attributed to them the highest compliment psychoanalytic thinking could offer, the power of the intellect, and in addition he sympathized deeply with the enormous price they had paid for their continuing commitment to tradition. As with Rome, he still could not allow himself to go over to the other side in his analysis, and on closer inspection he found Christianity equally if not more flawed than Judaism. He finally accused it of regression, of a return to a less-evolved consciousness and of adopting polytheism and mysticism. These were, as a matter of fact, the same accusations he had leveled against Jung, who he so desperately needed yet never fully trusted because of his Christian upbringing.

Thus, Freud had at last sorted out the threads of his Jewish ambivalence. He craved the release from the guilt, the strict morality, the renunciation of the senses, and perhaps most of all the anti-Semitism that Christianity had afforded its adherents. But he was not willing to pay the price that Christianity demanded. He was just not prepared to forfeit those special Jewish qualities that had allowed him to discover psychoanalysis nor to sacrifice his personal integrity by totally turning his back on his father and his tradition. His Jewishness was thus a dilemma with no obvious solution. Above all else he valued the intellect, and if that gift could be had only at the expense of the Jewish guilt and suffering, so be it. It was perhaps to this very feeling that he was referring when in *An Autobiographical Study* he wrote of his Jewish identity "My parents were Jews and I have remained a Jew myself,"[133] implying a resignation to the inevitable. But it had taken to the end of his days to figure out why.

In another sense Freud had found the fatal flaws in both Christianity and Judaism. In so doing, and by killing off the original Moses, he had set the stage for the emergence of a new Moses, that is, himself, and the introduction of a new and more advanced religion, psychoanalysis. The science of psychoanalysis in fact bore a strong resemblance to the third stage of human intellectual development hypothesized by Freud in the *Future of an Illusion*. Of it he had written: "A *Weltanschauung* erected upon science has, apart from its emphasis on the real external world, mainly negative traits, such as submission to the truth and rejection of illusions."[134] The problem of the Oedipal father and the guilt it caused would continue to haunt humanity, much in the same way that his own father had continued to haunt him throughout his life. But like the disciple Paul to whom he credited much of the actual creation of Christianity, Freud too had forged a new tool for addressing these eternal problems and for freeing the individual from the hold of the past. At the same time Freud's creation bore a strong resemblance to the very institutions it sought to replace. Various writers have in fact referred to the religious quality that surrounded the psychoanalytic movement. Max Graf for instance wrote the following:

> There was the atmosphere of a religion in that room. Freud himself was its new prophet who made the theretofore prevailing methods of psychological investigation appear superficial. Freud's pupils—all inspired and convinced—were his apostles.... After the first dreamy period and the unquestioning faith of the first group of apostles, the time came when the church was founded. Freud began to organize his church with great energy. He was serious and strict in the demands made of his pupils; he permitted no deviation from his orthodox teachings.... If we do consider him as a founder of a religion, we may think of him as Moses full of wrath and unmoved by prayers.[135]

It is even possible that *Moses and Monotheism* itself served as a vehicle for Freud's intention to become the new Moses. Repeatedly in the religion series he drew parallels between the psychic workings of the individual and the processes of human history. The Oedipal drama, for instance, played itself out both on the level of the individual human being and in the history of the species. If psychoanalysis could be applied to the situation of the individual, might it not also be applied to the phenomena of history? Freud's reasoning in the *Future of an Illusion* would certainly lead one to such a conclusion. It is then possible that Freud might have intended to apply his tools of therapy to the Jewish people, putting them on the psychoanalytic couch, so to speak? In individual psychotherapy an early trauma is overcome by being brought to consciousness. Might not the same be true of the historic trauma experienced by the Jews? This was in fact the contention of Kurt Eissler[136] vis-à-vis Freud and his book *Moses and Monotheism*. Eissler believed that by bringing to consciousness an awareness of the murder of Moses and before it the murder of the primal father through his last great work, Freud had been able to set his people free from their enormous guilt and a twenty-five-hundred-year-old destiny. By making the trauma conscious he had allowed the Jews finally to master it. There is also some question as to the psychic value of admitting guilt ritualistically, as in Freud's assessment of Christianity. According to some alternate interpretations, admitting guilt is more likely to lead to depression as opposed to greater health. Eissler further contended that *Moses and Monotheism* may even have laid the ground work for the founding of the modern state of Israel, and that through Freud's efforts the Jews were the first in history to achieve control of their own destiny through insight. While such contentions may seem rather far-fetched, Freud's vision was certainly far-reaching, and he was unshakenly committed to the therapeutic process he had discovered. And in the decades following the publication of *Moses and Monotheism*, Jewish history and the Jewish psyche did in fact take a rather radical turn.

While Freud may well have accomplished all of these different ends through his *Moses and Monotheism*, the transformations he wrought in its main character were clearly autobiographical and directed toward the very heart of his Jewish ambivalence. By making Moses into an Egyptian, Freud acknowledged his own desire for different, non-Jewish, and nobler origins. Like Moses in the biblical tale, he too had had two mothers—his own Amalie and one from the "other side," his nursemaid Resi Wittek. The latter had introduced him into the mysteries of the non-Jewish world, a lure he had never been able fully to transcend, and if his projections in *Moses and Monotheism* were any indication, he still craved her return. Freud had once before at the age of seven or eight transformed his real mother in fantasy into an Egyptian noblewoman. In *The Interpretation of Dreams* he reported the following dream. "I saw my beloved mother, with a peculiarly peaceful, sleeping expression on her features, being carried into the room by two (or three) people with birds' beaks and laid upon the bed."¹³⁷ The image of the bird people had probably been stimulated by the Egyptian woodcuts he had seen in his father's Bible. His father, on the other hand, he had transformed into the father of the great general Hannibal. As was so typical of Freud, he would later objectify these fantasies by raising them to the level of theory. He had noted on several occasions that neurotic patients and young children both tended to fabricate noble parentage for themselves in what he called the "family romance." As an adult, he would do the same, not only in relation to the biblical figure Moses but also in his analysis of Shakespeare to whom he attributed unrealistically noble parentage. It is also possible that Freud may have transformed Moses into an Egyptian in order to absolve the Jewish people and himself from the guilt associated with his murder. Killing an Egyptian Moses would clearly be a psychologically less culpable act and in fact a symbolic repetition of the Exodus story.

By attributing the creation of monotheism (and circumcision) to Akhenaten, Freud unconsciously brought to the surface his desire to convert and with it the guilt he felt in relation to his father. That Akhenaten had come to symbolize religious conversion for Freud was clear from an encounter with Jung and several other colleagues at the Psycho-Analytic Congress in Munich in 1912. During an argument over Akhenaten's motivation for obliterating his father's name from the great monuments of Egypt as a sign of his commitment to the new monotheistic religion, Freud fainted. The occasion for his extreme reaction was evidently Jung's contention that Akhenaten had not carried out the act because of Oedipal rage, as Freud and also Abraham believed, but rather due to a sincere desire to convert. Jung had probably come a bit too close to the truth about Freud's own desires and in response the latter withdrew temporarily from consciousness. Also likely at work in this scenario was a death wish toward Jung, for when Freud awoke he was quoted as having said: "How sweet it must be to die."¹³⁸ Of interest here also was the fact that Freud made no mention in *Moses and Monotheism* of Karl Abraham's 1912 paper on Akhenaten, which had no doubt first stimulated his interest in Egyptian monotheism. Abraham was Freud's primary Jewish confidant during this period, the only person with whom he shared his true feelings and concerns about anti-Semitism and being Jewish. It is likely that this omission was motivated by

Freud's uneasiness at the possibility of Abraham learning the truth about his mentor's secret desire.

With the death of Moses, Freud set into motion a complex intrapsychic scenario. Moses's demise, first of all, set the stage for Freud's own usurpation of his role in Jewish history. In telling Moses's story his own situation emerged with transparency. Both were at first deeply misunderstood, lonely founders who eventually found kindred spirits in the great Jewish prophets. Like Moses and also his more contemporary hero, Charles Darwin, Freud's ideas had met great hostility and had been violently rebuffed but were slowing gaining recognition. Perhaps he even dreamed of being buried beside Darwin in Westminister Abbey.

The murdered Moses in addition symbolized both Freud and his father simultaneously. By killing off Moses-Jacob he expressed the unconscious hostility he felt toward his father, hostility that was not merely Oedipal in the origin but also based in the very real trauma of his father's cowardice as a Jew. In *Moses and Monotheism* Freud defined a hero as "a man who stands up manfully against his father and in the end victoriously overcomes him."[139] Freud, the hero of this "family romance," was thus gaining a final heroic victory over his own Jewish father through Moses's demise. As the new Moses and in spite of his conversion fantasies he may have felt himself to be a better Jew than Jacob had been. Had not his father after all both refused to stand up for his people and turned his back on Orthodoxy early in his life? But nothing is simple in psychoanalysis. Freud at the same time identified with the murdered Moses in order to punish himself for this death wish toward his father, not to mention both for his own success through which he had handily surpassed his father and for his desire to convert. Freud's own impending death made such an identification all the more easy. A clue to the fact that Freud had been overcome by Oedipal guilt during the period of his writing *Moses and Monotheism* can be found in the reemergence of his fear of death (*Todesangst*) in the mid-1930s. Jacob and his stepbrother Emanuel had both died at eighty-one, and as Freud approached this age he evidently grew quite anxious that he might in fact outlive them both and in so doing "surpass" them. In 1935 Freud had been invited to contribute a paper to a volume honoring Romain Rolland. He decided to write a "short analysis of an 'experience of derealization' which overcame me in 1904 on the Acropolis in Athens. It is something quite intimate which has hardly anything to do with R. R."[140] In his interpretation of it Freud attributed the experience to a sense of guilt at having come such a long way and having thus surpassed his father. The critical link between that old memory and the present was the fact that during his visit to Athens he had also been seized by the same fear of death he was now experiencing.

There still remain two aspects of *Moses and Monotheism* that deserve some attention. The first is the question of why Freud felt the need to introduce two very different Moseses as well as two very different versions of the Jewish religion. While the historic Moses was in fact a highly enigmatic and changeable personality, Freud may well have introduced the two Moseses in order to give expression to two very different internal pictures he held of his father. The Jacob of Freiberg days was more like the Egyptian Moses: all-powerful, yet kindly and sensitive. The Jacob of his Vienna experience, on the other hand, was decidedly more tarnished. He was more like the Midianite shepherd as Freud portrayed him: psychologically weak and often taken to outbursts and expressions of anger and frustration. In the two aspects of the Jewish religion, one seen as an advance and other as a regression, he once again gave expression to his personal ambivalence over Judaism. The second question has to do with why Freud insisted on introducing the idea of the primal patricide when he could have accomplished the logical ending by merely killing off Moses, without recourse to the prehistoric myth. He was in fact rigidly insistent about the need to retain the very problematic notion of the survival of memory traces, that is, the inheritance of acquired characteristics, in spite of Jones's and other very strong efforts to dissuade him from such a course. Marianne Krull's suggestion that he needed this part of the story in order to distance himself from his own hostilities toward Jacob makes good sense here. One cannot after all be held responsible for an act that was both predestined and set into motion before one's own birth.

Not unexpectedly, *Moses and Monotheism* received very mixed reviews. It was lauded by dignitaries of the stature of Albert Einstein and H. G. Wells. In other quarters however Freud was likened to a "fanatical Christian in his hatred of Israel."[141] One young American had pleaded with him before its publication "not to deprive our poor unhappy people of the only consolation remaining to them in their misery." To this he could only sheepishly respond, adopting his usual reserved and self-effacing manner, "Can one really believe that my arid treatise would destroy the belief of a single person brought up by heredity and training in the faith, even if it were to come his way?"[142] Perhaps even at this late juncture in time he still remained largely unconscious of the inner struggle that had been played out under the guise of his last great work. In any case he had reached the "Promised Land" of England and could for the little time that remained finally allow himself to bask in the glory of yet another "Promised Land," that of his much overdue fame. To his amazement he was assailed in England by well-wishers expressing their joy over his escape as well as by "a horde of autograph hunters, fools, madmen, and the pious who sent tracts and gospels, want to save my soul, show the way to Christ, and enlighten me about the future of Israel. . . . In short, for the first time and late in life I have experienced what fame means."[143]

# 6
# The Jews and Gentiles of Psychoanalysis

As Freud emerged from the self-imposed isolation of his self-analysis, he began to attract a small circle of followers interested in his work. Although he was a private person by nature, rejection by Vienna's medical community had made him desperate for professional contact as well as an area in which to test out his new ideas. While his experiences as a Jew had prepared him for being "forced into the opposition," it made the process no less painful or isolating. In order to fill the void he anxiously sought out a succession of "fellow travelers" who would eventually disseminate his teachings. The vast majority of these were Jews. The few gentiles who did find their way into the movement were either highly sympathetic to the cause or quick to grow uneasy with its decidedly sectarian nature and disaffiliate.

During Freud's life, psychoanalysis would always remain his exclusive domain. Since his work overshadowed all else, it was not surprising, especially in the early days when the new science drew more opposition than support, that those who sought him out very quickly entered into personal relationships with him. He became their mentor and therapist, listened to their problems, and in whatever ways possible helped them further their careers. While the group was small, they gathered for the Wednesday night meetings in his apartment and afterward adjourned to local cafés for more informal discussions and gossip. Out-of-town guests always received invitations to dine with the Freuds, and "the Professor," as he was generally called, even at times entertained fantasies that certain of his special favorites might marry into the family. His correspondence with colleagues was chatty and highly personal, as filled with professional affairs, family news, and inquiries about the others' lives as with theoretical material. In short, private and professional lives were indistinguishable. One did not merely study psychoanalysis, one was totally immersed in it.

Psychoanalysis was from the beginning an "outlawed" movement—outlawed both because of its Jewish origins and because of Freud's questionable forays into sexuality. It understandably attracted a rather ragtag assortment of disciples. A small percentage joined the movement out of scientific interest or because Freud's ideas fit well with their own clinical experience. Most however were drawn by personal rather than scientific motives: either because of some indefinable intuitive sense that their fate was linked with Freud's, or in the hope of curing their own neuroses, or out of rebellion against the status quo, or because they identified with the rejection he and his theory were experiencing. These early followers freely projected their hopes, fears, and aspirations onto Freud and in turn competed with each other for his favors and attention. He in response controlled the movement with an iron hand: orchestrating discussions, suggesting future work, and planning strategies for gaining new adherents and greater professional credibility. His singular goal was to advance psychoanalysis, and he would not hestitate to use his followers in any manner he saw fit to further that cause.

Besieged by a hostile world, Freud felt the need for a supportive atmosphere in which to continue his work. This was clearly the purpose that the psychoanalytic movement was intended to serve. It was not meant to be, nor was it ever, a forum for the free exchange of ideas. Instead, its members were expected to subscribed to certain basic ideological notions, especially that of the supremacy of sexuality. Within these bounds, originality was welcomed and encouraged, but there was always the unspoken fear of apostasy, and so Freud had to remain ever vigilant to this possibility. Ironically, he eventually found himself caught in a trap of his own making. He was decidedly most attracted to those followers who were capable of creativity and independence of thought, because they were the ones most able to expand and refine his ideas. They were his favorites and the recipients of the majority of his energy and attention. This same group however was the least content with the atmosphere of unquestioned authority and the most likely eventually to defect. At the same time Freud was rather put off by those who would defer to him on every point, in spite of their assured loyalty.

It would not be accurate, however, to portray Freud as anything less than a commited scientist. As such, he paid serious attention to the opinions and concerns of those who gathered around him. Even when their ideas were in opposition to his own, he would patiently struggle to consider their point of view and then find some theoretical resolution or try earnestly to show them where they were in error. He only lost his usual clearsightedness and objectivity when he sensed that the scientific objections being raised in reality masked more personal reactions to him or his leadership. When this occurred, he could become highly rigid, dogmatic, and vengeful.

The history of psychoanalysis is punctuated by numerous inner struggles and subsequent defections. Each break with Freud involved first a serious theoretical disagreement followed by a rupture in the deep emotional ties that had developed between the professor and the exiting analyst. Deeply pained by each of these incidents, Freud would turn unmercifully upon the defector, rally support among his still-loyal followers, berate himself for not seeing the truth earlier, and cut off all further personal contact with the ingrate. This ambivalent pattern of the beloved friend or colleague turned hated enemy was a familiar one in Freud's life and in fact it characterized a number of his most significant relationships. He had a marked tendency to form exceptionally strong and dependent bonds with other people, but he would inevitably grow deeply disappointed in them. The magnitude of his response was typically out of proportion to the objective importance of any given precipitating factor, thus leading one to suspect the existence of powerful unconscious forces at work. Once a rift had occurred, he would sever all ties with the perpetrator, nurture an animosity that would seldom soften or alter with time, and in retrospect in his mind he would rewrite the history of the relationship in terms that fit his new mindset.

Freud himself attributed this tendency, of which he was well aware, to his early relationship with John, his nephew and boyhood friend in Freiberg. Their relationship, he believed, served as an unconscious model for all of those that would come later in life. According to Freud, he and John were both "inseparable friends" and often at odds, fighting and complaining about each other to their elders. In the years that followed his friends were in a certain sense "re-incarnations of this first figure. . . ." Freud always seemed to need both an "intimate friend and a hated enemy. Life circumstances in fact provided him with numerous candidates for both roles and not infrequently "the ideal situation of childhood has been so completely reproduced that friend and enemy have come together in a single individual."[1]

This explanation, while no doubt possessing some merit, served mainly to draw attention away from the more powerful antecedents of these friendship patterns. The first was his highly ambivalent relationship with Jacob, who had been transformed from a mighty and all-powerful adult into a cowardly Jew and who had further diminished himself in his son's eyes by his withdrawal from the role of family provider and strong father figure. The second involved the active remnants of his narcissitic scars from childhood. Freud would reenact this same drama in relation to Josef Breuer and Wilhelm Fleiss in early adulthood. In both of these men he unconsciously sought a less disappointing father figure. There had also been glimpses of the pattern during his engagement to Martha, visited at various times on her, or her mother, and especially on her brother Eli, who had once been Freud's closest friend and associate. The pattern would also emerge anew in relation to the various disciples who would eventually break with him. By this time in his life he had become the father in search of a less wayward and rejecting son that he himself had been and still was—the Jewish son who unconsciously wished to turn his back on the tradition of his ancestors.

\* \* \*

Most historians date the beginning of psychoanalysis from the publication in 1895 of Freud's and Josef Breuer's joint work *Studies in Hysteria*. The two men first met in the late seventies at Brucke's Institute of Physiology where Freud worked as a researcher. Because of common interests and a similar Jewish background they soon became intimate friends and colleagues. Freud, the young and aspiring medical student, was no doubt familiar with Breuer's reputation as a man of science and as one of Vienna's most highly respected physicians. He in fact had served as family physician for various university professors, including Brucke, Exner, and Billroth. The name Breuer was also familiar to Freud through his associations as a Jew. Breuer's father had written a text on Judaism that Freud most likely used during his religious education in the Gymnasium, and the Breuers lived in the same apartment building as the Hammerschlags. Freud was a frequent visitor to the home of his religious school teacher and friend during his Gymnasium and medical school years.

For more than ten years Josef Breuer, only fourteen years Freud's senior, served as a mentor and surrogate father to Freud at a time when his own father had become all but invisible in the life of his son. In this role Breuer lent Freud large sums of money, referred patients to him, provided personal and career counsel, welcomed him into his family circle, and was the one Freud turned to when he needed help or support. It was Breuer, for instance, whom he called upon for medical help in the middle of the night when his friend Ernst Fleischl developed delirium tremens with white snakes creeping over his skin in reaction to cocaine addiction. Fleischl had for several years suffered from an extremely painful terminal illness and upon Freud's concerned but naive advice turned to cocaine for relief.

Freud for his part idealized Breuer, who he felt was truly concerned about his welfare and who he saw as "a man who always understands one." He was a frequent visitor to the Breuer home, described them as "dear good understanding people,"[2] and had an equally strong attachment to Breuer's wife Mathilde, his eldest daughter's namesake, who had even helped him decorate his new apartment upon his return to Vienna from Paris.

Conservative and cautious by nature, Breuer nevertheless tolerated and even encouraged Freud's boldness as a scientist and thinker. On various occasions, such as the incident with Fleischl and cocaine, he had come to Freud's aid in spite of inner doubts about the path his younger colleague was pursuing. He even defended Freud's theories when they met substantial resistance among his own medical colleagues, a position that might well have jeopardized his own comfortable practice and highly esteemed reputation. Freud for his part deeply appreciated the fact of his friend's frequent, "fatherly" interventions. Without Breuer's powerful support it is questionable whether Freud would have felt secure enough to give rein to the adventurous and even reckless side of his nature that emerged at this point in his life. It was clearly a side of himself with which he was not altogether familiar, let alone comfortable, and he needed definite encouragement and support. In February of 1886 Freud wrote the following to his fiancée Martha. "Do you know what Breuer said to me one evening. That he had discovered what an infinitely bold and fearless person I concealed behind my mask of shyness. I have always believed that of myself, but never dared to say it to anyone. I have often felt as if I had inherited all the passion of our ancestors when they defended their Temple."[3] Freud could now venture forth into increasingly dangerous theoretical territory, for his surrogate father would serve as an alter ego guiding his way. When, for instance, he first undertook the exploration of the role of sexuality in the development of neurosis, he wrote: "Breuer will say that I have done myself a lot of harm."[4] Unspoken, however, was the accompanying thought that: "But he will still be there for me." There would soon come a time, however, when Breuer could no longer bring himself to risk his own circumstances for the younger man to whom he was so obviously deeply attached. Sadly, this would become the occasion when Freud would feel the need to reject him and his continued friendship.

The initial groundwork that ultimately led to Freud's discovery of psychoanalysis can be traced back to Breuer's work with a young Jewish patient, Anna O. Her real name was Bertha Pappenheim, and she was in fact an old friend of Martha Freud's who would in time become her relative. The patient suffered from a wide range of hysterical symptoms related directly to her father's fatal illness. Most interesting however was the discovery by Breuer that if the young woman could talk about her symptoms, she would gain some relief from them. In addition, if he had her relate the details of the first appearance of a symptom, it would completely disappear. This "talking cure" or "chimney sweeping," Bertha's own name for the process, became Breuer's primary mode of treatment with the young women. He would in time combine this process with hypnosis to create what he called the "cathartic method." Breuer had however developed a strong countertransference to this very interesting patient, and his wife became first bored and in time highly jealous of his continuous discussion of her symptoms. When he finally realized the source of his wife's growing unhappiness, he quickly terminated treatment. He was, however, called back that same evening to find Anna O. in the midst of an hysterical childbirth. This in turn had evidently developed as a consequence of an hysterical pregnancy that she had unconsciously created in response to Breuer's enormous concern and attention. He managed to calm her down through hypnosis and then fled the scene in a cold sweat. He was so personally shaken by what had occurred that he wished nothing more to do with the case. Anna O. never fully recovered, and in fact she fared much more poorly as a result of his efforts than

## The Jews and Gentiles of Psychoanalysis    153

Breuer was ever be able to acknowledge. But neurosis does not necessarily dampen the human spirit, and in time Bertha Pappenheim became Germany's first social worker and would undertake a number of dangerous expeditions to Russia, Poland, and Romania during World War II to rescue Jewish children whose parents had been killed in anti-Semitic pogroms.

The case of Anna O. made a very deep impression on Freud, who never tired of discussing its details with Breuer, in spite of the latter's general reticence. Three years later Freud went to Paris on a travel grant to study hysteria and hypnosis with Charcot. Charcot had demonstrated that hysterical symptoms such as paralysis, tremors, and anesthesias could be created through hypnosis. This fact in combination with Breuer's discovery that hysterical symptoms could be removed by merely talking convinced Freud of the psychogenic character of hysteria. He returned to Vienna excited and anxious to pursue this new approach to the treatment of hysteria. He was quickly dismayed however by the extremely cool reception his ideas received in medical circles, especially those which dealt with hypnosis and male hysteria. Chief among his critics was his former teacher, Theodor Meynert, who bore a strong antipathy toward Charcot that he generalized to Freud. In the heat of debate he had even referred to his former student as "only a hypnotist."[5] For several years thereafter Meynert waged war on Charcot through Freud and in the process poisoned the minds of many of his colleagues against him. Ironically, Meynert would confess to Freud on his deathbed that his opposition to the notion of male hysteria was highly personal: that he was himself a classic male hysteric and that in order to hide this fact he had fought the idea and its originator with all of his energy and might.

The rejection Freud experienced at the hands of critics such as Meynert was only exacerbated by a growing anti-Semitism in medical circles. He wrote the following to Fleiss in February of 1988: "There was a terrific row at the Medical Society yesterday. They wanted to force us to subscribe to a new weekly which is intended to represent the pure, elevated and Christian views of certain dignitaries who have long since forgotten what work is like. They will naturally carry their proposal through; I feel very inclined to resign."[6] These two sources of personal attack reinforced each other but only further steeled Freud's resolve to find a viable treatment for hysteria. They did however make Breuer's continued support all the more critical and necessary. Unhappily, Freud's growing defensiveness would simultaneously make him more dependent on Breuer and more demanding that his friend follow him into the unchartered territory he had set as his course. As was evident in relation to both his struggle with his Jewish identity and his prospective in-laws during the courtship with Martha, threat tended to push Freud into dicotimous thinking and into seeing the world in blacks and whites. It is not surprising then that Breuer's understandable and eventual reluctance would be interpreted as cowardice and outright opposition by Freud.

After his return from Paris, Freud had experimented with various treatments for hysteria. After a quick rejection of electrotherapy, the prescribed treatment of the day, because it had as much relation to reality as some "Egyptian dreambook,"[7] he turned to hypnosis and to Breuer's method of catharsis. But neither of these were sufficiently predictable and he slowly moved to suggestion and finally to free association. The idea for the latter had come to him from an essay written by Ludwig Borne entitled "The Art of Becoming an Original Writer in Three Days" that he had read during adolescence.

His cumulative clinical experience was increasingly convincing him of the critical nature of the doctor-patient relationship as well as the etiology of hysteria in childhood. He felt quite strongly that sexual experience played an important role in both. In the early 1890s Freud once again tried to revive Breuer's interest in hysteria. Realizing that much of his mentor's resistance revolved around the experience with Anna O., he shared with Breuer a similar incident in which one of his female patients had thrown her arms around him in an act of affection. This transference phenomena, he was convinced, was merely a characteristic of hysteria. His confession and analysis of what had happened seemed to calm Breuer and to assuage his feelings of personal guilt and reproach. He even agreed to work with Freud on *Studies in Hysteria*, which would include the case of Anna O., but only as long as his young friend would agree that sexuality would remain in the background.

The book was not well received and sold only 626 copies in thirteen years. But this was not what led to their ultimate break in the summer of 1894. Freud continued to press Breuer about the importance of sexual disturbances in the development of hysteria and Breuer in turn vacillated back and forth on the issue. He had once remarked to Freud that neurotic behavior was always connected with secrets of the marriage bed, but such a clinical anecdote was a far cry from scientific fact. He continued to publicly support Freud's views on sexual etiology, but he could not convince himself of it internally. Finally, in response to Freud's expression of thanks after once again voicing agreement with him at a meeting of the College of Physicians, Breuer could bear it no longer and turned away from Freud with the confession: "I don't believe a word of it."[8]

Freud would never again personally acknowledge Breuer, although he was always quite careful to pay an intellectual debt to him for having brought psychoanalysis into being. Freud had put up an impregnable wall that would never again be breeched. He was especially tormented by the inability to repay his financial debts to Breuer and doubly frustrated by his former friend attempting to write them off against medical services Freud had provided to a relative of his. A year later he wrote to Fleiss, who had replaced his former friend as confidante and intimate, that the very sight of Breuer would make him inclined to emigrate.[9] In *The Psychopathology of Everyday Life* he offered a thinly veiled reference to a change in his attitude toward the M. family: "Our intimate friendship later gave place to a total estrangement. . . . I fell into the habit . . . of also avoiding the neighborhood and the house . . . as if it were forbidden territory."[10] And there was finally the very sad story told by Breuer's daughter-in-law, who remembered walking with Breuer when he was a very old man. Suddenly he saw Freud coming toward him on the street and instinctively opened his arms. Freud passed right by, pretending he had not seen him.[11]

Mere intellectual differences could not explain the bitterness that Freud felt toward his once intimate friend and colleague nor why his admiration and idealization had so fully turned into hatred and loathing. The relationship with Breuer had obviously reignited certain deep inner conflicts that he had unconsciously projected onto Breuer. The most likely candidate was Freud's enormous ambivalence over dependency, which was an undisguised throwback to his unresolved Oedipal feelings for Jacob. One side of Freud's personality desperately craved the all-powerful and giving father, a role that his own father had never been able adequately to fulfill. Breuer, on the other hand, was everything Jacob was not. He could provide clear and decisive advice when needed; unlike Jacob who, though deeply dedicated to his son, could only be vague and distant. Breuer had made a great success of his life and was a figure to emulate; again the opposite of Jacob, who was in his son's eyes a failure in all aspects of his existence. And he had the resources and abilities to intervene in the world on behalf of his surrogate son; unlike Jacob who had for some time been actively withdrawing from it.

Freud had willingly placed himself in debt to Breuer, first financially and then intellectually. The habit of borrowing money to survive had begun with his old Hebrew teacher Samuel Hammerschlag, who sympathized from his own youth with Freud's financial straits and offered a loan to ease the situation. Freud found the solution almost magical, but needed a justification that would allow him to overcome his feelings of indebtedness and dependency. He summarized the resulting logic for Martha as follows. "I intend to compensate for it by being charitable myself when I can afford it. . . . At first I felt very ashamed, but later, when I saw that Breuer and he agreed in this respect, I accepted the idea of being indebted to good men and those of our faith without the feeling of personal obligation. Thus I was suddenly in the possession of fifty florins."[12] Jewish law in fact made it incumbent upon those who were able to help those in need, and it was at the same time quite clear in its dictate that such giving must occur in a manner that underplayed any sense of indebtedness. The recipient was believed to have provided the donor an opportunity to fulfill an important commandment and thus had given as well as received. By thus claiming an aspect of his birthright as a Jew, Freud was able to solve, temporarily anyway, a knotty intrapsychic dilemma.

But this financial indebtedness did weigh heavily on his mind at least unconsciously, for he reported on several different occasions experiences that he called "*schnorrer* fantasies," that is, dreams of coming into large sums of money purely by accident. A *schnorrer* is Yiddish for a beggar who refuses to feel any obligation for what he receives. Evidently, a side of Freud identified strongly with this figure, which offered a fantasied means of escaping his dilemma. In Paris, for instance, he met an Austrian doctor and his wife, the Richettis, who were both childless and quite fond of him. He often fantasized of inheriting large sums of money from them. He also had daydreams of stopping a runaway horse and being rewarded substantially for his heroic act. All were clearly magical solutions to his very real poverty and accumulating indebtedness.

Freud was also in Breuer's debt for the insights that the case of Anna O. had afforded him. His desire to collaborate with

## The Jews and Gentiles of Psychoanalysis    157

Breuer in the continued exploration of hysteria was a perfect solution to his indebtedness. It not only allowed him a means finally to pay back his mentor in the form of a scientific accomplishment of his own initiation, but at the same time it guaranteed him Bruer's continued support and protection. Freud was no doubt also somewhat shocked by the content of his discoveries and anxiously sought the possibility of shared responsibility. Hiding behind Breuer's reputation, even in the smallest way, must have afforded him a well-appreciated sense of paternal comfort and support. Yet in their work together Freud was clearly the dominant and moving force. He in fact referred to this period as a time when Breuer "submitted to my influences."[13] Freud's enormous daring, drive, and persistance were no doubt simultaneously attractive and frightening to the more conservative Breuer. He was definitely ambivalent about the whole project and was thus more than willing to play a subservient role. In the summer of 1895 he characterized their relationship in a letter to their mutual friend Fliess as follows. "Freud's intellect is soaring at its highest. I gaze after him as a hen at a hawk."[14]

Yet as his dependency on Breuer increased, its opposite in the form growing rebelliousness and a need to be dominant and to assert his independence also emerged. This aspect of his Oedipal conflict could tolerate no weakness, dependency, or indebtedness. As long as Breuer would yield to his demands and willingly adopt the secondary role in their collaboration, all was well. But as soon as the older physician began to hesitate and vacillate, he became a threat to Freud's feelings of independence and control and had to be summarily rejected. In Breuer's hesitancy to swallow whole the primary and exclusive role of sexuality in the development of neurosis Freud perceived great cowardice. Referring to Breuer's occasional references to the importance of sexuality he wrote. "It is one thing to give utterance to an idea once or twice in the form of a passing *apercu*, and quite another to mean it seriously—to take it literally and pursue it in the face of every contradictory detail, and to win it a place among accepted truths."[15] This charge of cowardice could not help but reverberate back unconsciously to the critical incident of Jacob and the anti-Semite. Its deep scar, as in the current situation with Breuer, would always sensitize Freud to the possibility of disappointment in those upon whom he depended. So sensitized, he would inevitably discover these traits in those whom he allowed to come close. And with that disappointment, as Freud now felt toward Breuer, inevitably came the feelings of anger and rejection at the loss of the all-powerful and protecting father.

\* \* \*

At about the same time as his estrangement from Breuer, Freud entered into yet another, even more intense relationship: this time with Wilhelm Fliess, a nose and throat specialist from Berlin who was two years Freud's junior. Ernest Jones called this relationship the "only really extraordinary experience in Freud's life." By way of explanation he wrote: "For a man of nearly middle age, happily married and having six children, to cherish a passionate friendship for someone intellectually his inferior, and for him to subordinate for several years his judgement and opinions to those of that other man: this . . . is unusual. . . . But for that man to free himself by following a path hitherto untrodden by any human being, by the heroic task of exploring his own unconscious mind: that is extraordinary."[16]

The two men first came to know each other, ironically enough, through Breuer. Fleiss had been visiting Vienna in 1887 for some postgraduate study when he encountered Breuer, who suggested he attend some lectures being given by Freud. The two hit it off immediately and initiated an correspondence that grew increasingly regular and personal as Freud's break with Breuer proceeded.[17] Fliess was clearly an unconscious replacement for the dependency he had expressed toward Breuer. In many ways however Fliess was even better suited to the job, for he neither balked at the topic of sexuality nor felt any inhibition or hesitancy in pursuing the most radical or farfetched ideas. Those who knew him described Fliess as a highly attractive and "fascinating"[18] personality: an accomplished conversationalist, impressive in his appearance, with a wealth of biological knowledge, an imaginative grasp of medicine, and a penchant for far-reaching speculation. On the negative side, however, was a tendency dogmatically to hold to ideas once formed and to eschew all criticism. Only Karl Abraham, who had the uncanny ability to perceive faults from the start in those who would eventually come into conflict with Freud, was less than impressed with Fliess.

The two shared many characteristics and interests in common. Both were young medical specialists in the process of establishing practices and raising families. Fliess had somewhat of an easier time of it, however, for he had married a wealthy Viennese wife[19] and found practice in Berlin far freer and less constricted than Freud's in Vienna. Both shared an interest in literature and history that found frequent expression in their correspondence. There were in addition great similarities in the ideas they were pursuing. Fliess had hypothesized the existence of the "nasal reflex neurosis," a complex of symptoms that bore a striking resemblance to Freud's notion of neurasthenia and that could be relieved by the application of cocaine to the nose. Related also was his theory that there was a biological connection between the nose and the female genital organs. Freud would in fact ask him on several occasions to perform operations on the nasal cavities of female hysteric patients in the hope of providing relief from their symptoms. Fliess also believed in the idea of periodicity, that is, of recurrent life periods or cycles that determined the stages of human growth, the dates of illnesses, and the date of one's eventual death. Lastly, he placed enormous emphasis on the bisexuality of human beings. This idea would eventually find its way into Freud's own conception of sexuality. At the height of their relationship Freud even hoped that Fliess's theories would lead the way to a discovery of the anatomical correlates of the psychological phenomena he was unearthing.

As with Breuer, Freud identified with Fliess as a fellow Jew. Freud's letters[20] were amply sprinkled with Yiddish phrases, allusions to Jews, Jewish jokes, and biblical references as well as commentary on current events of Jewish interest. Both for instance followed the unfolding Dreyfus case in France with great interest and emotion. Of it Freud wrote the following: "Zola keeps us breathless. He is a fine fellow, a man with whom one could get on. The disgusting behavior of the French reminded me of what you said on Breslau bridge about the degeneracy of France, which at first I could not believe."[21] Finally Fliess's penchant for numerology, like Freud's, had its origins in their shared ethnic past.

Because of the physical distance that separated them, the major part of the relationship took place through letters. Their correspondence covered a period from 1887 to 1902: from Freud's growing disappointment in Breuer through the completion of his self-analysis and the beginnings of the psychoanalytic movement proper. When possible the two met in person—most often in Vienna because of Fliess's wife's family there, occasionally in Berlin, and when possible elsewhere for two- or three-day meetings, which Freud fondly called their "congresses." They shared the details of their work, emerging theories, and private lives. Freud, more than Fliess, desperately sought the contact. He called Fliess "his sole public."[22] This was in fact not far from the literal truth, for by then not only had his unorthodox ideas cut him off from most of his old medical acquaintances, but his avoidance of Breuer had served to sever ties with the few colleagues who had remained friendly.

Many writers have commented on the great passion Freud expressed toward Fliess, even subtly hinting at the existence of homosexual overtones in the relationship. Speaking of their forthcoming congress in 1896, for instance, Freud wrote that he "panted" for it "as to a slaking of hunger and thirst" and after it felt "in a state of continual euphoria and working like a youth." Another congress was described as "a proper wish-fulfillment, a beautiful dream that will become real." And further: "After each of our Congresses I have been newly fortified for weeks, new ideas pressed forward, pleasure in the hard work was restored, and the flickering hope of finding one's way through the jungle burned for a while steadily and brilliantly."[23] While the great passion that infused these letters may have at some level reflected homosexual yearnings, it simultaneously showed Freud's desperate need for emotional support and intellectual contact. What he longed for, in short, was a strong figure upon whom he could depend and from whom he could gain succor and comfort in this particularly difficult emotional time in his life. His break with Breuer had only exacerbated his enormous dependency needs, which were continuously fed by growing isolation and shortly would be activated anew by the death of his father.

So great were Freud's needs in fact that he unconsciously magnified and distorted Fliess's abilities and concern. He called him "the Kepler of biology,"[24] saw him "as an even greater visionary than I,"[25] and likened him to the "Messiah"[26] if only his work on periodicity could solve the problem of predicting safe intercourse. He also felt enormous emotional support from Fliess. "People like you should not die out, my dear friend; we others need the like of you too much. How much have I to thank you for in consolation, understanding, stimulation in my loneliness, in the meaning of life you have given me, and lastly in health which no one else could have brought back to me. It is essentially your example that has enabled me to gain the intellectual strength to trust my own judgment . . .

and to face with deliberate resignation, as you do, all the hardships the future may have in store."[27] Fliess became, in short, a blank screen for Freud's unconscious needs, and as Paul Roazen suggested, an "uncomprehending" one at that.[28] Although the doctor from Berlin in actuality no doubt possessed certain gifts, he was far from Freud's intellectual equal and by all accounts much too self-absorbed to either truly grasp what Freud had undertaken or to lend the therapeutic support Freud so desperately craved. The idea of Fliess playing the role of emotional mentor and intellectual guide to the would-be father of psychoanalysis was objectively nothing short of ludicrous. In reality, Freud's wish list represented yet another attempt to find an adequate father-substitute.

In the mid-1890s Freud was emotionally on the edge: squarely in the grip of his psychoneurosis and shortly to undertake his self-analysis as a means of treatment. In this too Fliess played an unknowing yet critical role. Through Freud's frank and often uncensored self-disclosures and sharing of the material that emerged from the analysis, he put Fliess into the position of being a sounding board and therapist. It is even possible that a transference neurosis of sorts was established between the two. Never before or again would Freud, who was usually rather self-contained, disclose so much of himself to another human being. The fact that their friendship survived in this rather unusual form for over ten years depended no doubt on the limited personal contacts that distance afforded. This barrier actually allowed for and encouraged Freud's enormous projection. Ironically, however, if Fliess had in fact been able to provide Freud any of what he craved, he probably would not have been driven into the self-analysis or the realization of his own abilities and intellectual prowess, not to mention the great discoveries that grew out of it. Freud had in sum created a fantasized parent who gave him the courage to accomplish something which he was clearly capable of doing but lacked the confidence to carry out on his own.

Of particular importance to Freud was the hope that Fliess with his supposed vast knowledge of biology and anatomy would serve as a check on the scientific validity of his theories. Freud would send Fliess the latest version of a theory or idea and wait anxiously for acknowledgment of its empirical acceptability. If it was deemed credible, he could continue, assured that he was on a proper track and had not fallen into some logical trap or strayed into erroneous territory. Fliess's positive assessment of his work seemed absolutely critical to Freud. He likened Fliess's praise to "nectar and ambrosia," and equally telling, he wrote the following in 1890. "I feel very isolated, scientifically blunted, stagnant and resigned. When I talk to you, and saw that you thought something of me, I actually started thinking something of myself, and the picture of confident energy which you offered was not without its effect."[29] The substantial credence Freud paid to Fliess's judgment cannot help but make one wonder whether he might not at this point in his career have been experiencing some serious doubts about his creative abilities or the validity of the course he was pursuing. If he had such doubts, it would not have been at all surprising. His ideas had after all been for several years now publicly attacked by the bastions of the Viennese medical world, including many of those who had been his teachers. And of late even Breuer, as much father as colleague, had seen fit to reject him because of his growing obsession with sexuality. In spite of the usual bravado and arrogance, he could not have been other than deeply hurt and torn by serious doubts about his work. Even the most self-confident man, and this was clearly not Freud, would doubt under such circumstances. Thus, the more Freud could inflate the knowledge and critical judgment of his lone critic, the more able he was to ward off self-doubt and self-recrimination.

But the psychological picture was even more complicated than this, because since adolescence Freud had experienced concern over his strong tendencies toward uncontrolled speculation. To allay these fears he had become a zealous convert to science and its most demanding expression, radical empiricism. He had not found a comfortable niche for himself at the university until he joined Brucke's Institute of Physiology. There he worked under the direction, guidance and, perhaps most important, the censorship of one of the world's foremost empircists. Even in his research efforts Freud was careful to a fault and would always require excessive proof before drawing any conclusion. This fear had in fact cost him dearly, for on two different occasions—the first his research on the physiology of the neuron and the second on cocaine—his hesitation to publish prematurely had allowed others to gain fame for ideas he had discovered much earlier. Even as he ventured into the new realm of psychology, he felt a compulsion and strong need to support his ideas with data from neurology and physiology. Even in *Moses and Monotheism* he had been driven to postulate a biological mechanism to explain the transmission of memory of the primal murder from generation to generation.

## The Jews and Gentiles of Psychoanalysis 163

Fliess, like the many mentors and teachers who had preceded him, was expected to keep a tight rein on Freud's tendency to speculate. One of the works that he had submitted to Fliess for comments and critique was *Project for a Scientific Psychology*. It was in fact Freud's effort, and a masterful one at that, to explain psychological functioning in terms of neurological activity. The choice of Fliess for this role was particularly ironic. He was, first of all, too engrossed in his own ideas and theories to be able to function objectively at any level. What he provided Freud instead were equal amounts of hollow praise and suggestions on grammatical structure, style, and discretion and the appropriateness of the material. Second, Fliess possessed a tendency toward wild and unsubstantiated speculation himself, which in actuality made even Freud's greatest fears about himself pale in comparison. Yet ironically Freud valued those very qualities in Fliess that he found so objectionable in himself. "For your revelations in sexual physiology I can only bring breathless attention and critical admiration. I am too circumscribed in my knowledge to be able to discuss them. But I surmise the finest and most important things and hope you will not refrain from publishing even conjectures. One cannot do without people who have the courage to think new things before they are in a position to demonstrate them."[30] In addition he attributed to Fliess intellectual characteristics he himself possessed in abundance and that his friend sorely lacked: good judgment, basic scientific knowledge, and sheer intellect. All he felt were necessary in someone near to him in order to balance his own speculative tendencies. Sadly, by imbuing Fliess with such extraordinary qualities, he robbed himself of his own virtues and in the process of his self-confidence. Herein however resided one of the true benefits Freud would derive from his self-analysis: relief from his great dependency on others. Only when he could trust himself enough to stand on his own would he be able to forgive his father for disappointing him (and not being there to stand up for him) and thus let loose some of the repressed anger. Only then could he begin to value and nurture rather than fear his greatest intellectual gift and genius: his ability to speculate and enter into new and previously unexplored regions of the mind. After Fliess and his self-analysis, Freud was able to serve the critical function for himself. One can in fact identify in subsequent works an internal dialogue that he created with himself and his reader. After his self-analysis, Freud also seemed less in need of an external father figure. He had instead begun to transform the dependency need into a need to be depended upon by others, thus opening the way for the creation of a movement to support his work.

Related to his intellectual insecurity was Freud's surprising attraction to superstitious beliefs. He felt, for instance, a strong inner attraction for Fliess's notion of periodicity and for the numerology he practiced to prove its validity. Even after he had grown disillusioned with Fliess himself,[31] he retained into old age an almost obsessive concern for predicting the age at which he would die. As each milestone passed, he would create a new one. Fliess had predicted, for example, that Freud would die at age fifty-one. When this did not come to pass, he changed the critical date to sixty-one or sixty-two, reasoning as follows. In 1899 Freud was given a new telephone number: 14362. Since he was forty-three at the time, the remaining digits probably signified the "real" date of his death. Freud also entered into similar numerological speculations in *Psychopathology of Everyday Life.* Freud would also periodically set upon these superstitious beliefs. When his seriously ill daughter, Mathilde, took an unexpected turn toward health for example, he was compelled to throw a slipper against the wall, an act that he interpreted as a sacrificial behavior, performed in thanksgiving.

Freud was put off, however, by what he labeled as "mysticism" in others. He used the term pejoratively to refer to all nonrational and unscientific phenomena, which included superstitious behavior and magical thinking of the sort he himself practiced, as well as mental telepathy, acausal events, and spiritual faith and knowledge. He especially accused Jung of straying into the realm of the mystical as the latter's ideas moved further and further afield from the primacy of sexuality. Yet Freud could never completely suppress his own fascination with the subject nor rid himself of his own superstitious beliefs or behaviors.

In 1909 Freud confided in Jung that his fascination with numerology confirmed "the specifically Jewish character of my mysticism."[32] This confession offers an interesting possibility for understanding the roots of his ambivalence in this area. The Eastern European and Galician Jews of his ancestry were particularly superstitious and mystical in their approach to life and to Judaism. Numerology was in fact widely practiced. An early exposure to such beliefs in the home of Jacob and Amalie would not be at all out of the question and this was very likely the source of his own lingering superstitions, such as those related to the date of his death. This same concern may well have been reinforced intrapsychically and gained power through the unconscious guilt Freud felt over the possibility that he might surpass his father and ancestors by giving up their ways. It is further possible that this same ambivalence toward the nonrational might be related to the fear of wild speculation that had early on attracted him to radical empiricism. His adolescent rejection of traditional Jews and Judaism could well have included a discomfort with their superstitious, unscientific, and undisciplined ways and beliefs. To the extent that he perceived similar tendencies in himself, he might have become fearful that they might hold him back, keep him imprisoned forever in the ghetto and mark him as different and as Jewish, like the clumsy boy in the Biergarten or his traveling companions on the train from Freiberg to Vienna. If there is any truth to this contention, it offers yet another powerful connection between him and Fliess as Jews. Interestingly enough, in this regard David Bakan in what was probably the first major work on Freud's Jewish identity, *Sigmund Freud and the Jewish Mystical Traditional*, argued that both Freud and Fliess were significantly affected in their ideas by Jewish mysticism and elements of the Kabbala.

Perhaps not surprisingly, as Freud moved through his self-analysis, he progressively lost the need for his dependency on Fliess. When the break finally occurred,[33] which was inevitable given the incompatibility of their views, it was nowhere nearly as painful for Freud as his estrangement from Breuer had been. From Freud's perspective the discovery of the dynamic workings of the psyche from his self-analysis made Fliess's deterministic notions of the laws of periodicity increasingly untenable. Fliess for his part attributed Freud's "violence toward me"[34] to his colleague's envy. Freud also laid some blame for the break-up on himself and his in retrospect unwise attempt to psychoanalyze his former friend. Especially hurtful to Freud was Fliess's contention that psychoanalysts merely projected their own thoughts into the minds of their patients.

A final parting conflict involved Fliess's accusation that Freud had leaked his theory of bisexuality to a patient, Herman Swoboda, who had in turn communicated it to Otto Weininger. The latter had published a highly successful book with bisexuality as its theme. Evidently Fliess was generally correct in this matter, but Freud was too embarrassed to acknowledge the truth. And to make matters even worse, he evidently had some unconscious thoughts of his own of pilfering the idea. Unfortunately, the whole matter got out of hand with accusations and counteraccusations and ended up first in print and then in the courts. Although Freud would always acknowledge Fliess's contributions to psychoanalysis, he remained bitter about the break-up to the end, and when in 1925 Fliess sent him greetings through Karl Abraham, his comment was: "This expression of sympathy after twenty years leaves me rather cold."[35]

Almost as fascinating as the story of the relationship between Freud and Fliess was the saga of what happened to their letters. Freud had destroyed all of the letters Fliess had written him, but Fliess had preserved Freud's. After Fliess's death in 1928, his widow sold them to a Berlin bookseller, Reinhold Stahl, but with the instruction that they not be passed on to Freud himself. Stahl fled to France to escape the Nazis and there sold the letters to Marie Bonaparte, who was at that time in analysis with Freud. She told Freud of the letters and he immediately grew angry and gave her advice in his characteristic form of a Jewish joke. "How do you cook a peacock?" "You first bury it in the ground for a week and then dig it up again." "And then?" "Then you throw it away."[36] He insisted she destroy the letters and offered to pay half of the expenses incurred in getting them. But she refused and deposited them in the winter of 1937–38 in the Rothschild Bank in Vienna. Fearing for the security of Jewish banks after the Nazi invasion of Austria, she immediately returned to retrieve them. Because she was royalty, she was allowed to make a withdrawal from her safety deposit box but under the watchful eye of the Gestapo. Luckily, they did not inquire into the box's contents. She was forced to leave the letters in the Danish Embassy in Paris, but again luck would have it that the Danish Legation in Paris had been spared and was not rummaged through. The letters faced a final hurdle in crossing a mine-filled English Channel, but at last they reached London intact and unharmed, wrapped in waterproof and floatable materials just in case of disaster.

* * *

Freud's continuing need for a sympathetic audience and sounding board, especially in light of the disillusionment he suffered with Fliess, brought him to the Jewish fraternal order of the B'nai B'rith, which he joined on 29 September 1897. The Wien chapter had been established only two years earlier but was experiencing unprecedented growth. As the anti-Semitism in Vienna worsened, it attracted more and more Jews who felt the need for a safe haven away from the social and professional hostility that had become increasingly common. At its induction into the international order in fact the Wien chapter had already attracted almost fifty members. Freud was at this point in his life isolated from the medical world, in the midst of his bout with psychoneurosis and desperate enough soon to begin his self-analysis. The pressure of isolation, both as a radical theorist and as a Jew, was likely a motivation for his participation in B'nai B'rith. "I soon became one of you, enjoyed your sympathy, and almost never neglected to go to the place, surrounded by hostility, where I was certain to find friends."[37] Many of the men he met in the meetings were old acquaintances from school days, and like the majority of them he had ventured off into the gentile world but was perhaps now wondering whether it was not more prudent to remain among one's own people. Freud had previously felt this sense of secret sympathy with Hammerschlag and Breuer when he had first encountered anti-Semitism at the university and later he felt it with Fliess. Like so many others, when Freud was faced with the ugly realities of anti-Jewish hatred, he too tended to disassimilate, that is, loose the desire to be part of the gentile world. Martin Freud recalled that during this period he "can hardly remember a non-Jewish person among the many guests at our home."[38]

But the B'nai B'rith was more than merely a safe haven from anti-Semitism. In addition it sought to perpetuate Jewish values and identity in its members. A sense of its mission can be found in the following excerpt from the organization's statement of purpose.

> Formed out of an inner urgency, the Humanitarian Societies of B'nai B'rith embark courageously and consciously upon their difficult and as yet unfulfilled tasks: to work on "elevating the mental and moral character of the people of our faith," to arouse and perfect the inherent virtues of our people, to eliminate as far as is humanly possible the defective influences which seize every nation, and thus to work on behalf of mankind. For good reasons we therefore bear the sublime word humanity in our name.[39]

Such a message did not fall on deaf ears, for the same impulse that had brought so many new members to the B'nai B'rith was also causing them to rethink their positions in society and the meaning of their identities as Jews. A group affiliation that had previously seemed merely irrelevant was suddenly being reexamined with great seriousness for what it might offer by way of self-definition. Freud remained within this milieu, an active and committed member of B'nai B'rith, for over five years,[40] and there is no reason to believe that he too did not enter into a similar process of soul-searching and was not swayed by these same forces, especially given the kind of personal insights vis-à-vis his feelings about being a Jew that his self-analysis was dredging up.

With time and no relief from anti-Semitism, the B'nai B'rith slowly yet consistently changed its position in relation to its gentile neighbors. Although it continued to espouse a philosophy of universalism and concern for all humanity, its programs of charity—including agencies for finding jobs for recent Jewish immigrants, lending money, treating illness, and caring for Jewish orphans—were for Jews alone. The justification: "This restriction exists only by necessity. It is a restriction based on the fact that the poor and oppressed Jew is not only poor and oppressed because this is his common human destiny, but is in a much more deplorable situation and is more oppressed than even the destitute of other faiths because he is a Jew."[41]

Many members had also begun to develop an increasingly chauvinistic attitude about their Jewishness. To them the ideals of Judaism had in fact become a source of personal uniqueness and superiority. Gone were the days of unbridled enchantment with all things German. Anti-Semitism flew squarely in the face of dreams of full equality and the possibility of truly amicable relations between Jew and gentile. The only solution, and this seemed to be the direction that the B'nai B'rith advocated, was a withdrawal from the hostility and intolerance that was part and parcel of the Christian world and a cessation of further efforts to gain acceptance into it.

This position was a radical departure from the one taken by Jews a generation earlier. The parents of those currently involved in B'nai B'rith found it impossible to believe that the great hopes of full citizenship and equality that had seemed so close only a decade ago were not going to be realized. Typical of this position was Freud's one-time mentor, Josef Breuer. Breuer had been particularly critical of the growing Jewish chauvinism and many Jews' refusal to submit to the insults of anti-Semitism. He had written the following to *Kadimah*, a Jewish fraternity whose student members had grown particularly belligerent in their physical responses to anti-Semitism. "Our epidermis has almost become too sensitive. I would wish that we Jews had a consciousness of our own value, which would make us indifferent to the judgement of others, rather than this unwavering, easily insulted, hyper-sensitive *point d'honneur.*" To emphasize his dual identity he signed the letter "Josef Breuer, Jew by origin, German by nature."[42] As Freud's mentor, Breuer had counseled him to remain a Jew, but to do so with dignity. This meant to emulate neither those Jews whose moral weakness or self-doubt pushed them to conversion, nor those, and this was perhaps even more objectionable to Breuer, who stooped to undignified displays of chauvinism and self-defense. If Freud's attitudes about Jewish self-expression had in fact been changing along similar lines as those of his brothers in the B'nai B'rith, his growing distance from Breuer's position may well have been another, though unstated, reason for their break. Also possible in Freud's perception of Breuer's position as a Jew was an association to Jacob's cowardice.

As a member of B'nai B'rith, Freud attended meetings regularly, was active in recruiting new members and establishing a second Vienna chapter, led discussions on the mission of the order, and delivered twenty-one lectures to the group between 1897 and 1917, mostly before 1902. With the exception of Fliess and two talks given to the Judische Akademische Lesehalle in 1896 and 1897, the B'nai B'rith was his exclusive audience during this period. Many of his early ideas in fact first saw the light of day at these weekly meetings. His first two lectures, for example, given on 7 and 14 December 1897 were on the interpretation of dreams, and the response was highly "enthusiastic," as shown by "unrestrained applause."[43] Freud was so delighted with the reaction to the first lecture that he blurted out "I shall continue it next Tuesday."[44]

In time the order would proudly celebrate Freud as one of its own. The ideas he put forth were highly provocative, and many of those who had first been introduced to psychoanalysis in this manner would later join the movement itself. In a sense the B'nai B'rith functioned as a launching pad for it, what Dennis Klein called the "prefiguring"[45] for the organization that Freud would in time create. His participation in B'nai B'rith had bolstered his intellectual confidence, offered him a forum for refining his ideas, and provided an initial vehicle for attracting a following. It had also provided a safe environment for struggling with the meaning of his Jewish identity and an opportunity to discover a relationship between his emerging work and his ethnic origins. Just as the brothers of the order came increasingly to see Jews as the "champions of the ideal of humanity"[46] and as a bastion of the ideals of peace and democracy, so too did Freud see his work as visionary of the future and the Jews within it as performing a pioneering function. To those within the Society there was little doubt that Freud's efforts in the creation of psychoanalysis were squarely within the tradition of Judaism, "genuinely Jewish," as Ludwig Braun put it. In his address to the order on the occasion of a celebration honoring Freud, Braun further stated: "Can anyone even imagine Freud as not Jewish?"[47] Braun went on to define the meaning of Jewishness as being comprised of an independence of spirit, the willingness to do battle with an unjust society, and a vision of the whole of nature and humanity. All, he suggested, were intimate aspects of Freud's personality and liberally infused in his work. These remarks impressed and pleased Freud greatly. They "cast a spell over the whole audience, including my family,"[48] he wrote, and in response he drafted his statement to the B'nai B'rith quoted earlier. At times however Freud's ambivalence would emerge and he would grow uncomfortable with references to himself as a Jewish hero or model. He wrote to Arthur Schnitzler shortly after the B'nai B'rith celebration: "From all sides and places, the Jews have enthusiastically seized me for themselves" and he went on to share his embarrassment at being treated as if he were "a God-fearing Chief Rabbi" or "a national hero."[49]

In spite of such discomfort he would continue, even after he became less active in B'nai B'rith in 1902 in order to form his own study group, to surround himself with Jews. From 1902 to 1907 in fact, the year Carl Jung and Ludwig Binswanger first met with Freud in Vienna, all of his followers, by then twenty in number, were Jewish. Leonard Konigstein, Oscar Rie, and Eduard Hitschmann, all recruited by Freud for the B'nai B'rith, came with him to form the core of his early study group. Rudolph Urbantschitsch, the first Viennese non-Jew to join the psychoanalytic circle, did not do so until 1908, followed the same year by Ernest Jones. Freud would in fact confess to feelings of discomfort and "strangeness"[50] when the first non-Jews joined the movement.

\* \* \*

The Psychoanalytic movement per se began in 1902 when Freud sent postcards to four Viennese physicians who had shown some interest in his work. They included Alfred Adler, Wilhelm Stekel, Max Kahane, and Rudoph Reitler. He invited them to meet with him in his home to discuss matters of mutual scientific concern. These four were joined by several of Freud's brothers from the B'nai Brith to form what became known as the Psychological Wednesday Society. The society met weekly in Freud's waiting room and surrounded by his collection of antiquities discussed a variety of topics—recent books, case material, evolving theory—all loosely related to psychoanalysis. Coffee and cigars were served as a regular ritual. In 1908 the group, whose ranks had grown to over twenty members, was renamed the Vienna Psychoanalytic Society to emphasize itself as one of the centers of the movement's increasing international composition. By then Freud had been joined by Max Eitingon and Karl Abraham from Berlin, Carl Jung and Eugen Bleuler from Zurich, Ernest Jones from England and A. A. Brill from the United States. All were established physicians in their own right.

As psychoanalysis attracted an increasingly talented group of young disciples from beyond the borders of Austria, Freud's hopes for the future were encouraged. In response he redoubled his efforts to construct a viable organization for the dissemination of psychoanalytic thinking. These efforts in turn served to highlight his own growing frustration with his Viennese group and their incessant backbiting, petty jealousies, and rivalries for his attention and favors. They were, as suggested earlier, a mixed group of local physicians and laymen, drawn to Freud for a variety of personal reasons, not all scientific. Although their support at the beginning had been invaluable and he owed them a considerable debt, he could not help but notice now how their abilities paled in comparison with the more recent arrivals. He had no choice but to conclude that the future of psychoanalysis must lie elsewhere and with non-Viennese disciples. If nothing else, Freud was a pragmatist to the core who would do whatever was necessary to promote his young science, including forsaking old relationships and debts. Besides, he could not help but be aware of the fact that the Viennese were all Jews like himself and thus unable to exert any real influence in international circles. In relation to this concern, Freud's long-standing Jewish ambivalence would soon emerge to leave its full impact on the very development of the movement. Perhaps yet another dimension of his negativity toward the Vienna group was a projection onto them of his own frustration at Vienna's continued indifference to his ideas, even though his theories were gaining acclaim everywhere else. In any case the Viennese in turn, headed by Adler and Stekel, were feeling more and more sleighted and passed over in the distribution of power and status within the movement.

The matter came to a dramatic head at the second International Psychoanalytic Congress held at Nürnberg in March 1910 with Freud's decision to choose Jung as president of the International Association. The nomination was made, at Freud's request, by Sandor Ferenczi from Budapest, who unfortunately added salt to the wound by also suggesting that Zurich become the next headquarters for the movement. The Viennese were obviously hurt and outraged, and when Freud heard that a protest meeting was being held in Stekel's hotel room, he showed up there and made an impassioned plea in response to their angry criticism. He asked for their continued support, given the realities of the situation. "Most of you are Jews and therefore incompetent to win friends for the new teaching. Jews must be content with the modest role of preparing the ground. . . . I am getting on in years and am weary of being perpetually attacked. We are in danger. They won't leave me a coat on my back. This Swiss will save us—will save me and will save you as well."[51]

As a token of appeasement and in order to promote a truce, Freud retired from the presidency of the Vienna Society and allowed Adler to succeed him and Stekel to become its vice president. He also proposed the creation of a new journal, the *Zentralblatt für Psychoanalyse*, with Adler and Stekel as its editors. Neither gesture made any real difference in the end, however, for Adler would leave the movement in five months and Stekel two years later. It was Adler's contention that Freud had grossly overestimated the "perils"[52] faced by psychoanalysis because of his own sense of inferiority. And perhaps there was some truth in Adler's allegation, for anti-Semitism had in fact temporarily waned after the turn of the century, and it was certainly possible that Freud, so long embittered and embattled against it, could no longer discriminate subtle changes.

Adler was the first major figure to defect from the movement. Like those who would follow a similar path in the future, his ideas slowly diverged from those of Freud and eventually reached a point where they no longer fell within the confines of psychoanalysis as Freud defined it. By the time Adler left the movement, for example, his interests were clearly focused on ego or conscious functioning as opposed to the unconscious, and he stressed aggression, derived from feelings of inferiority, not sexuality, as the central motivator in human behavior. Freud rightly saw Adler's work, as he would that of future defectors, as no longer part of psychoanalysis. By strongly asserting a clear definition of the boundaries of his theories, he was contributing to the maintenance of their integrity. He was after all well versed in the psychology of groups and aware of the tendency of followers to dilute the essence of an idea in order to make it their own. He thus felt the need vigilantly and aggressively to protect his ideas against outside corrosion. In this spirit he wrote at about the time of Adler's defection. "Even today no one can know better than I do what psychoanalysis is."[53] Freud would not however deny Adler, or anyone for that matter, their place in the sun. "There is room enough on God's earth, and anyone who can has a perfect right to potter about on it without being prevented; but it is not a desirable thing for people who have ceased to understand one another and have grown incompatible with one another to remain under the same roof."[54]

As suggested earlier, it was only when Freud sensed that theoretical disagreement in reality masked personal issues, in Adler's case a sense of insufficient recognition, that he grew rigid and combative. That the two men spent nine years in close association, given the enormous differences in their personal styles and values, is an amazing fact in itself. This longevity was probably due primarily to Freud's efforts and his desire for established and respected colleagues early in the history of the movement. To keep Adler content he willingly and carefully cultivated his support, even when this meant feeding substantial ego needs. He had for example referred his brother Alexander's wife to Adler for psychoanalysis, and it was rumored that he always sat Adler at his right hand during the early meetings of the Vienna Society in order to show everyone present the special regard he had for him. Freud's efforts to placate Adler after Jung's choice as head the International Association were evidently part of a longstanding pattern required of Freud in order to keep peace within the Vienna group.

Characterological differences could not help but fuel the fires. While Freud was emotionally reserved, formal in his manner, and highly organized in his thinking and personal habits, Adler was his opposite: aggressively outgoing and at times even "rambunctious,"[55] indifferent to his appearance, and not at all the systematic thinker or theorist. Adler was in fact rather indifferent to putting ideas down on paper, which was a real passion and art form for Freud. He instead preferred to share his thoughts verbally and in the context of social interaction with colleagues. For Freud, as has become repeatedly apparent, nothing or no one took precedence over his work. Adler was much more easygoing in this regard. Adler projected himself forcefully into the world. He was an ardent socialist, along with his Russian-born wife, who was an intimate of such Russian revolutionaries as Trotsky and Joffe, and Adler felt more at home applying psychoanalysis in the real world, as in the fields of education and preventative mental health, than in theorizing about it, which was Freud's major passion. These tendencies and a bruised ego later led Freud to suggest that Adler had only "slight talent for the estimation of the unconscious material."[56]

Adler's great sensitivity to rejection and his need for recognition had their roots in childhood. Short, stocky, and rather homely in appearance, he had been both a sickly and unloved and rejected child within the family complex. The residue of these early experiences, combined with a lifelong rivalry with an older brother who had been his mother's obvious favorite, led Adler to overcompensate later in life in the form of an aggressive and overstriving personality. Not surprisingly, he drew upon his own inner experiences to posit the notion of the inferiority complex around which he organized the majority of his theories. Ironically enough, his brother's name had been Sigmund, and Adler may well have displaced some of his sibling jealousy upon Freud, as has been suggested by several writers.

After the second international congress, the gap between the two men widened significantly. Adler grew increasingly hostile toward Freud in the weekly Wednesday night meetings, and Freud began to lose his characteristic reserve in his frustration with the latter and his cohort Stekel. He wrote for example: "I am having an atrocious time with Adler and Stekel. I have been hoping it would come to a clean separation, but it drags on and despite my opinion that nothing is to be done with them, I have to toil on. It was often much pleasanter when I was alone."[57] In early 1911 Freud decided to bring the matter to a head. On two subsequent Wednesday evenings Adler was invited to present his views to the Vienna group. Freud would respond at the following two meetings. According to several witnesses, the debate turned into a trial and Freud was nothing short of unrelenting and, to quote Hanns Sachs, "did not spare his opponent and was not afraid of using sharp words and cutting remarks."⁵⁸ According to Freud, what seemed new in Adler's theory was trivial and the remainder was taken from his teacher without proper recognition. The outcome of these meetings was that Adler was asked to leave the society. He willingly agreed and was joined by nine others. The sense of the ensuing situation was that members were forced to choose between the two antagonists, and Adler, who at the beginning of these sessions had no real followers, found himself the center of a exiting core of former members. The feud split the society in half. Longstanding friendships were destroyed and lifelong animosities created. Freud is rumored never to have forgiven those members of the society who defected with Adler. Paul Klemperer, for instance, a member of this group, claimed that Freud would not even acknowledge his presence on the street.

In response Adler formed his own group and gave it the rather insulting name of the "Society for Free Psychoanalysis." The conflict grew so severe and personal that it eventually became a source of curiosity and a topic of gossip within the intellectual world of Vienna. Adler became "little Adler,"⁵⁹ and Freud claimed that he had "made a pygmy great."⁶⁰ He described Adler as "venomous," "a loathsome individual," and attributed to him "an ungovernable mania for priority."⁶¹ Adler in turn would describe psychoanalysis as that "filth" and "fecal matter,"⁶² and its founder by such names as "swindler, sly, schemer . . ."⁶³ and the like—all the result of old wounds and sensitivities. For Freud the experience reawakened old feelings associated with Fliess's departure. "I had quite got over the Fliess affair. Adler is a little Fliess come to life again. And his appendage Stekel is at least called Wilhelm."⁶⁴ In addition to their enormous egos Adler and Fliess shared a great sensitivity for priorities, that is, for getting appropriate recognition for their original work. For Adler his relationship with Freud had stimulated his deepest psychic scars. "Do you believe," he once asked Freud, "that it is such a great pleasure for me to stand in your shadow my whole life."⁶⁵

Of special interest was a remark made by Freud to Arnold Zweig upon Adler's sudden death during a trip to Aberdeen, Scotland. Freud's response: "I don't understand your sympathy for Adler. For a Jew boy out of a Viennese suburb a death in Aberdeen is an unheard-of career in itself and a proof of how far he had got on. The world really rewarded him richly for his service in having contradicted psychoanalysis."⁶⁶ In this remark, which the Freud family tried unsuccessfully to censor, one senses yet another area of possible tension possible between the two men—that of their common ethnicity and the very different ways in which they chose to relate to it. Why else would Freud choose to identify Adler's Jewishness and do so in such a cruel way as his parting comment upon his first significant supporter? There is in fact no other reference in the literature by Freud to Adler's ethnicity. Nor were such outbursts at all common for the very reserved and ever-appropriate Freud.

A possible explanation can be found in the circumstances surrounding Adler's identity as a Jew and Freud's likely, though unstated, reaction to it. In 1904, two years after the beginning of their association, Adler had himself and his two daughters baptized as Protestants.[67] The reason given by one biographer for the conversion was that he "resented the fact that the Jewish religion was only for one ethnic group and preferred to 'share a common deity with the universal faith of man.'"[68] A more reasonable explanation, however, based on the limited biographical information that is currently available, was that Adler might well have felt great negativity about his Jewishness and converted in order to further distance himself from his ethnic roots. As in the case of Freud's biographers, those who chronicled Adler's life have tended to obscure and underplay the significance of his Jewishness by portraying it as a highly peripheral fact that he was able to shed without personal consequences. A more careful reading of the available biographical materials in light of some of the principles of ethnic dynamics presented earlier, however, leads one to a rather different picture.

Adler's family came from Burgenland, a province in Hungary where Jews enjoyed greater prosperity and less persecution than did their counterparts, like the Freuds, in the Austrian Empire. Adler's biographers have pointed to this fact as an explanation for his general indifference to his Jewishness. Their arguments suggest that since he did not grow up with the mentality of a persecuted minority, he would not develop the same kind of Jewish sensitivities and attachments as did Jews like Freud. Adler was however born in Vienna and spent his formative years moving from suburb to suburb in response to the changing economic plight of his family. From the ages of seven to ten he lived in the Leopoldstadt, the same Jewish immigrant district to which the Freuds moved after leaving Freiberg. For a short period of time in fact he even attended the same school in which Freud had previously been a student. It is highly unlikely that young Alfred could have avoided exposure to anti-Semitism in this environment nor would he have been spared the experience of a persecuted minority group member during this period. We have already discussed the negative impact that life in the Leopoldstadt had on Freud's Jewish identity and we are aware that by the time of Adler's residence there anti-Semitism had grown significantly worse. Adler's boyhood years in Leopoldstadt are not mentioned by most of his biographers, and there is some suggestion that this period held unpleasant memories that he wished neither to remember nor discuss. It is equally significant that Adler never introduced the topic of anti-Semitism in any of his writings. Anti-Semitism was after all a significant phenomena in turn-of-the-century Vienna. For someone like Adler, whose interests were so squarely centered on the impact of social phenomena on personality development and whose writings have had such significant impact on minority psychologists, consistently to omit any reference to anti-Jewish hatred in all of his work does not seem like an accidental act.

There were also other indications that point to the possibility of identity conflict in Adler. Two early experiences may have set the stage for a negative identification. Once, at the age of five, while attending synagogue with his parents, he pulled at a piece of material sticking out of a cupboard and caused the entire cupboard to fall with a resounding crash. Later during a Passover celebration at home and at an age when he was obviously beginning to question the veracity of Jewish rituals, he substituted leavened bread for unleavened and watched the entire night to see if there would be any negative effects. While the Adlers evidently retained some ritual in the home while their son was growing up, it seems unlikely that it had any significant impact. Two of his younger brothers would later convert to Catholicism, he to Protestantism, and his oldest brother would leave the Jewish community without declaring a religious preference.

Such widespread identity rejection does not emerge from a vacuum, and it is likely that the family environment either fostered a decidedly negative attitude toward Jewish tradition or at best stimulated an ambivalent connection. It is known, for example, that Adler's father was highly assimilated by the end of his life. A grandson wrote: "Grandfather Leopold Adler was a rather elegant, good-looking gentleman who held himself erect and was particular about his dressing. . . . In the last few years of his life he had his meal in the Rathauskeller at lunch, always with a glass of wine, then a ham sandwich at 5 p.m. and to bed at 6 p.m."[69]

After leaving the Leopoldstadt when he was eleven, Alfred's family moved to an area of Vienna that had far fewer Jews, and one biographer reported that he grew up in the streets, playing and fighting with non-Jewish boys from lower-class origins. It was in this non-Jewish world that Adler seemed to feel most comfortable and with which he would subsequently identify himself. He chose to work clinically with this same working-class population and evidently, according to certain biographical anedotes, he felt rather uncomfortable both in manner of dress and personal style in the bourgeois Jewish world that Freud frequented.

From what is known of Freud's expressed feelings about conversion and his own unconscious identity conflict, it is highly unlikely that he would have looked kindly upon Adler's decision to convert. In 1904, the year of Adler's conversion, however, Freud was very much in need of his continued support and may well have been able temporarily to repress his feelings in the service of continued positive relations. When their association had finally grown problematic and ultimately ended, it would not have been unlikely for Freud then to draw upon these old negative feelings as a further impetus for his dislike and rejection of Adler. It is equally possible that Freud's conscious identification as a Jew and the movement's early Jewish flavor, not to mention the professor's own bit of anti-Semitism in his overestimation of Jung, may have all unconsciously stimulated Adler's discomfort with his own Jewishness and ultimately contributed to his break with Freud and to his decision to leave the psychoanalytic establishment.

\* \* \*

Even more riddled with racial tensions was Freud's relationship with Carl Jung and his Swiss contingent. In 1906 Freud received letters from Jung and his mentor at the Burgholzli[70] Eugen Bleuler. Both praised his work and expressed interest in a possible collaboration. Freud's reaction was nothing short of ecstatic. "Contrary to all expectations, the situation changed suddenly at one stroke,"[71] he wrote after an early meeting with Jung. Freud could for the first time breathe a slight sigh of relief. He had at last found substantial support beyond his own Viennese group who because of their ethnicity could be of little real assistance in the actual dissemination of psychoanalysis. So desperate was he for non-Jewish support that he would grossly misread the situation. He would overestimate what the Swiss could and would contribute to the movement. In their pursuit he would permanently alienate many of his earlier and most loyal followers. Perhaps most important, he would blind himself, at least at first, to the anti-Semitism that the Swiss could not help but bring with them. As will become apparent shortly, these factors would all conspire to create yet another heart-wrenching schism in the movement, with Jung and his Swiss followers defecting seven years after their initial contact with Freud to create their own competing school of psychology.

The relationship that developed between Freud and Jung was clearly one of surrogate father and son. Repeatedly Freud engaged this very metaphor in his description of the relationship with Jung. Jung was his adopted "son and heir,"[72] his "successor and Crown Prince,"[73] "This is my beloved son, in whom I am most pleased,"[74] he wrote on yet another occasion. In a similar vein he incorporated Jung into his unconscious identification with Moses. According to Jones, for instance: "Jung was to be the Joshua destined to explore the promised land which Freud, like Moses was only permitted to view from afar."[75] The phrase: "because he was a Jew" should perhaps be added to Jones's quotation for emphasis. What Freud had finally found and had so desperately wished for was not merely a son, for he already had three by birth in whom he took great pleasure. Rather he had procured for the movement a Christian son, who could successfully carry on his life's work and who would, as he suggested in his speech to his disgruntled Viennese group at Nürnburg, ultimately "save me and save you as well." It will be remembered that Freud had strongly discouraged his own sons from following in his footsteps because of anti-Semitism and in an effort to protect them from their own Jewishness. But that left him without an heir and out of desperation and through magical thinking he created an all-powerful one for himself in the person of Carl Jung. Freud's great tendency toward dependency seemed to have been reengaged by the relationship with Jung and in characteristic fashion he would pin all of his hopes not only for psychoanalysis but also for the safety of himself, his family, and his Jewish followers on him. To this end he wrote: the "assurance that the children will be provided for, which for a Jewish father is a matter of life and death, I expected to get from Jung."[76]

The relationship, however, was reciprocal, for Freud became, for a time anyway, the substantial and satisfying father figure Jung had never had. Jung's father, a pastor of the Reformed Church and a biblical scholar, was evidently a tyrant who gave his son a strict religious education and upbringing, but little else. Jung had once remarked that his parents belonged to the Middle Ages. Outwardly an obedient child, Jung rebelled emotionally against his father and the church he represented, but not against religiousity per se, which would in fact permeate his later work. Freud would later refer to this as his bent for "mysticism." At twelve, for example, Jung reported having a dream in which God had caused great pieces of excrement to fall upon and destroy the cathedral in his hometown of Basel. Jung would describe his first meeting with Freud as the most exciting event of his life and would later speak of the knowledge he gained from Freud in terms of eating from the tree of life in paradise.

This mutual dependency lasted for over five years, with each man unconsciously feeding the other's inner deprivations and simultaneously overlooking the enormous temperamental and intellectual differences of which only they were unaware. Both in addition had within them psychic time bombs that would eventually be set off by the other. We are well aware, first of all, from the models of Breuer and Fliess, of Freud's pattern of excessive dependency followed by violent upheaval when that dependency became frustrated by disappointment. While Jung would go to great lengths on several different occasions to reassure Freud that he would never leave him, early scars are not so easily overcome, and Freud would remain ever-vigilant for signs of rejection or defection. Jung for his part as a boy had been the victim of a sexual assault by a man he had deeply worshipped, another father-substitute. Given this bit of history, one would expect some uneasiness and discomfort as his "veneration" and "religious crush"[77] for Freud deepened. Even Freud sensed the volitility in this area. He in fact wrote to Jung: "a transference on a religious basis would strike me as most disastrous; it could end only in apostasy."[78]

Freud's own sensitivity to anti-Semitism proved yet another, though initially unspoken, source of discomfort. It is perhaps not surprising, given his own history, that he would doubt or at least feel some uneasiness vis-à-vis Jung's feelings about his being a Jew. He had in addition himself chosen the Swiss psychiatrist as a successor primarily on the basis of race. There is even some evidence that Freud suspected Jung of a disguised anti-Semitism from the very beginning of their relationship, but he hid these feelings from himself in order to carry on his plans for the dissemination of psychoanalysis. Only after Jung's loyalty first came into doubt could he begin to acknowledge his true fears. He would later write of his early concern for "the theological pre-history of so many of the Swiss,"[79] no doubt including Jung among them, for he was the son of a pastor. Freud also would refer to Jung's decision "for my sake to give up certain racial prejudices"[80] and in a more hurt and angry mood after their break had occurred of Jung's "anti-Semitic condescension towards me."[81]

Although Freud would not allow himself to be aware of it, there was actually friction between the Swiss and the Viennese from the very beginning. The seeds of jealousy at the special treatment accorded the newcomers that erupted violently at the second international congress were already evident among Freud's Jewish followers at the first international congress held in Salzburg. The Swiss had evidently acted in a condescending and superior manner and treated the Viennese as socially inferior. Jung even went so far as to characterize them as a group of "artists, decadents and mediocrites."[82]

It was however Karl Abraham, the Jewish psychiatrist from Berlin, who first came into direct conflict with Jung. As a young doctor, Abraham had studied in Zurich and came away from that experience with a bad taste in his mouth: mistrustful of the Swiss and their tendencies toward unscientific thinking and suspicious of their anti-Semitic leanings. These attitudes paved the way for his immediate friction with Jung. The initial source of conflict was a differing view of dementia praecox. Both had presented papers on the subject at Salzburg. Abraham stuck closely to Freud's psychogenic view of the disease as a consequence of massive blocking of the feeling process. Jung for his part reverted back to a more regressive view and described it as organic in origin. More importantly, Abraham had not referred to the previous contributions of Bleuler and Jung in his paper and Jung was insulted by this omission. Anxious to reinstitute harmony immediately and fearful of so soon alienating his new associate, although he did not agree with the Swiss position, Freud asked the young disciple from Berlin to contact and placate Jung, for his sake. The movement, Freud argued, was still much too small to tolerate internal disagreements and besides Jung, although clearly drawn to psychoanalysis, was still vacillating between it and his earlier organic position and needed time to come around completely.

At this point Freud appealed to Abraham as a fellow Jew:

> Be tolerant and don't forget that really it is easier for you to follow my thoughts than for Jung, since to begin with you are completely independent, and then racial relationship brings you closer to my intellectual constitution, whereas he, being a Christian and the son of a pastor, can only find his way to me against great inner resistances. His adherence is therefore all the more valuable. I was almost going to say it was only his emergence on the scene that has removed from psychoanalysis the danger of becoming a Jewish national affair.[83]

Abraham did as Freud asked but received no reply from Jung. In his next letter to Abraham, Freud again reiterated his earlier theme in response to further criticism of Jung. "We Jews have an easier time, having no mystical element." And in a subsequent letter he wrote:

> I will do all I can to put matters right when I go to Zurich in September (1908). Do not misunderstand me: I have nothing to reproach you for. I surmise that the repressed anti-Semitism of the Swiss, from which I am to be spared, has been directed against you in increased force. But my opinion is that we Jews, if we want to cooperate with other people, have to develop a little masochism and be prepared to endure a certain amount of injustice. There is no other way of working together. You may be sure that if my name were Oberhuber my new ideas would, despite all the other factors, have met with far less resistance.[84]

And this pattern would continue until the time of the actual break with Jung. Abraham would bring to Freud's attention each instance of Jung's growing divergence from psychoanalysis, and Freud would in turn make excuses for his Swiss associate. He would then ask Abraham once again to control his reactions for the sake of the movement. Foremost in Freud's mind, until he could no longer deny the reality of what was actually transpiring with Jung and his Swiss followers, was their importance to his work. The world's press was continuing erroneously to attribute psychoanalysis' obsession with sexuality to its origins in Vienna, and this only reinforced Freud's desire to find a new geographic center for the movement. But even in these stereotypes of Vienna he saw lurking his old foe. "I have sometimes been inclined to suppose that the reproach of being a citizen of Vienna is only a euphemistic substitute for another reproach which no one would care to put forth openly."[85] Freud was at this point in early 1909 still so obsessed with his belief in the Swiss as saviors of psychoanalysis that he continued to be blinded to the racial under currents. "Our Aryan comrades are quite indispensable to us," Freud would reiterate to Abraham, "otherwise psychoanalysis would fall a victim to anti-Semitism."[86] At first he attributed Abraham's feelings about Jung to "personal complexes," and a belief that Abraham had "a rather excessive dislike" of Jung because of "a trace of a persecution complex."[87] Only eventually and not until 1913 would he be able fully to acknowledge the great disparity that by then existed between his own views and those of Jung. It would take him equally as long to admit the existence of significant anti-Semitism among the Swiss themselves.

According to Paul Roazen, the final dawning of clarity for Freud did not occur until after he experienced his depression at the competion of *Totem and Taboo* in 1913. As suggested earlier, the work was an unconscious response to Jung's growing mystical tendencies and Freud's effort to show him that he need not stray beyond the psychoanalytic framework. Evidently, it simultaneously served to free him from his obsession with the Swiss. The signs of a coming break were there for everyone except Freud to see. Although Jung had never been completely comfortable with the professor's extreme position on sexuality and would unconsciously waver whenever possible, he began overtly to repudiate it after his second trip in 1911 to the United States, where he had been well-received in his own right. At Fordham University, for example, he paid Freud the backhanded complement that "we must be glad that there are people who are courageous enough to be immoderate and one-sided," but that "obtaining pleasure is by no means identical with sexuality."[88] In the same context he went on to object to "the incorrect terminology and the boundless extension of the concept of sexuality"[89] as practiced by Freud. Equally objectionable to Freud would be Jung's mystic tendencies, which would eventually take the form of an overextension of the concept of the unconscious into the idea of the collective unconscious.

A significant turning point in the emotional separation of Freud and Jung occurred in Munich in November of 1912 with Freud's famous fainting episode. It will be remembered that the incident was stimulated by a disagreement between Jung and Abraham over the correct interpretation of Akhenaten's removal of the name of his father from the royal Egyptian monuments. Jung's interpretation clearly flew in the face of the Oedipal complex and evidently Freud was so overcome with anger that he lost consciousness. Jung's interpretation of the event focused on Freud's oversensitivity to criticism and his inability to accept any challenge to his authority, which was in many ways correct. His own anger at Freud, not to mention his male chauvinism emerged however when he likened his teacher to "a woman. Confront her with a disagreeable truth: she faints."[90] Less obvious to Jung was his own Oedipal lashing out at his surrogate father.

By the time of the fourth international congress, the lines of battle had already been drawn. Racial tensions were by now out in the open and being directly addressed by Freud. Maeder for instance had written to Ferenczi to suggest that the differences between the Swiss and Viennese were racial in nature and resulted from the latter being Jews and the former "Aryans." According to Jones, Freud had instructed Fereczi to respond in the following manner. "Certainly there are great differences between the Jewish and the Aryan spirit. We can observe that every day. Hence there would assuredly be here and there differences in outlook on life and art. But there should not be such a thing as Aryan or Jewish science. Results in science must be identical, though the presentation of them may vary. If their differences mirror themselves in the apprehension of objective relationships in science there must be something wrong."[91]

The incident that precipitated the final break was Jung's manner of presiding over the congress. By limiting presentation time and expanding the opportunity for discussion, he seemed to be trying to provoke argumentation and conflict. As a protest, Abraham with Freud's backing proposed that those who were no longer comfortable with Jung's leadership abstain from voting for his reelection. A third of the body present followed this course. This was the final straw and marked the beginning of the end of Swiss involvement in psychoanalysis. Jung and Freud would never see each other again after this meeting. Freud wrote: "We took leave from one another without feeling the need to meet again."[92] In the following year Jung would resign first from his presidency and journal editorship and then from the association altogether. As if to acknowledge his superior insight throughout the affair and Freud's own culpability in the whole matter, Abraham was appointed temporary president

## The Jews and Gentiles of Psychoanalysis 185

of the international association. And as if to place a final exclamation point behind the racial roots of the conflict, Ernest Jones, himself a non-Jew, would report that at the conclusion of the congress Jung had turned to him and said in an accusing tone: "I thought you were a Christian."[93]

A particularly interesting and insightful glimpse into the deteriorating relationship between Freud and Jung can be found in a series of documents recently brought to light by Aldo Carotenuto. The central figure in this material, which includes a personal diary and letters exchanged with both Jung and Freud, was a young Russian Jew named Sabina Spielrein. She had been treated for hysteria by Jung, first at the Burgholzli Clinic and then in private practice, and later became his lover. After gaining sufficient relief from her analysis, she completed her education, received a degree in medicine, pursued training in psychoanalysis and in time became a personal acquaintance and associate of Freud's in the Psychoanalytic Society. The period spanned by these events was 1904–23, and within the various interactions which the documents highlight one can clearly discern the changing tenure of relations between the two men, in particular along the dimension of racial conflict.

Sabrina Spielrein was the eldest child of a wealthy, Jewish family from Rostov-on-Don in Russia. In early childhood she exhibited a rich inner fantasy life, which later gave way to frightening hallucinations and nightmares. These in term were accompanied during adolescence by fits of depression and wild mood swings. In 1904 when Sabrina was twenty her parents took her to Zurich both for the purpose of gaining treatment and of continuing her education. It was at this point that she first entered treatment with Carl Jung, who diagnosed her condition as a "psychotic hysteria."[94] A strong transference and countertransference developed between the two over the course of their work together, and after ceasing formal treatment, Jung and Spielrein became lovers and remained so for a number of years in spite of his marriage. Jung's attraction to the younger woman derived largely from the fact that she was a Jew, and he evidently was fascinated by Jewish women. He had earlier fallen in love with a cousin of his who had pretended to be Jewish and to this previous infatuation he attributed his current attachment to Spielrein. Spielrein also suggested that Jung's attachment to her may have been a replacement for an earlier attraction to Freud's eldest daughter, Mathilde. It appears from her diary that Spielrein too was obsessed with Jewish-gentile relations and wished somehow magically to effect an integration of the two. This wish would later take concrete form first in a desire to give birth to a child by Jung who would bridge the gap between their Jewish and Aryan pasts and later in her wish somehow to professionally integrate the "Jewish theories" of Freud and the "Aryan ones" of Jung. Thus she wrote in a letter to Jung. "My Sigfried[95] problem . . . might just as well yield a real child as a symbolic Aryan-Semitic child—for instance, a child that resulted from the union of your and Freud's theories."

Freud first entered the scenario in 1906 when Jung consulted with him about the case. Jung again sought advice several years later after the situation had taken a decidedly personal turn. Spielrein's first contact with Freud was in 1909 when she asked him to intercede in the affair. Jung had recently contacted her mother and in what in retrospect seems rather poor judgement asked her for a fee in exchange for his ending the personal relationship with her daughter and reestablishing a professional one. From 1909 to 1923 Freud remained in close personal contact with Spielrein. As Freud's own relationship with Jung worsened, he increasingly advised her to take control of her feelings and to sever her connections with Jung. In particular he was offended by her desire for a mixed-race child. In 1912 he wrote. "My wish is for you to be cured completely. I must confess, after the event, that your fantasy about the birth of the Saviour to a mixed union did not appeal to me at all. The Lord, in that anti-Semitic period, had him born from the superior Jewish race. But I know these are my prejudices."[96] During that same year he encouraged her to develop a connection with Karl Abraham as an alternative to Jung. "It would please me very much if you were to associate yourself more closely with Abraham. There is much to be learned from him, and his sober manner is a good counterweight to the many temptations to which you are exposed in your work."[97] It may well be that by such a move Freud hoped to reconnect Sabrina with a more Jewish world. In 1913 Freud gave the first indication in their correspondence of the growing rift with Jung. "My personal relationship with your German hero has definitely been shattered. . . . Since I received that first letter from you, my opinion of him has greatly altered."[98]

Not long before this last letter, Spielrein had informed Freud that she was pregnant. She had in June of 1912 married Dr. Paul Scheftel. This fact obviously pleased Freud, who wrote:

## The Jews and Gentiles of Psychoanalysis 187

"As far as I am concerned, that means that you are half cured of your neurotic dependence on Jung."[99] In response to the pregnancy he confessed his concern that her fantasy of a mythic mixed child not interfere with her subsequent relationship with the real child. At this point his anger at Jung emerged in only slightly veiled form as a surge of Jewish chauvinism.

> I am, as you know, cured of the last shred of my predilection for the Aryan cause, and would like to take it that if the child turns out to be a boy he will develop into a stalwart Zionist. He or it must be dark in any case, no more towheads. Let us banish all these will-o'-the-wisps! . . . We are and remain Jews. The others will only exploit us and will never understand or appreciate us.[100]

After the birth of a daughter he wrote: "Well, now, my heartiest congratulations! It is far better that the child should be a 'she.' Now we can think again about the blond Siegfried and perhaps smash that idol before his time comes."[101]

In June of 1914 Freud asked Spielrein, as he had done with all analysts in the association, to make a choice between himself and Jung. With her however there was clearly a flavor of the therapeutic in the request as well as a final effort to win her allegiance:

> Please let me know if you want to appear on the masthead of our journal. . . . It would be the clearest sort of partisanship if your name was placed on it now. . . . Don't stand on ceremony, but whatever you decide to do, do it unreservedly. Of course I want you to succeed in casting aside as so much trash your infantile dreams of the Germanic champion and hero, on which hinges your whole opposition to your environment and to your origins. . . . There will be a warm welcome for you if you stay with us here, but then you will have to recognize the enemy over there.[102]

She would in the end remain associated with Freud but could never fully give up her emotional attachment to Jung. In 1923 she returned to Russia to practice psychoanalysis and she founded a home for disturbed children. Unfortunately, the home was closed in the 1930s and the practice of psychoanalysis banned under the influence of Stalinism. In spite of this she continued to live in Rostov, to teach and care for a younger daughter. Her eldest daughter was then a promising violoncellist studying in Moscow. According to her niece, Spielrein perished during the Nazi invasion of the Soviet Union. During the early stages of the occupation, all the Jews in the city had been taken to the synagogue and shot. According to one version, Sabina in characteristic fashion went up to a German officer and introduced herself in German, the tongue which had become her second language. "It could have ended only one way, for her and her daughters."[103]

Perhaps the most disturbing episode in the continuing racial conflict between Freud and Jung and around psychoanalysis in general took place with the Nazi rise to power. Because of his activities during this period, Carl Jung has been accused by many, Jews and non-Jews alike, of actively collaborating with the Nazis. The accusation had two aspects. The first was that his beliefs about racial differences between Jews and Aryans helped provide scientific credence and support to Nazi theories of racial differences and in turn the systematic destruction of European Jewry. Increasingly, and especially after his break with Freud, Jung wrote and spoke in terms of racial group differences and of their roots in the collective unconscious. In particular he seemed obsessed with the differences between Jewish and Aryan psychologies. The following appeared as part of an article in 1934 entitled "On the Present Situation Of Psychotherapy." It is worth quoting at length.

> Freud and Adler have beheld very clearly the shadow that accompanies us all. The Jews have this peculiarity in common with women; being physically weaker, they have to aim at the chinks in the armour of their adversary, and thanks to this technique which has been forced on them through the centuries, the Jews themselves are best protected where others are most vulnerable. Because, again, of their civilization, more than twice as ancient as ours, they are vastly more conscious then we of human weakness, of the shadow-side of things, and hence in this respect much less vulnerable than we are. Thanks to their experience of an old culture, they are able, while fully conscious of their frailties, to live on friendly and even tolerant terms with them, whereas we are still too young not to have 'illusions' about ourselves. Moreover, we have been entrusted by fate with the task of creating a civilization—and indeed we have need of it—and for this 'illusions' in the form of one-sided ideals, convictions, plans, etc., are indispensable. As a member of a race with a three-thousand year-old civilization, the Jew, like the cultured Chinese, has a wider area of psychological consciousness than we. Consequently it is in general less dangerous for the Jew to put a negative value on his unconscious. The 'Aryan' unconscious, on the other hand, contains explosive forces and seeds

of a future yet to be born, and these may not be devalued as nursery romanticism without psychic danger. The still youthful Germanic peoples are fully capable of creating new cultural forms that still lie dormant in the darkness of the unconscious of every individual—seeds bursting with energy and capable of might expansion.

The Jewish race as a whole—at least this is my experience—possesses an unconscious which can be compared with the "Aryan" only with reserve. Creative individuals apart, the average Jew is far too conscious and differentiated to go about pregnant with the tensions of unborn futures. The "Aryan" unconscious has a higher potential than the Jewish; that is both the advantage and the disadvantage of youthfulness not yet fully weaned from barbarism. In my opinion it has been a grave error in medical psychology up till now to apply Jewish categories—which are not even binding on all Jews—indiscriminately to Germanic and Slavic Christendom. Because of this the most precious secret of the Germanic peoples—their creative and intuitive depth of soul—has been explained as a morass of banal infantilism, which my own warning voice has for decades been suspected of anti-Semitism. This suspicion emanated from Freud. He did not understand the Germanic psyche any more than did his Germanic followers. Has the formidable phenomenon of National Socialism, on which the whole world gazes with astonished eyes, taught them better? Where was that unparalleled tension and energy while as yet no National Socialism existed? Deep in the Germanic psyche, in a pit that is anything but a garbage-bin of unrealized infantile wishes and unresolved family resentments. A movement that grips a whole nation must have matured in every individual as well. That is why I say that the German unconscious contains tensions and potentialities which medical psychology must consider in its evaluation of the unconscious.[104]

In these words, which appeared in 1934 in Germany's then most prestigious psychology journal, one can identify reverberations of the same basic sentiments and unrestrained anger that had begun to appear among Jung and his disciples as they parted company with their former Jewish colleagues. In his own defense, Jung argued adamantly that he was not against the Jews but only against Freud and the application of his theories, which in his mind were decidedly Jewish, to non-Jews. In any case there is no denying that he was clearly guilty as Clarence Karier has suggested "of cultivating the intellectual climate through which the 'final solution' was ultimately made possible."[105] In a similar manner his assessment of Hitler and National Socialism as an expression of the German unconscious led him to counsel others against resistance. "To protest is ridiculous—

how protest an avalanche? It is better to look out. Science has no interest in calling down avalanches; it must preserve its intellectual heritage even under the changed conditions."[106] And again in relation to his own personal situation. "There is no sense in us as doctors facing the National Socialist regime as if we were a party. As doctors we are first and foremost men who serve our fellows, if necessary under all aggravations of a given political situation. We are neither obliged nor called upon to make protests from a sudden access of untimely zeal and thus gravely endanger our medical activity."[107]

It was in this very spirit that Jung undertook the activities that would lead to the second aspect of the charges of collaboration leveled against him. In 1933 he agreed to serve as president of the International General Medical Society for Psychotherapy, a former organization of psychotherapists which would shortly be cleansed of its Jewish members. Its purpose became that of promoting the superiority of Aryan psychology over that of the Jew, and its members were expected to be fully conversant with *Mein Kampf* so that their professional work would perpetuate the goals outlined within it. After two years, Jung resigned from this position. He also agreed in 1936 to accept the post of editor of the Aryanized journal *Zentralblatt für Psychotherapie*, which he shared with Matthias Göring, the cousin of Hermann Göring and the most influencial psychologist in the Third Reich. In retrospect, Jung claimed that he had used these positions to help individual Jews and was himself attacked and blacklisted by the Nazis, both of which were in fact true. But to quote Giovanni Costigan. "Be this as it may, it does not excuse him for having failed to protest when pernicious racial theories were being propagated in the guise of psychotherapy, nor does it exonerate him from having placed his great international prestige at the service of the Nazis at a time when it was most valuable to them."[108]

After the Nazi downfall, Jung repudiated his Aryan leanings in favor of a more benign Swiss identity. He also began to interpret the phenomenon of Hitler and Nazi Germany as an aberration as opposed to a natural consequence of uncontrollable unconscious forces. He would never admit any culpability in these matters nor see any connection between his enormous anger at Freud, the father, and his own theories of a "Jewish psychology." He in fact remained to the end rather proud of what he had accomplished. "I am grateful to my theological forebears for having passed on to me the Christian premise, and I also admit my so-called 'father complex': I do not want to knuckle under to any 'fathers' and never shall."[109] The great reaction his behavior had elicited would in turn also remain a puzzlement to him. "I must confess my total inability to understand why it should be a crime to speak of 'Jewish' psychology."[110] It is finally interesting that Freud never commented publicly upon this controversy over Jung's alleged collaboration. His only statement, when visited by a follower of Jung in 1932, was that Jung had been "a great loss"[111] to psychoanalysis.

\* \* \*

Those closest to Freud grew increasingly concerned about the impact Jung's eventual defection would have on him and the movement. Sensing a need to fill the void that would soon be left by Jung, Ernest Jones spoke with Sandor Ferenczi and Otto Rank in July of 1912 about the possibility of forming an inner circle of followers upon whom Freud could depend, no matter what the future would bring. The group would also serve to relieve Freud of much of the administrative drudgery that he so disliked and had hoped Jung would ultimately remove from his shoulders. The idea was presented to Freud, and it was received quite enthusiastically. "What took hold of my imagination immediately," he wrote to Jones, "is your idea of a secret council composed of the best and most trustworthy among our men to take care of the further development of psychoanalysis and defend the cause against personalities and accidents when I am no more. . . . I daresay it would make living and dying easier for me if I know of such an association existing to watch over my creation."[112] The proposal provided Freud relief on a number of different fronts. There were those, first of all, who he could surely count upon in the continuing struggles with Jung and the Swiss. He could also expect concrete and substantial assistance in the administrative activities necessary for the dissemination of psychoanalysis. Finally, with such a structure in place he could trust that his creation would be carried on by others and could then actually begin to withdraw into himself, as he would in fact do after World War II. The idea of such a committee may well have rekindled warm memories of the years when he was active in the brotherhood of the B'nai Brith. He had even used similar words then to describe what membership had meant to him at the beginning of his work. Perhaps not surprisingly, all with the exception of Jones would be Jews.

Freud would suggest the inclusion of Karl Abraham and Hanns Sachs in the group and six years later the addition of Max Eitingon. These five, according to Jones, would be the last close friends that Freud would ever make. Each was at least a generation younger than him: Ferenczi the oldest, Sachs the youngest. Of them Freud would write. "You cannot imagine what pleasure the cooperation of five such men gives me."[113] At their first meeting in the summer of 1913 Freud presented each with an antique Greek intaglio from his collection, which he had set in a gold ring similar to the one he himself wore.

While the members of the committee varied in emotional closeness to Freud, he was able to carry on a distinct and personal relationship with each of them. Ferenczi, whose Hungarian Jewish family name had originally been Fraenkel, was clearly Freud's favorite and probably the warmest and most human of the group. He was a regular traveling companion for Freud on his holidays and was for some reason allowed liberties with the professor that no one else would have dared take. While Freud received fewer and fewer guests with age, he would always willingly sacrifice his much-beloved seclusion to welcome Ferenczi. During their relationship Freud wrote him over twenty-five hundred letters and even discussed health problems with the Hungarian. This was a kind of personal sharing that was exceedingly rare for Freud. Perhaps it was the fact that Ferenczi was himself a bit of a hypochondriac. In 1926 he was so concerned about Freud's emotional state that he offered to psychoanalyze him as a means of providing some relief. This proposal, which if it had come from anyone else would have elicited enormous anger, moved Freud deeply. So close did Freud feel to Ferenczi that he had secretly harbored hopes at one point that the Hungarian doctor would marry his oldest daughter, Mathilda.

Two characteristics were probably responsible for the close emotional ties. Ferenczi, first of all, felt an insatiable hunger for Freud's fatherly attention, and Freud for his part seemed more than willing to accommodate him in this regard. He even addressed him in several letters with the salutation: "son." On another occasion Freud wrote. "I must admit that I should prefer to have a self-confident friend, but when you make such difficulties then I have to treat you as a son." Ferenczi evidently gave off a certain sense of boyish helplessness that seemed to engage rather than offend Freud. Freud had tried briefly to analyze him on two different occasions but without much success.

Ferenczi would in fact remain rather neurotic throughout the relationship. He suffered, for instance, from chronic indecision, and it took him eighteen years to decide to marry. Freud however never seemed to tire of his young friend nor of his unending insecurities and need for support. It is likely that Freud even saw a bit of himself and his own personal struggles in the likeable Hungarian. The following desciption, for example, seems to ring true. "Your struggle for independence need not take the form of alternating between rebellion and submission." he once told Ferenczi. "A man should not strive to eliminate his complexes, but to get in accord with them: they are legimately what directs his conduct in the world."[114] Freud would even forgive Ferenczi clear professional misconduct until he could no longer ignore it. Out of his insatiable need to be loved, Ferenczi had taken to encouraging female patients to fall in love with him and to kiss him during the analytic hour as a therapeutic device. This practice marked the beginning of a pattern of deteriorating mental health for the Hungarian. With Hitler's rise to power, Ferenczi became more and more apprehensive about anti-Semitism. He begged Freud to leave Vienna and considered emigrating himself from Hungary to Switzerland. He developed paranoic delusions and began to believe that even Freud bore him ill will. He subsequently underwent serious personality changes and he died suddenly, hopelessly insane. In spite of these troubles, however, he had singlehandedly constructed a psychoanalytic organization in Hungary and served for several years as the president of the international society. Of his friend's passing Freud wrote: "Ferenczi takes with him a part of the old time; then with my departure another will begin."[115]

Otto Rank, the second of Freud's followers to affirm Jones's idea of an inner committee, came from much humbler circumstances than the rest, what has been referred to in the literature as the "lower social stratum."[116] He grew up with an alcoholic and irresponsible father, whose authority he and his brother rejected when Rank was sixteen. As an act of defiance, he changed his name from Rosenfeld to Rank. This name change was evidently in addition symptomatic of an inner conflict over his Jewish identity, for in 1903 he formally repudiated Judaism in favor of the writings of Friedrich Nietzsche. Trained in a technical school, he took on a variety of menial jobs in order to support himself and his mother. He was extremely bright and in spite of the external demands upon him managed to read voraciously and at the same time to complete three novels by the age of twenty. Emotionally, he was rather depressed. Not only was he weighed down by circumstances but also a sense of loneliness and isolation brought on by extreme shyness. He was in addition evidently taken to constant brooding over his life situation and the possibility of suicide. At the age of twenty-two and with the help of his physician, Alfred Adler, he was able to meet Freud and present him with his essay "The Artist." Freud was immediately taken with Rank and his great unschooled potential and became his mentor. He supported him financially much of the time, encouraged him to get a Ph.D. at the university and helped nuture his daring ideas in the realm of mythology. Freud may well have been attracted to Rank because of his lack of formal background and his future potential in the movement once trained properly. Such a possibility might have been particularly compelling, given Freud's general dissatisfaction with most of his Viennese pupils. One of Rank's earliest papers dealt with the relationship of Jews to psychoanalysis. It is likely that finding a suitable calling in psychoanalysis and father figure in Freud allowed him to disassimilate enough to consider the subject of his ethnic past, which he may have, like Freud, negatively associated with his father and rejected.

As part of an arrangement to help support him financially, Rank became Freud's general assistant and did what whatever was needed within the emerging formal organization of the movement. He kept the minutes of the Vienna Society, proofread manuscripts, did research at Freud's behest, and was available as needed. Anecdotes have it that he even fetched water for Freud and lit his cigars at the weekly meetings. In time Rank even took on responsibility for managing Freud's personal financial affairs, evidently much to the unhappiness of Freud's son Martin, who assumed that role with Rank's defection from the movement. To Freud he was "a most faithful helper and collaborator" and "invaluable, his person irreplaceable."[117] Rank was treated like a member of the Freud family, as was his Polish wife, Tola, after he married. But unlike Ferenczi, who sought Freud's genius as a personal therapist, Rank tended to keep his emotional distance. For example, he refused ever to be personally psychoanalyzed.

During World War I, Rank served in the military in Krakow and edited a newspaper. These experiences combined with the positive consequences of married life evidently served to make him substantially more self-confident and independent. The change was actually quite dramatic but would have severe consequences for his relationship with Freud. In 1924 he published *Trauma of Birth*, which attributed to the birth trauma and the child's relationship to the mother primary significance in early personality formation. Freud did not at first experience Rank's diminution of the Oedipal complex as heresy, but merely as erroneous. He in fact continued for a time to encourage Rank's boldness and richness of thought. The eventual conflict was actually precipitated by other members of the committee, especially Abraham and Jones. Whether out of personal jealousy or merely in the role of protectors of the faith, they pushed Freud on the issue of Rank's discordant views. Freud had always contended that "my pupils are more orthodox than I,"[118] and in this case his astute observation was more than borne out. Rank went to the United States in 1924 and there found encouragement for a serious departure from classical psychoanalytic positions, especially in the realm of treatment. He would, for instance, radically shorten the timeframe for therapy, abandon the analysis of childhood experience and eventually focus exclusively on the transference relationship between patient and therapist. Of these innovations Freud once quipped that Rank's method was well suited to American life. An apologetic Rank however sought a reconciliation with Freud upon his return from America. Freud readily accepted him back and blamed his waywardness on a psychiatric condition. But Rank, evidently in the thores of inner forces beyond his control, once again defected, and after this Freud refused to take him back. Rank would eventually die in New York, only five weeks after Freud's own death.

Freud, however, never forgot Rank, who was in all likelihood his most creative and promising pupil. In *Moses and Monotheism* he presented a short case study that he later identified as Rank. "A young man whose fate it was to grow up beside a worthless father, (who) began by developing, in defiance of him, into a capable, trustworthy and honorable person. In the prime of life his character was reversed, and thenceforward he behaved as though he had taken this same father as a model. In . . . the beginning of such a course of events there is always an identification with the father of early childhood. This is afterward repudiated, and even overcompensated, but in the end establishes itself once again."[119] The reason for its inclusion in Freud's highly autobiographical work on the Jews is unclear.

Was he perhaps talking about himself as well as Rank? Was he still seeking to show Rank the errors of his way by pointing out the Oedipal presence in his own life? Or might it have to do with the ethnic theme of the work and its relevance to Rank's own struggle with Jewish identity?

Karl Abraham received his training in psychiatry in Switzerland and in 1907 settled in Berlin where he would practice until his untimely death in 1925. During this period and with the support of Hanns Sachs, Franz Alexander, Sandor Rado, and Max Eitingon, he turned Berlin into what became widely acknowledged as the finest training center for psychoanalysis that then existed. It quickly surpassed all others in terms of the number of candidates, the quality of their work, and financial resources. After Jung's departure, Freud came increasingly to rely on Abraham and his good judgment, steadfastness, great integrity, and skill in organizational matters. One story has it that in order to mediate a conflict between several warring factions from different national groups, he spoke with the participants in Latin, one of the eight languages in which he was fluent.

Abraham was by far the most normal and consistent of the group. Personally, however, he was not Freud's favorite. Calm, courteous, very reserved, exceedingly thorough and reliable, his very lack of eccentricity and neuroses, while a clear boon to the movement, seemed to leave Freud rather cold. On one occasion Freud described Abraham as "too Prussian"[120] and on another as having "no dash."[121] Freud in general seemed more drawn to the artistic and temperamental sorts like Ferenczi, Jung, and Rank, though in the end they proved most problematic. He was also frankly bothered by Abraham's unstinting optimism, both about human nature and the future of psychoanalysis. Only once did Abraham come into disagreement with Freud and assert himself over a contrary position; on all other occasions, as with Jung, he had always deferred to Freud's wishes. The conflict situation revolved around the making of a movie about psychoanalysis, shortly before Abraham's unexpected death. Freud had refused to consider a very lucrative offer from Samuel Goldwyn. According to Sachs, this refusal had created an even bigger sensation in New York than had *The Interpretation of Dreams*. Abraham felt that it was wiser to oversee the creation of such a picture than to leave it to the supervision of some "wild"[122] analyst, for such a movie would surely be made in any case. Freud refused to relent,

## The Jews and Gentiles of Psychoanalysis       197

and the unofficial version of the picture that did eventually appear created quite a stir, not to mention further conflict between the two. Abraham, once again correct in his prediction, saw fit to remind Freud of his previous perceptiveness in the matters of Jung and Rank, and Freud countered that there was no reason why he should always be right. But the exchange in no way permanently interfered with their continued cordial relations. Abraham contracted lung cancer and died on Christmas Day of 1925 at the age of forty-eight. This event totally unsettled Freud. It may be that his abrupt passing made Freud aware of the depths of his true attachment for Abraham, not to mention his own mortality. Freud had by then come to see Abraham as the future leader of the movement. Although Freud found excess displays of emotion distasteful, he was moved enough during the funeral ceremony to describe his friend with a rather poetic phrase from Horace: "A life of integrity and free from blemish." These were the same words he had spoken at the death of his dear friend from medical school days, Ernest Fleischl. So stricken was Freud by Abraham's death that Sachs reported a conversation with Freud several months later. "And how is Abraham?" Freud asked him in passing. "Noticing my astonishment, he look at me with an expression in his eyes which made my heart tremble and murmured, 'I still cannot believe it,' and turned away."[123]

Although he was deeply attached to Abraham, the question remains as to why Freud could not experience more personal warmth toward him. Again, one can only generate hypotheses. It may have had something to do with Abraham's role as the censor in the movement. On several different occasions he felt the need to warn Freud of potentially problematic situations of which he seemed largely unaware, as in the cases of Jung and Rank. Unconsciously, Freud may have blamed him for what had transpired, as if to kill the messenger who bears bad news. Or Freud might have unconsciously associated Abraham with his own Jewishness and thereby experienced some of the same ambivalence toward him. Throughout the affair with Jung, Abraham had become Freud's primary confidante on matters of race and ethnicity and thus he may have become a transferential object for his feelings. Freud's very obvious omission of reference to Abraham and his work on Amenhotep in *Moses and Monotheism* would support such a conclusion. Or perhaps it was merely the fact that Abraham was so intellectually independent and emotionally self-contained that he really did not need Freud in the same emotional ways as did the others. In this regard Jones has suggested that Abraham felt equally close to all members of the committee.

Ernest Jones, the only non-Jew within the group, was both its initiator and its unofficial chairperson. His status as a gentile and an Anglo-Saxon made his position somewhat problematic. He joined the Psychoanalytic Society in 1908 after reading Freud's work for several years and finally deciding to forsake a career in neurology after being passed over for an academic post to which he felt entitled. An early interpretation of *Hamlet* won him Freud's initial intellectual respect. As Jones slowly earned Freud's trust, the professor more and more came to see in him those very qualities—justice, fair play, and tolerance—he had always found so appealing in the English. A fiery little man with a military demeanor and at times a quarrelsome disposition, he was somewhat of an enigma to the Viennese. For a long time in fact Freud tended merely to take him for granted. Slowly, however, Jones proved himself not only highly trustworthy, but even more important, decidedly masterful in all aspects of organizational activities. He was for instance a highly proficient writer, who was able to make Freud's ideas more generally accessible and also a masterful publicist.

Jones stood steadfastly on the side of the Viennese Jews during the Jung affair. He had even hoped that Freud might consider him as a replacement for Jung in the role of representative and disseminator of psychoanalysis to the non-Jewish world. Unfortunately, this episode had only reinforced Freud's basic mistrust of non-Jews, which in turn made him more susceptible to the warnings to those among the Viennese who continued to be suspicious of Jones, both personally and racially. The Englishman thus had once again to redouble his efforts in order to gain full acceptance. Even within the committee itself there were lingering doubts and mistrust, especially on the part of Ferenczi and Rank. Jones did feel that the Jews on the committee, Freud least of all, showed a rather heightened sensitivity to anti-Semitism and mistrust of non-Jews. Add to these cautions a general suspiciousness of anyone with originality and a forceful personality might rebel and found his own competing school, and one can begin to appreciate the kind of resistance that Jones must have encountered. He stood his ground, however, and earned the committee's respect both in small ways and later by his persistence and bravery in rescuing and finding refuge in England for over fifty German and Austrian refugee analysts, including Freud himself and his family. Jones' only hesitancy in this regard had been over helping Theodor Reik, then practicing in Holland, gain entry into England. The reason: he felt Reik to be a very real rival for leadership of the British Society.

Jones's willingness to tolerate his treatment as an outsider and to feel comfortable in this all-Jewish environment grew out of his own experience as a minority as well as his frequent previous contacts with Jews. Of this he himself wrote. "Coming myself of an oppressed race it was easy for me to identify myself with the Jewish outlook which years of intimacy enabled me to absorb in a high degree. My knowledge of Jewish anecdotes, wise sayings, and jokes became under such tutelage so extensive as to create astonishment among other analysts outside this small circle"[124] As a young doctor, he had worked in a hospital in the Jewish section of London's East End, and after his first marriage failed, he had married a Jewish woman, Katherine Jokl. He felt a kinship with Freud and the others, who were torn between their identities as Jews and Germans, for he himself experienced great ambivalence over his hyphenated Welsh-English identity and saw a commonality in the manner that oppression, misfortune, and suffering tended to invoke a sense of inferiority. Finally he seemed to enjoy Jewish company. He confessed that his Welsh mind became "a little impatient of Anglo-Saxon complacency and slowness of imagination" and "responded gratefully"[125] to the liveliness, wit, and alertness he found in Jewish society.

In the end Jones would actually fulfill his wish to replace Jung at the center of the psychoanalytic world. He would create an empire in England, which would in time welcome Freud with open arms during the last years of his life. He would write the definitive biography of Freud,[126] he delivered the eulogy at his funeral, and he served for twenty-three years as president of the International Psychoanalytic Association.

The fifth member of the committee was Hanns Sachs. Originally a lawyer, he had been in the Vienna Society for nine years when he decided to forsake the law entirely to begin practice as a lay analyst. The following year he moved to Berlin to become part of the training center that Abraham had developed there. Outgoing and rather loquacious, he was the epitome of the Viennese Jewish intellectual. He was a longtime bachelor, enjoyed good food and female company, frequented Vienna's many cafés, and continually entertained his associates with an "endless stock of the best Jewish jokes."[127] Short and rotund in appearance, his detractors said he bore a strong resemblance to an owl. His interests fell in the arena of the literary application of psychoanalysis, and he coauthored the journal *Imago* with Rank. In the politics of psychoanalysis and its dissemination he evidently had little interest and perhaps for this reason was Freud's least favorite on the committee. In 1932 he emigrated to Boston to become a training analyst there, but his remaining years were to be difficult ones. He encountered various problems with the Boston medical establishment, which did not recognize the practice of lay analysts, as well as with local analysts for his less-than-organized methods of procuring trainees. Finally, however, he was able to obtain a teaching appointment in the Harvard Medical School. He would also experience heart trouble as well as a serious depression that lasted until the end of his life over the loss of many friends and relatives to the Nazi Holocaust. Like many in the movement, Sachs worshipped Freud and hung on his every word. In Berlin it was said that his "couch was placed in such a way that the analysand faced a portrait bust of Freud standing on a high wooden pedestal."[128] In his personal manner he emulated the master in every way possible, even down to his habitual cigar-smoking and neurotic anxiety over train travel.

Max Eitington was the last member to join the committee, which he did in 1919, and he was in fact a replacement for the wealthy Hungarian brewer Anton von Freund who had fallen ill and who died unexpectedly the following year. He was the only analyst in the group who possessed private financial means and was always more than generous in his support of various psychoanalytic projects and undertakings. Shy, modest, and rather reserved due partially to a lifelong stammer, he, like Sachs, was a true worshipper of Freud. Eitington was Freud's first training analysand and the analysis evidently was completed during a series of nightly walks around Vienna.[129] Remembering these early days, Freud wrote to Eitingon: "You were the first to come to the lonely one."[130] In time he too moved to Berlin and almost singlehandedly financed the Berlin Polyclinic and its associated Berlin Psychoanalytic Institute. His psychoanalytic work centered almost exclusively around formulating international standards for training analysts. Eitingon had been born into a very wealthy, Orthodox Jewish family and never gave up his connection to tradition. He was an ardent Zionist, who according to Jones related to Freud's ideas with too much of a biblical attitude. This, according to Jones, accounted for his general unwillingness to entertain innovations in the method. In 1910 he visited Palestine, where his family had purchased land, and he emigrated there in 1933. More than any of the others, he feared the repercussions of Hitler's rise to power and its eventual impact on Freud and psychoanalysis. In 1932 he made a special trip to Vienna to see Freud in person to discuss the plight of the Berlin Institute, but he was only encouraged by Freud to hold on as long as possible. A decree by the new German government forbade foreigners[131] from sitting on the committees of any medical societies, so he was forced to resign from the institute. In Palestine he sought to create an institute of psychoanalysis at Hebrew University but was refused because it was "premature to introduce . . . psychoanalysis before a Chair in Psychology has been established."[132] Undaunted, he established a private institute with a library furnished with the personal books he had managed to rescue from the Berlin Institute. He died in 1943 and was buried on Mount Scopus outside of Jerusalem.

* * *

With the committee in place to look after the details of organizational empire-building and with psychoanalysis gaining wider acceptance and even new spheres of application, Freud could finally step back and appreciate all that had been accomplished. He was already well over sixty when the committee was formed and probably past due developmentally to begin the withdrawal inward that is typical of late adulthood and approaching old age. Much to his own adolescent chagrin, his father had entered into this same process quite prematurely, and it was not likely that Freud would have allowed himself to do the same or even begin until he was quite confident that there were those who could be trusted to carry on his work.

Unhappily, these last years would not be peaceful ones for Freud. Instead, he would experience a series of painful personal tragedies as well as witness the horror of two world wars and the systematic destruction of his own people. Heroically and without complaint he faced the fate that awaited him, but not without progressively sinking into the depths of emotional depression. Over the course of these years he grew extremely dismal about the worth of humanity and in time secretly longed for the relief that death would bring. He had always been an insular man, but old age and physical suffering caused him to draw even further into himself. Because of what he believed, the isolation had to be faced alone and without the comfort of any religious support. In his final years he took pleasure in the small things: the companionship of his dogs, a few personal honors that were of significance to him, such as Thomas Mann's visit, his ability to continue working and, perhaps above all else, the company of his daughter Anna.

World War I marked a turning point in Freud's personal psychology through a resurrection of old ghosts from the past in the form of renewed concerns over anti-Semitism, the safety of his family, and poverty. Like so many other Jews raised on the unrealistic hopes of the seventies and eighties, he too was devastated by the social realities that the war brought to crystal clarity. In its wake the dreams of Jewish equality and fair treatment, let alone acceptance into the Christian world, were finally and unequivocally shattered. The Jews were once again unwanted outsiders. Closer to home, Freud feared for the very well-being of his family. He was especially beset by continual worries about his sons, who were then fighting in the war, and Martin, who had been captured and was a prisoner of war in Italy. Finally, the postwar economic depression proved a devastating blow to Freud and his family's finances. Always fearful of impending financial doom, he watched helplessly as inflation devoured his life savings and turned an insurance policy he had purchased to protect Martha into worthless paper. The inflation also reduced to almost nothing a very large bequest made to the Psychoanalytic Association by von Freund in 1918, causing it to hover on the brink of insolvency. Thus at sixty-two Freud found himself once again with nothing more than the money he earned through his daily practice.

The year 1920 ushered in a series of personal tragedies and losses from which Freud would never recover emotionally. In January of that year his second daughter Sophie died unexpectedly at twenty-six of influenza in an epidemic that swept across Europe and had almost taken Martha as well. Sophie left behind a happy marriage and two small boys. Since no trains were at the time running between Vienna and Hamburg, Freud was even denied the opportunity say goodbye or grieve at her funeral. In August of 1922 death again touched Freud in the person of his niece, Caecilie Graf, to whom he was quite attached. She was the only daughter of his sister Rosa, whose only other child, a son, had been killed in the war. But this was not the end, for his grandson Heinz Rudolph, Sophie's youngest son, lovingly referred to as "Heinerle," would die at the age of four-and-one-half of tuberculosis during a visit to Vienna. Of him Freud once wrote. "He was indeed an enchanting little fellow, and I myself was never aware of having loved a human being, certainly never a child, so much."[133] On no other occasion had Freud ever been observed to weep openly. This series of wrenching events evidently served permanently to destroy Freud's capacity for pleasure. In a letter to Binswanger, who had only recently informed Freud of the death of his own son, he summarized his inner state.

> I am writing out of an inner urge, because your letter has awakened a memory in me—absurd, for after all, this memory has never been asleep. I lost a beloved daughter . . . but bore this remarkably well. That was in 1920, when we were crushed and miserable, after years of war. . . . [Referring to the lost of Heinerle] To me this child had taken the place of all my children, and other grandchildren, and since then . . . I don't care for my grandchildren any more, but find no joy in life either. That is the secret of my indifference . . . towards the danger to my own life.[134]

During this same period Freud also had to bear the pain of watching his fellow Jews suffer increasing hardships and threat as Nazism cast an ever-widening shadow over the European continent. His final assessment of human nature bore the imprint of these experiences. In 1918 he had written to his Swiss friend Pfister: "On the whole I have not found much of the 'good' in people. Most of them are in my experience riff-raff, whether they proclaim themselves adherents of this or of that ethical doctrine, or of none at all."[135] In 1929 to Lou Andreas-Salome he wrote: "In the depth of my heart I can't help being convinced that my dear fellow men, with a few exceptions, are worthless."[136]

A final cruel affront to Freud's person came in the form of cancer of the jaw and palate. He was operated on for the condition first in April 1923. Because the operating surgeon had neglected to take proper precautions against tissue shrinkage, Freud had to wear a painful prosthesic device in his mouth for the next fifteen years. In all, he would suffer through thirty-three operations, the slow and progressive loss of the ability to eat and speak, and the embarrassment of a progressive physical distortion of his face. Never, however, would he consent to the use of drugs until the very end. So important to him was the retention of his mental acuity and awareness that he repeatedly refused to trade it for the cessation of physical pain.

* * *

With the rise and coming to power of National Socialism in Germany, the attack and persecution of psychoanalysis and its Jewish adherents intensified. The Berlin Institute, for instance, was the simultaneous target for psychiatrists from the nearby Charity Hospital, Alfred Rosenberg's Battle Group for German Culture, and propagandist Julius Stricher, who was fondly referred to as the "Jewbaiter of Nuremberg." All vied for power and position within the chaotic structure of the Third Reich, and anti-Semitism was a proven weapon in this struggle. To further his own aims Streicher introduced a new paper whose concern was health policy. Its first issue introduced a feature entitled "The Role of the Jew in Medicine" that described psychoanalysis as a Jewish "poisoning of the soul" whose purpose was to: "remove the last ethical support from the patient's soul in its battle over control of its instinctual life, and cast it down before the Asiatic world view, 'Eat, drink, and be merry, for tomorrow you die!' And that was Freud's aim, or perhaps his assignment, for he lined up dutifully with other Jewish endeavors to strike the Nordic race at its most sensitive spot, its sex life." Psychoanalysis was a "foreign body within the German nation,"[137] and Freud was in turn guilty of all manner of crimes against the German people including perpetuating Jewish entrepreneurship, perverting the work of the Aryan creators of depth psychology, and destroying the reality of the heroic, soldierly German.

Max Eitingon visited Freud three days before Hitler's ascension to the chancellorship and expressed his concern about the future plight of the institute. By April a decree had been issued barring all foreigners including Jews from executive functions of medical societies. This included the Berlin Institute. Within a month Freud's works were being burned at German universities, and Jewish analysts along with many candidates and students at the institute were doing what they could to escape the country. The Nuremberg race laws were instituted by September 1935 and the following March the warehouse of the International Psychoanalytic Press in Leipzig was confiscated. The Reich Physicians Decree of 1936 ushered in a series of laws aimed at entirely eliminating the Jewish practice of medicine. According to Hitler: "The Führer regards the cleansing of the medical profession as far more important than, for example, of the bureaucracy, since in his opinion the duty of the physician is or should be one of racial leadership."[138] Jewish analysts who did not escape in time ended up in concentration camps, and what followed was a systematic collection of Jewish mental patients for exportation to the same camps. The Austrian Anschluss, which would occur in March of 1938, marked the beginning of the end of the Vienna Psychoanalytic Institute and the introduction of a similar process in Austria. Its story marked the beginning of the final saga of Freud's escape.[139]

\* \* \*

On 15 March 1938, four days after the Nazi invasion of Austria, Ernest Jones flew to Prague and then rented a small monoplane to reach Vienna. His intent was to try and convince Sigmund Freud to leave his lifelong home for a safer haven. Jones found the Austrian capital's airport and the skies above it filled with German planes and its streets teeming with roaming tanks and roaring crowds shouting "Heil Hitler." He immediately contacted Anna Freud who advised him to go directly to the Verlag, the psychoanalytic publishing firm. It was hoped that his presence as a foreigner asserting its international character might protect it from a Nazi takeover. Jones wrote the following of what he found there. "The stairs and rooms were occupied by villainous-looking youths with daggers and pistols, Martin Freud was sitting in a corner under arrest, and the Nazi 'authorities' were engaged in counting the petty cash in a drawer."[140] Jones was immediately arrested but released an hour later and was able to find his way to the Freud residence.

The Freuds had also been visited by a similar gang of Nazi thugs. Mrs. Freud, with characteristic demeaner, had invited the sentry to be seated and then placed her household money on a table saying: "Won't the gentlemen help themselves." Anna then escorted them to another room and opened the family safe. At this point Freud himself appeared, "frail and gaunt," with "blazing eyes that any Old Testament prophet might have envied."[141] His powerful presence combined with the extreme civility they had been afforded must have completely unhinged the visitors, for they left immediately. The Gestapo would return a week later and carry out a complete search under the guise of seeking anti-Nazi documents, but they did not enter Freud's rooms. They did however take Anna Freud away with them.

Jones did his best to convince Freud that he must leave Vienna, but the professor was bent on staying. After finally acknowledging that his life might be of some importance to others, Freud argued first that he was too weak to travel and then that no country would allow him to enter. The parrying continued back and forth, but he finally agreed that Jones should return to England to see if emigration there for him and his family could be arranged. A related problem was securing the Nazis permission for him to leave Vienna. To help with this task Jones contacted W. C. Bullitt, then American ambassador to France with whom Freud had coauthored a psychoanalytic study of Woodrow Wilson. Bullitt in turn contacted President Roosevelt directly, and the political wheels were set into motion. In Paris, Bullitt called on the German ambassador to France and "let him know in no uncertain terms what a world scandal would ensue if the Nazis ill-treated Freud."[142] Edoardo Weiss, an Italian pupil of Freud's, had also gotten Mussolini, then especially in Hitler's good graces, to intercede on Freud's behalf.

On 13 March the board of the Vienna Society met and it was decided that everyone would try to escape if possible and that the new site of the society would be wherever Freud eventually settled. Freud, his sense of Jewish history obviously stimulated, drew a biblical analogy: "After the destruction of the Temple in Jerusalem by Titus, Rabbi Jochanan ben Sakkai asked for permission to open a school at Jabneh for the study of Torah. We are going to do the same. We are, after all, used to persecution by our history, tradition and some of us by personal experience," adding jokingly and pointing to Richard Sterba, the only non-Jew present, "with one exception."[143] Sterba, too, however had decided to escape and left for Switzerland several days later. He subsequently would refuse requests by German analysts to return as director of the Vienna Institute and Clinic. The Germans had hoped to take over and "Aryanize" the institute as they had in Berlin, but as Jones so graphically put it "there was not even a rump for the Germans."[144] All that could be salvaged by them was the society's library and the Verlag.

Marie Bonaparte arrived from Paris on 17 March so that Jones could leave immediately for England to see to arrangements there. It was strongly felt that the Freuds would remain far

## The Jews and Gentiles of Psychoanalysis  207

safer if a powerful foreigner remained in their presence. Upon arrival in London, Jones contacted William Bragg, president of the Royal Society, which had honored Freud only two years earlier, in order to seek that lofty organization's intercession with the British government. Bragg at once complied, but completely unsettled Jones when he naively asked: "Do you really think the Germans are unkind to the Jews."[145] Home Secretary Sir Samuel Hoare in turn fully supported the plan and allowed Jones to get travel permits for Freud, his family, his servants, his personal doctors, and a limited number of pupils and their families.

What remained was gaining permission from the Nazis for the Freuds to leave. This would clearly be costly. The process took three anxious months. By a lucky coincidence, a Dr. Sauerwald, a Viennese Nazi, had been chosen to oversee the arrangements, in particular the financial ones. It turned out that he had studied with and developed a great respect for Professor Herzig at the University, a lifelong Jewish friend of Freud. These feelings he now extended to Freud and suppressed at great personal risk the fact that the family had money abroad until they were physically out of the county. The Nazis did demand a particularly large sum of money under the guise of an income tax and threatened to confiscate Freud's library and collection in lieu of payment. Marie Bonaparte advanced the necessary sum. Throughout the negotiations Martin was repeatedly called to Gestapo headquarters but he was never detained. Most frightening, however, was the day Anna was arrested and kept all day by the Gestapo. Freud spent the day "pacing up and down and smoking an endless series of cigars to deaden his emotions," no doubt with visions of his "precious"[146] daughter being tortured and deported to a concentration camp, as was so often the case during those days. All were ecstatic when she finally returned unharmed. It was later discovered that throughout this period the American chargé d'affaires Mr. Wiley had kept a close eye on these events and had in fact intervened on behalf of Anna. He also saw to it that a member of the American legation traveled with Freud from Vienna to Paris.

In May Freud wrote the following to his son Ernest, already in London. Again, he felt compelled to draw upon his Jewish heritage for analogies. "In these dark days there are two prospects to cheer us: to rejoin you all and—to die in freedom. I sometimes compare myself with the old Jacob whom in his old age his children brought to Egypt. It is to be hoped that the result will not be the same, an exodus from Egypt. It is time for Ahasverus [the wandering Jew] to come to rest somewhere."[147] From 5 May on individual members and families were issued permits and allowed to emigrate. The first was Minna Bernays, who was taken from a sanitarium and escorted to England by Dorothy Burlingham, an American analyst and Anna's closest friend. After signing the famous document in which he "heartily recommended the Gestapo,"[148] Freud, his wife Martha, Anna, and two servants were issued exit visas on 4 June. After a joyous but uneventful journey they arrived in the "Promised Land" by a night ferryboat to Dover on 5 June 1938.

Freud would spend the next year living and working as a free man: writing on psychoanalysis, finishing his *Moses* novel, receiving distinguished friends and visitors from throughout the world, and basking in some of the glory he so richly deserved but had been denied for so long in anti-Semitic Austria. By September 1939 the cancer had become unbearable and Freud was near death. On 21 September he spoke candidly to his doctor and friend. "My dear Schur, you remember our first talk. You promised me then you would help me [with sedation] when I could no longer carry on. It is only torture now and it has no longer any sense." Schur pressed his hand and agreed. Freud thanked him and added: "Tell Anna about our talk."[149] After the injection the next morning, he sighed with relief, slipped into a peaceful sleep, and died before midnight the next day. Ironically, he had died on Yom Kippur, the holiest day of the Jewish year. True to his lifelong ambivalence, he was cremated and had his ashes placed in a Grecian urn, all contrary to the Jewish laws of burial.

# 7
# Psychoanalysis and Its Jewish Connection

The case study just presented argues that Freud's life experience and personality were significantly shaped by the fact of his Jewishness and all that that implied in turn-of-the-century Vienna. Anti-Semitism, although at times perhaps overestimated, was an ever-present and oppressive reality for him, which shaped the very core elements of his life, including his relationship with Jacob his father, his career choices and advancement, his efforts in the creation of psychoanalysis, and his very beliefs about the world and human nature. Freud grew up in the midst of an old world, yet assimilating Jewish family, the first-born favorite son of a smothering and demanding yet indulgent mother and a loving but distant and inaccessible father. Certain critical developmental events—including a disruption in the early attachment to a caregiver, a discontinuity in the basic security of a home environment, disillusionment with the Oedipal father, and anxiety over selection of a mate and fatherhood—came to be inextricably bound up with Freud's feelings about being Jewish. As a result of these events, his Jewish identity took shape into its basic ambivalent form that included: flouting Jewish tradition and ritual, efforts to protect his children from anti-Semitism, ambivalence over Zionism, an unconscious desire to convert, as well as a fierce chauvinistic pride, a preference for association with Jews, and an identification with biblical figures. Because of various inner changes in this identity, stimulated first by his own psychoanalysis and later by the break with Carl Jung and occasioned by an unconscious desire to integrate the disparate aspects of his Jewishness, he was ultimately led to the creation of much of psychoanalysis.

It is also important to note that these various aspects of his psychology intertwined and reinforced each other to give shape to his basic identity, not only as a Jew but also as a person. While it is perhaps tempting to isolate a single element as the most crucial in defining the connection between Freud's Jewishness and psychoanalysis, as has been the case with most previous writers—be it Carl Schorske's emphasis on Freud's political frustrations as a Jew, Martin Bergmann's notion of his ambivalent identification, or Marianne Krull's focus on Freud's feelings of guilt for surpassing his father and rejecting his tradition, to list only three, each certainly correct in its own right—such an approach invariably leads to oversimplification and distortion. Personal history is after all the product of various interacting factors: intrapsychic, social, cultural, political, and intellectual. It is only out of a consideration for their totality that an accurate picture of human experience can emerge. Freud's Jewish connection must be sought then not in any single factor, but rather in a synthesis of their individual effects. Only in this manner can one come to fully appreciate the profound influence of a phenomenon such as ethnicity.

Having said this much, however, one is still left with a rather important question. It has to do with the relationship between Freud's Jewishness and the product of his life's work, psychoanalysis. Is there in fact anything decidedly Jewish about the body of knowledge and theories that Freud and his disciples came to create? Ironically, with this question we find ourselves faced once again with the very concern that unconsciously and unmercifully haunted Freud—that of psychoanalysis' status as a "Jewish Science." His critics certainly thought so. Carl Jung, for instance, warned of the "grave error" of applying "Jewish categories . . . indiscriminately to Germanic and Slavic Christendom,"[1] and William McDougall in 1921 offered a similar caution. "It looks as though this theory which to me and to most men of my sort seems to be strange, bizarre and fantastic, may be approximately true of the Jewish race."[2] Freud, for his part, while acknowledging "differences between the Jewish and Aryan spirit,"[3] argued also for the universality of his ideas. Such positions and counterpositions, however, as has been suggested earlier, seldom in actuality have much to do with the pursuit of scientific truth. Rather, they tend to mask very personal issues and concerns. In the case of Jung, for instance, and perhaps McDougall as well, the underlying issue might well have been anti-Semitism and a fear of the Jew. In Freud's case it was a desperate and unquenchable desire for recognition and acknowledgement, stimulated in part by his own sensitivities as a Jew. A far more productive approach, which does not immediately call forth race-related responses, is to ask whether there is anything about psychoanalysis per se that brands it as particularistic, that is, Judeocentric. Or, put somewhat differently: Is there any aspect of its content or structure that would lead it to be limited in its application?

The question, in short, is one of Freud's role as a transmitter of culture. The case study presented makes it clear that he was in fact thoroughly Jewish: in his values, temperament, modes of thought, and lifestyle. Could he still, however, given this indisputable reality, generate a method for understanding human nature that transcended the particularism of his own experience? And if not, what parts of his theory are guilty of culture-boundness and must thus be called into question as appropriate for application to the situation of other cultural groups?

A careful examination of psychoanalytic theory leads one to the realization that much of its substance was drawn from Freud's own early experience and that his referent for this was the Eastern European Jewish family with its strong bonds between mother and son and father and daughter, tensions between same-sexed parents and child, repressed sexuality, strict incest taboos, and the inferior status of women. Upon this very template Freud superimposed the more unique aspects of his own family situation. This included, for instance, a young and very attractive mother and an older, more distant and patriarchal father. The Oedipal drama in turn became an apt and engaging metaphor for this very personal situation. It is perhaps fair to suggest that this central component of psychoanalytic theory and all the concepts that issued forth from it—Freud's descriptions of the psychology of men and women, the theory of psychosexual stages and development, the theory of psychological fixations and types, and his descriptions of the development of human society—must all be held suspect in regard to their universal applicability. Routinely to apply this model to patients from other cultures, especially ones having radically different value systems and family patterns, would be both ill-advised and inappropriate. If, however, one chooses, as was in fact the case with many neo-Freudians, to interpret the Oedipal conflict more metaphorically, as for instance representing the prototypic struggle for independence (be it from authority, parents, or a cultural past), then one can begin to approach more universal relevance.

What does seem universal in Freud's work and remains today as the very core of all depth psychology is what he referred to as his metapsychology, that is, the structure and processes that define the general workings of the psyche. In his concepts of the id-ego-superego, the unconscious, instinct and need, anxiety and defenses, and psychoanalysis as a treatment process one finds what is truly universal in psychoanalytic theory. Not surprisingly, these are the very elements that have tended to be retained in the theories of those who have chosen to follow Freud's general lead. Where his successors have differed has been in relation to how much of the more cultural material, most specifically the Oedipal complex, is retained and where in the id-ego-superego system one tends to place major control for the determination of behavior.

A related phenomenon that deserves attention because it has been used so often as a justification for rejecting psychoanalysis as a Jewish enterprise is the fact that Jews have always been disproportionately represented among the ranks of its practitioners and patients. The first eighteen members of the psychoanalytic movement were in fact Jews, and gentile analysts would remain a very decided minority until after Freud's death and the relocation of the movement's centers to England and America. Even today the numbers are still very much slanted. A 1970 study of mental health professionals carried out by the University of Chicago, for instance, showed that 76 percent of all practicing male psychoanalysts were Jewish.[4]

The fact that Jews have been disproportionately represented within psychoanalytic circles does not, however, in and of itself imply a narrowness in its realm of application. Such a relationship might well reflect elements having nothing to do with the question of generalizability, for example, the existence of intraethnic association patterns, or limited career options for Jews, or even an avoidance of psychoanalysis by gentiles. Each of these phenomena has in fact been evident in the history of the psychoanalytic movement. But again none necessarily implies particularism in relation to the basic ideas it espouses. The findings of the Chicago study showed that factors such as these seemed to predispose both Jewish and gentile psychoanalysts toward careers in the profession. Specifically, it was found that five personal characteristics were related to a choice of psychoanalysis as a career: parental attitudes toward socioeconomic mobility, areligiousity, personal leanings toward liberal politics, a sense of social marginality, and an introspective cognitive style.

More to the point is the possibility of the existence of certain parallels or similarities between psychoanalysis and Judaism, wherein being Jewish would either by nature or upbringing provide some familiarity, comfort, or other advantage in the practice of psychoanalysis. David Bakan, for instance, saw psychoanalysis as rooted in Jewish mysticism with the two systems sharing such similarities as the role of the demonic, the meaning and interpretation of dreams, the role and use of sexuality, and the use of similar interpretive techiques. Arnold Meadow and Harold Vetter, for their part, have enumerated a series of parallels between Judaic core values and central concepts in psychoanalysis. These included similar attitudes toward worldliness and bodily pleasure, the importance of rationalism, the role of authority, and the place of the mother. Mortimer Ostow added yet another candidate to this growing list: a shared emphasis on salvation through special knowledge. Finally, Karl Menninger saw in the Jewish family characteristics that laid the groundwork for psychoanalytic work: a high value placed on the verbal expression of feelings, the scholarly organization of thought, and an emphasis on the importance of psychological as well as physical reality. Freud himself expressed a similar conviction in his letters to Karl Abraham where he stressed the intellectual similarities the two shared and their differences with their non-Jewish colleague Carl Jung. "Please be tolerant," Freud wrote to Abraham, "and do not forget that it is really easier for you than it is for Jung to follow my ideas, for in the first place you are completely independent, and then you are closer to my intellectual constitution because of racial kinship. While he as a Christian and a pastor's son finds his way to me only against great inner resistances."[5]

But the possibility of such parallels does not negate non-Jewish involvement in psychoanalysis; it only implies that gentiles may have a more difficult time learning or growing comfortable with the system. Again, however, to avoid the trap of invidious racial comparisons, it is more useful to pursue a description of those specific personal characteristics and skills that seem to underlie successful psychoanalytic thinking and practice. In addressing the contributions of his own Jewishness, Freud took just this tact. "Because I was a Jew I found myself free from many prejudices which restrict others in the use of the intellect" and "As a Jew I was prepared to be in opposition and to renounce agreement with the 'compact majority.'"[6] Thus for Freud what was essential was first a certain degree of intellectual freedom, that is, an ability to transcend conventional patterns of thought and prejudice, especially those which tend to defend against self-insight. It will be remembered that one of Freud's greatest discoveries was the individual's ability to avoid self-knowledge. Secondly, Freud pointed to the value of social marginality. In doing so, he implied that socially marginal people tended to be freer of established values and attitudes and also to possess a superior ability, developed through social experience, to resist conformity, be it social or clinical in nature. While such abilities are probably most typically found in members of minority and excluded groups because of their position as perpetual outsiders, there is no reason to believe either that individual circumstances cannot created them in others or that they cannot be developed with adequate time and training. This was certainly one of the distinct purposes of the training analysis.

It is interesting to note in this vein that some biographers have suggested that psychoanalysis was itself a collective response to Jewish marginality and a covert assault on the society that systematically excluded Jews and treated them as less than human. Rothman and Isenberg, for one, described Freud's creation as an indirect attack on Catholic majority culture that served to create equality through universalism. According to their argument, the experience of marginality provided Jews particular insight into the workings of the dominant culture, and it was this awareness that infused Freud's work. John Cuddihy took a somewhat different tact when he pointed to a direct correspondence between Freud's description of the psyche and the situation of Jews who had assimilated into civilized culture. By equating the unassimilated Jew with the id, Freud was able to attack Christian culture at its most vulnerable core—civilization leads inevitably to neurosis; all peoples, Jews and gentiles alike, share a common inner structure and are thus the same; and perhaps most damning of all, there is a Jew (in the form of the id) buried deep within the psyche of every gentile.

To the extent that psychoanalysis did in fact emerge in relation to forces now facing all human groups, not just the Jews, such as alienation and fragmentation, then it would have a more general relevance both as a critique and as a possible palliative. It is in this general sense that Orlando Patterson suggested that modernity has made Jews of us all, that is, has placed humanity as a whole in a state of perpetual alienation, a condition once the exclusive legacy and birthright of the Jewish people. Writers, such as Rothman and Isenberg, Cuddihy, and Schorske, who took such a position, see psychoanalysis as a measured, although unconscious response to the psychological circumstances with which assimilating Jews were faced: the social marginality and alienation, the impersonal facade of civility, an out-of-control political and social world. Similarly, psychoanalysis has been viewed as a much-needed palliative to this new human condition. It has created equality and a sense of human belonging through universalism. It has destroyed social categories that tended to define inferiority and isolation. It has provided a vehicle for the attainment of inner freedom and peace. Perhaps psychoanalysis' great attraction in the modern era has been its response to the new set of human circumstances posed by contemporary living.

A final perspective on the qualities that might predispose one to a facility for psychoanalytic work is offered by Karl Menninger. According to him, the gifted psychiatrist or psychologist is able to experience very directly the emotions and pain of others. This occurs because "in the suffering of other people there is awakened in him some recollections of his own suffering as a child, a suffering which was perhaps never completely assauged; in this case, his wish to help the other person. His wish to see into the other person's problems and to set him aright, is in part an acting out of a wish that he himself might be saved or have been saved this pain."[7] Thus there is something in the analyst's own suffering as a child that can be transformed into a greater understanding of such a state in others and thereby offers the possibility of help. Obviously, not all suffering can be transformed in this manner, and the critical difference seems to be whether the person is somehow able to sublimate and socially exploit that early trauma, that is, channel its energy outwardly and constructively, or must continue to experience it masochistically throughout life.

As briefly described in an earlier chapter, Menninger believed that the Jewish child was more likely to become scarred emotionally than was the gentile child. Because of circumstances in the Jewish family brought about by external prejudice and anti-Semitism, the child cannot help but become hyperaware of his or her own group membership. This in turn "results in certain reactions with reference to nonmembers of the group, attitudes of hostility, fear, distrust, and repudiation mixed with wishful and uncertain longings to be liked and to be assimilated by other groups, and reaction formations against these wishes."[8] Jewish parents for their part respond to their plight by overemphasizing the family bond and by overprotecting and being overly demonstrative toward their children. This solicitousness eventually takes its toll emotionally and creates not only "terrific aspiration and a compulsive striving toward superiority," but also a heightened sense of superiority and specialness. The inflated sense of superiority leads not only to a social discomfort with others and a sense of separatism and social isolation but also to a predisposition to a "mounting sense of disappointment and disillusionment. . . ." as the child "discovers that his parents, being human, were not entirely sincere in their adulation and demonstrativeness.[9] The overprotected and overestimated child cannot help but experience indifference or even the least bit of inattention, (first on the part of the parent and later from the world in general), as tragic rejection. In the process he or she learns the painful lesson that "no one can be implicitly and completely trusted."[10] The result of this complicated scenario is wounded self-esteem and basic mistrust of humankind. This attitude, if not somehow corrected, is carried into the world and into the arena of intergroup relations. The child so predisposed psychologically cannot help but overestimate existing dangers, and the resulting fear either impels him or her "to forestall this danger by befriending the Gentile in an obsequious manner" or defy it "by being aggressive and provocative,"[11] which in turn often invokes an in-kind response.

Such a child grows up amazingly attuned to the world and to the reactions of others, albeit perhaps irrationally expecting the worst. To the extent that young Jews can learn to understand and control the heightened sensitivity and feelings of insecurity, to develop sufficient detachment to become more objective, analytic, and discerning in their judgment of others, they can ultimately "turn to account" in their work with others the "perception of unseen motives with telling effect,"[12] as is routinely done in psychoanalytic work. What Menninger has described, again, is not necessarily the sole and exclusive property of Jews, but rather a family scenario that tends to appear with unusual frequency in Jewish homes, creating a narcissistic child who may if he or she is lucky subsequently learn to transcend and sublimate his or her innermost tendencies in the service of others.

## Psychoanalysis and Its Jewish Connection

What is particularly ironic about Menninger's portrayal is how closely it fits Freud's own early biography or rather what we know of it. He was by all accounts the prototypical narcissistic child: pampered, indulged, and imbued with the myth of his own specialness and of the great things he would ultimately accomplish in life. Out of these early expectations grew an unrelenting drive for recognition and an almost grandiose need to leave his mark upon the history of humanity. This desire of Freud's perhaps found its greatest expression in his identification with Moses and in his work *Moses and Monotheism*. His early years were also marked by great interpersonal disillusionment: the loss of his nursemaid and the familiarity and comfort of his Freiberg home and as well as the great disappointment he experienced at the cowardly behavior of his father in response to an anti-Semitic insult. These early experiences were echoed in kind later in life by an almost unending series of disappointments—the slow advancement of his medical career, the less than enthusiastic reception his ideas received, and the sequence of friendships, first with mentors and later disciples that always somehow turned sour. His great sensitivity to rejection, often masked by a blustery bravado or deep cynicism especially during adolescence, emerged most clearly in his courtship of Martha and the unending tests and acts of exclusive attention that he demanded of her.

From early adolescence Freud exhibited a sensitivity around his Jewishness. He vacillated between a desire to placate, which eventually gained consciousness through his self-analysis, and an equally strong tendency to stand up to and even provoke non-Jews, a clear motive for his work on religion. He tended to overestimate the negative impact of anti-Semitism and had even collapsed before it until he was finally made bold by his long-delayed visit to Rome. He always preferred the comfort and safety of Jewish comrades. This was especially true in times of great personal stress as with his membership to the B'nai Brith. He even unconsciously made the early psychoanalytic movement into a decidedly Jewish enterprise, although he would periodically rebel against its particularism. With age, growing recognition, and the perspective he had gained first through his self-analysis and later through his writing on religion, he was in time able to find a certain comfort with himself in general and his Jewish identity in particular.

It is tempting to suggest that out of Freud's own efforts to deal with his own inner suffering, which took the form of an insatiable narcissism and enormous sensitivity to rejection—to gain some distance from it, to see it more clearly and to sublimate and exploit it—grew the system of therapy that he would ultimately give to the world. His gift of intuitive perception and concern for the unhappy and suffering souls who found their way to his office developed directly out of his own inner experience and pain. What he sought to create, then, was a method for curing others like himself, Jews and non-Jews alike, of the early wounds unintentionally created in them by loving, yet fearful parents. So insightful was his mind, so deep his hurt and so desperate his search, that it would eventually transform an entire world and that world's perception of itself.

# Notes

Works frequently cited have been identified by the following abbreviations:

Freud/Abraham    Sigmund Freud and Karl Abraham. *A Psychoanalytic Dialogue: The Letters of Sigmund Freud and Karl Abraham, 1907–1926.* Edited by Kilda C. Abraham and Ernst L. Freud. Translated by Bernard Marsh and Hilda C. Abraham. New York: Basic Books, 1965.

Freud/Jung    Sigmund Freud and Carl G. Jung. *The Freud/Jung Letters.* Edited by William McGuire. Princeton: Princeton University Press, 1974.

Freud/Pfister    Sigmund Freud and Oskar Pfister. *Psychoanalysis and Faith: The Letters of Sigmund Freud and Oskar Pfister.* New York: Basic Books, 1963.

Freud/Zweig    Sigmund Freud and Arnold Zweig. *The Letters of Sigmund Freud and Arnold Zweig.* Edited by Ernst L. Freud. New York: Harcourt Brace Jovanovich, 1970.

Letters    Sigmund Freud. *The Letters of Sigmund Freud.* Edited by Ernst L. Freud. Translated by Tania and James Stern. New York: Basic Books, 1960.

Origins    Sigmund Freud. *The Origins of Psycho-Analysis: Letter to Wilhelm Fliess, Drafts and Notes 1887–1902.* Edited by Marie Bonaparte, Anna Freud, and Ernst Kris. Translated by Eric Mosbacher and James Strachey. New York: Basic Books, 1954.

S.E.    Sigmund Freud, *The Standard Edition of the Complete Works of Sigmund Freud,* Translated under the general editorship of James Strachey in collaboration with Anna Freud. 24 vols. London: Hogarth Press and the Institute of Psychoanalysis, 1953–74.

## Chapter 1. The Politics of Ethnicity

1. Frederic Grunfeld, *Prophets without Honor* (New York: McGraw-Hill, 1973), p. 56.
2. Ibid., p. 63.
3. Ernest Jones, *The Life and Work of Sigmund Freud,* abridged edition (New York: Basic Books, 1961), p. 518.
4. Sigmund Freud and Karl Abraham, *A Psycho-Analytic Dialogue: The Letters of Sigmund Freud and Karl Abraham, 1907–1926,* ed. Helda C. Abraham and Ernst L. Freud, trans. Bernard Marsh and Hilda C. Abraham (New York: Basic Books, 1965), p. 34; henceforth cited as *Freud/Abraham.*

5. Paul Roazen, *Freud and his Followers* (New York: Alfred A. Knopf, 1971), p. 22.

6. Dennis Klein, *Jewish Origins of the Psychoanalytic Movement* (New York: Praeger, 1981), p. vii.

7. Sigmund Freud, *The Letters of Sigmund Freud*, ed. Ernst L. Freud, trans. Tania and James Stern (New York: Basic Books, 1960), p. 368; henceforth cited as *Letters*.

8. Gregory Zilboorg, *Psychoanalysis and Religion* (New York: Farrar, Straus and Cudahy, 1958), p. 5.

9. This theme has been recently picked up and amplified by Paul Vitz in *Sigmund Freud's Christian Unconscious* (New York: Guilford Press, 1988). Vitz's work offers yet another instance of the distortion of ethnic materials, in this case through selective misinterpretation. Vitz, like Gregory Zilboorg, whom he acknowledges as the one who "gave me the first glimpse of the importance of the present topic" (p. vii), argued that Freud had a strong and intense attraction to Christianity. However, his evidence attested more to the vissisitudes and far-reaching gymnastics of Jewish identification than to any substantial, pro-Christian bent in Freud's character. That Freud was ambivalent about his identity as a Jew does not imply that he was necessarily drawn to Christianity, as Vitz's work suggested repeatedly. Nor does the fact that he was familiar with Christian mythology and dogma as well as the works of various Christian writers indicate anything beyond his being a voracious reader, not to mention a young and aspiring Jew who was desperate to gain knowledge of mainstream culture and the world beyond the Jewish ghetto so that he might somehow win a place within it. Vitz in pursuit of his hypothesis refused to take Freud at face value, as for instance when he asserted that "I have no attraction to Christianity and its 'lie of salvation,'" (Sigmund Freud, *The Origins of Psycho-Analysis: Letters to Wilhelm Fliess, Drafts and Notes 1887–1902*, ed. Marie Bonaparte, Anna Freud, and Ernst Kris, trans. Eric Mosbacher and Mames Strachev [New York: Basic Books, 1954], p. 336; henceforth cited as *Origins*), or when he commented to Oskar Pfister that "my judgment of human nature, above all of the Christian-Aryan variety, has little reason to change" (Freud, *Letters*, p. 418).

10. Zilboorg, *Psychoanalysis and Religion*, p. 42.

11. Ibid., p. 4.

12. Mortimer Ostow, *Judaism and Psychoanalysis* (New York: KTAV, 1982), p. 150.

13. Theodore Lewis, "Freud, the Jews and Judaism," *The Jewish Spectator* (March 1958): 11–14.

14. The "Jewish Question" was a euphemism for the concern shared by Jews and gentiles alike as to whether Jews were capable of transforming themselves sufficiently to make themselves indistinguishable from gentiles and thus to assimilate fully into mainstream society.

15. Sigmund Freud, *The Standard Edition of the Complete Psychological Works of Sigmund Freud*, trans. under the general editorship of James Strachey in collaboration with Anna Freud, 24 vols., (London: Hogarth Press and the Institute of Psychoanalysis, 1953–74), 22:168; henceforth cited as *S.E.*

16. Ostow, *Judaism and Psychoanalysis*, p. 150.

17. *S.E.*, 8:xv.

18. Ernest Jones, *The Life and Work of Sigmund Freud*, vols. 1, 2, and 3 (New York: Basic Books, 1953, 1955, 1957), 2:36 and 1:260.

# Notes

19. *Origins*, p. 237; Sigmund Freud, *The Complete Letters of Sigmund Freud and Wilhelm Fliess 1887–1904*, ed. Jeffrey M. Masson (Cambridge: Harvard University Press), p. 285.
20. Ibid., pp. 295, 370.
21. Jones, *Life and Work*, p. 18.
22. Joseph Wortis, *Fragments of an Analysis with Freud* (New York: Simon and Schuster, 1954), p. 144.
23. Juliet Mitchell, *Psychoanalysis and Feminism* (New York: Vantage Books, 1974), p. 434.
24. For a fuller treatment of Arendt's concepts, see Hannah Arendt, "The Jew as Pariah: A Hidden Dimension," in *The Jew as Pariah: The Case of Hannah Arendt 1906–1975*, ed. Ronald Feldman (New York: Grove Press, 1978).
25. Exemplary works include: Ralph Ellison, *The Invisible Man* (New York: Random House, 1972); James Baldwin, *Notes of a Native Son* (Boston: Beacon Press, 1984); Richard Wright, *Black Boy* (New York: Harper and Row, 1969).
26. Exemplary works include: Franz Fanon, *Black Skins, White Masks* (New York: Grove Press, 1967); Kurt Lewin, *Resolving Social Conflicts* (New York: Harper and Row, 1948).

## Chapter 2. The Assimilated Jews of Vienna

1. Kurt Lewin, *Resolving Social Conflicts*, (New York: Harper & Row, 1948) pp. 153–55.
2. Galacia became a part of Austria in 1772 when Poland was partitioned. This division followed the invasions by Chmeilmicki that served to break the Polish aristocracy's power. Galacia did not gain independence from Austria (at which time it again became part of Poland) until after World War I.
3. Hasidism is a popular, nonrationalistic, and mystical approach to Judaism. Rabbinic Judaism is a continuation of traditional and rationalist Orthodoxy. Haskalah was a movement to reform and modernize Jewish religious ideas, forms, and practices.
4. Children from traditional Jewish families who rejected Jewish identity and practices were viewed and treated as if they were dead.
5. Klein, *Jewish Origins*, p. 6; cited in Walter B. Simon, "The Jewish Vote in Austria," *The Leo Balck Institute Yearbook* 16 (1971); p. 106.
6. Sigmund Mayer, *Die Weiner Juden: Kommerz, Klutur, Politik 1700–1900* (Vienna and Berlin: Lowit Verlag, 1917), pp. 469–70.
7. Hendrik Ruitenbeek, "The Professor," in *Freud as We Knew Him*, ed. Hendrik Ruitenbeek (Detroit: Wayne State University Press, 1973), p. 17.
18. Arthur Schnitzler, *The Road to the Open*, trans. by Horace Samuel (New York: Alfred A. Knopf, 1923), p. 250.
9. Grunfeld, *Prophets without Honor*, pp. 1–35.
10. Peter Gay, *Freud, Jews and Other Germans* (New York: Oxford University Press, 1978), pp. 194–95.
11. Ibid., pp. 189–230. Using the case of German-Jewish conductor Hermann Levi as an example, Gay offers an excellent study of the viscissitudes of Jewish self-hatred.
12. Ibid., p. 199.

13. Stanley Diamond, "Kibbutz and Shtetl: The History of an Idea," *Social Forces* 5 (Fall 1957): 71–99.
14. Ibid., p. 92.
15. Martin Bergmann, "Moses in the Evolution of Freud's Jewish Identity," *Israel Annals of Psychiatry and Related Sciences* 14 (March 1976): 8.

## Chapter 3. The Dynamics of Jewish Identity

1. The period novels of Stefan Zweig and Arthur Schnitzler offer various instances of the former, while Theodor Lessing's book *Der jüdische Selbsthass* (Berlin: Zionistischer Bücher-Bund, 1930) and Kurt Lewin's papers on the German Jews as a minority in *Resolving Social Conflicts* provide excellent examples of the latter.
2. See, for example, Judith Weinstein-Klein, *Jewish Identity and Self-Esteem*, Ph.D. diss., Berkeley, The Wright Institute, 1977.
3. Ibid.
4. Marian Radke Yarrow, "Personality Development and Minority Group Membership," in *The Jews: Social Pattern of an American Group*, ed. Nathan Sklare (New York: Free Press, 1958), pp. 451–74.
5. A useful schema for distinguishing different forms of Jewish identity formation is offer by Klein; see note 2. Positive identification implies a full integration of the individual's various Jewish self-images into a generally coherent and positive whole. Ambivalent identification implies only a partial integration of Jewish self-images that exists side-by-side with negatively toned and rejected aspects of the Jewish self. Negative identification, finally, implies a preponderance of disowned and rejected Jewish self elements. The term identity-rejection refers to either of the latter conditions. Jewish self-hatred, although at times used synonymously with ambivalent and negative identification, also implies a rejection of aspects of the personal self as a consequence of disowned ethnicity.
6. Hector Myers and Larry King, "Mental Health Issues in the Development of the Black American Child," in *The Psychosocial Development of Minority Children*, ed. Gloria Powell (New York: Brunner-Mazel, 1985), pp. 275–306.
7. See, for instance, William Grier and Price Cobbs, *Black Rage* (New York: Basic Books, 1968).
8. Sex roles in traditional Jewish culture gave men the major responsibility for religious obligations.
9. Karl Menninger, "The Genuis of the Jew in Psychiatry," in Karl Menninger, *A Psychiatrist's World* (New York: Viking Press, 1959), pp. 415–24.

## Chapter 4. Growing Up Jewish

1. Willy Aron, "Notes on Sigmund's Freud's Ancestry and Jewish Contacts," *YIVO Annual of Jewish Social Sciences*, 11 (1956–57): 288.
2. S.E., 20:7–8.
3. *Letters*, p. 395.
4. The Jewish Enlightenment movement, which aimed to renovate Judaism.

5. The traditional fur-lined hat and robe worn by Orthodox, Galacian Jews.

6. Josef Sajner, "Sigmund Freuds Beziehungen zu seinem Geburtsort Freiberg (Pribor) und zu Mahren," *Clio Medica* 3 (1968): 167–80.

7. It should be remembered that the mid-eighteenth century witnessed a short period of liberalism throughout Austria and its neighboring provinces.

8. Sajner, "Sigmund Freuds Beziehungen," pp. 143–52.

9. Emanuel Freud was by then married with a family of his own.

10. Judith Heller, "Freud's Mother and Father," in *Freud as We Knew Him*, ed. Hendrik Ruitenbeek (Detroit: Wayne State University Press, 1973), p. 419.

11. Martin Freud, *Sigmund Freud: Man and Father* (New York: Vanguard, 1958), p. 10.

12. Jones, *Life and Work*, p. 5.

13. Ibid., p. 4.

14. Ibid.

15. Heller, "Freud's Mother and Father," p. 337.

16. Ibid., p. 338.

17. Martin Freud, *Sigmund Freud*, p. 11.

18. Jones, *Life and Work*, p. 5.

19. Heller, "Freud's Mother and Father," p. 339.

20. Eli Bernays was in fact the brother of Sigmund's future wife Martha.

21. Martin Freud, *Sigmund Freud*, p. 16.

22. Of all ethnic characteristics, family patterns tend to be the most resistent to change and often require several generations for internal acculturation to occur. Thus, one would not expect to see assimilated patterns of child-rearing or family interaction in the home of Freud's parents or even in his own, but rather in those of his children and children's children.

23. This data was first presented publicly as case material Freud included in his early writings, especially in *The Interpretation of Dreams* (S.E., 4 5: 1–338, 339–621), to document various aspects of his emerging theory and privately in his correspondence with Wilhelm Fleiss. The possibility of unconscious distortion and the temptation unconsciously to fit facts to theory is just too strong to draw sound conclusions from these rememberances alone. Only to the extent that they can be supported by additional data and fit logically into an emerging psychological picture of Freud's inner psychology and outer life can their veracity be trusted.

24. At a broader interpersonal level, for instance, Freud would feel throughout his life more comfortable and safer interacting with Jews as opposed to gentiles. In relation to the impact of individual personalities, he would refer on several different occasions for example to the impact of his relationship with John as a paradigm for later adult interactions, especially with mentors and younger colleagues. There will be more to say about the accuracy of this assessment in chapter 6.

25. Part of the amnion still covering the head.

26. *S.E.*, 4:192.

27. Ibid., p. 216.

28. *S.E.*, 5:424–25.

29. Anna Bernays, "My Brother Sigmund Freud," *American Mercury* 51 (1940):337.

30. *S.E.*, 17:156.

31. Marianne Krull, *Freud and His Father* (New York: W. W. Norton, 1986). p. 117.
32. *S.E.*, 22:133.
33. Heller, "Freud's Mother and Father," pp. 337–38.
34. Jones, *Life and Work*,: p. 7.
35. Ibid., p. 16.
36. Aron, "Notes," p. 289.
37. *S.E.*, 4:216.
38. Ibid., p. 248.
39. Ibid.
40. Shortly after the move both Emanuel and Phillip emigrated to England, thus providing some support for this particular contention.
41. *S.E.*, 3:314.
42. *Origins*, p. 237.
43. Martin Freud, *Sigmund Freud*, p. 19.
44. *S.E.*, 3:312.
45. Jones, *Life and Work*, p. 14.
46. *S.E.*, 4:205.
47. Arons, "Notes," p. 289.
48. *S.E.*, 20:8.
49. Ibid., p. 253.
50. *Origins*, p. 162.
51. Bernays, "My Brother," p. 336.
52. *Letters*, pp. 96–97.
53. This attribution is specifically made by Freud in his 1926 letter to the B'nai Brith lodge and further amplified in chapters 5 and 7.
54. *Letters*, p. 215.
55. Sigmund Freud, "Sieben Briefe und zwei Postkarten au Emil Fluss," *Psyche* 24 (1970):21.
56. *Letters*, p. 4.
57. Reuben Rainey in *Freud as Student of Religion* (Missoula, Mont.: Scholars Press, 1975) has reconstructed the curriculum in Jewish education to which Freud was likely exposed during his adolescent school years.
58. Ibid., p. 37.
59. For a flavor of the kind of Judaic materials Freud was specifically exposed to during his gymnasium years, the reader is referred to Rainey, *Freud as Student of Religion*, pp. 44–45, in which the author reproduced the entire curriculum taught during that period by Freud's religious instructor, Samuel Hammerschlag.
60. Ibid, p. 50.
61. Jones, *Life and Work*, I:179.
62. Rainey, *Freud as Student of Religion*, pp. 41–42.
63. *S.E.*, 19:291.
64. See, for example, novelist Arthur Schnitzler, *My Youth in Vienna*, trans. Catherine Hutter (New York: Holt, Rinehart and Winston, 1970) or Franz Kafka, "Letter to His Father," in *Dearest Father: Stories and Other Writings*, trans. Ernest Kaiser and Ethne Wilkins (New York: Schocken Books 1954).
65. *S.E.*, 4:197.
66. Jones, *Life and Work*, p. 19.
67. *Letters*, p. 78.

68. Martin Freud, *Sigmund Freud*, pp. 70–71.
69. Ibid., p. 165.
70. Sigmund Freud, "Some Early Unpublished Letters of Freud," ed. Ernest L. Freud *International Journal of Psychoanalysis* 50 (1969):422.
71. Ibid., p. 424.
72. *Letters*, p. 6.
73. Freud, "Some Early Unpublished Letter," p. 420.
74. Ibid., p. 423.
75. Quoted in Rainey, *Freud as Student of Religion*, pp. 40–41. Unpublished letter to Eduard Silberstein, 18 September 1874.
76. *S.E.*, 20:9.
77. *Letters*, pp. 131–32.
78. Quoted in Krull, *Freud and His Father*, p. 174. Unpublished letter to Eduard Silberstein, 9 September 1875.
79. Martin Freud, *Sigmund Freud*, pp. 12–13.
80. Jones, *Life and Work*, I:37–38.
81. *S.E.*, 20:10.
82. Roazen, *Freud and His Followers*, p. 49.
83. Erich Fromm, *Sigmund Freud's Mission* (New York: Harper and Row, 1959), p. 18.
84. Jones, *Life and Work*, I:130.
85. Jones, *Life and Work*, p. 79.
86. The first time occurred in relation to an argument over whether his brother Alexander, who was apprenticing with Eli, should be paid; the second time when Eli supported his mother's plan to return to Hamburg; and the third time was in relation to Eli's possession of part of Martha's dowry.
87. Jones, *Life and Work*, p. 78.
88. Ibid.
89. Martin Freud, *Sigmund Freud*, pp. 13–14.
90. Martin Freud, "Who Was Freud?" in *The Jews of Austria: Essays on Their Life, History, and Destruction*, ed. Josef Fraenkel (London: Valentine and Mitchell, 1967), p. 203.
91. Jones, *Life and Work*: p. 86.
92. Jones, *Life and Work*, I:228.
93. Monster. Quoted in Peter Gay, *A Godless Jew* (New Haven: Yale University Press, 1987), p. 153.
94. Ralph Steadman, *Sigmund Freud* (New York: Paddington Press, 1979), p. 65.
95. *Letters*, p. 22.
96. Jones, *Life and Work*, p. 101.
97. Quoted in Giovanni Costigan, *Sigmund Freud: A Short Biography* (New York: Macmillan, 1965), p. 14.

## Chapter 5. Freud's Jewish Identity

1. Interestingly enough, Freud's parents, Jacob and Amalie, had previously done the same thing. Specifically, they adopted the birthdates of Bismark and Emperor Franz Josef, respectively. For this reason it might be assumed that Freud followed a similar custom.
2. Martin Freud, *Sigmund Freud*, p. 190.

3. Jones, *Life and Work*, p. 102.
4. Roazen, *Freud and His Followers*, p. 58.
5. Theodor Reik, "Years of Maturity," *Psychoanalysis* 4, 1 (1955):27.
6. Jones, *Life and Work*, p. 357.
7. This will become especially apparent in his later interaction with Breuer, which would eventually bring forth deep feelings of dread and anger in regard to the dependency he felt.
8. Jones, *Life and Work*, p. 362.
9. The picture appeared in the front of Martin Freud's book, *Sigmund Freud: Man and Father*.
10. Ibid., pp. 100–01.
11. *S.E.*, 20:73.
12. *S.E.*, 5:73.
13. Theodor Herzl, *The New Ghetto* (Vienna and Berlin, 1920), p. 45.
14. *S.E.*, 5:442.
15. *S.E.*, 4:197.
16. Both Zionist student organizations.
17. *Freud/Abraham*, p. 264.
18. Ernst Simon, "Sigmund Freud the Jew," *Leo Baeck International Yearbook* 11 (1957):275.
19. *S.E.*, 13:xv.
20. Quoted in Costigan, *Sigmund Freud*, p. 272.
21. Jones, *Life and Work*, 3:83.
22. As a writer, for example, Zweig, who was most comfortable in his native German, found it excessively restricting that Hebrew was the only language allowed for publication.
23. Sigmund Freud and Arnold Zweig, *The Letters of Sigmund Freud and Arnold Zweig*, ed. Ernst L. Freud (New York: Harcourt Brace Jovanovich, 1970), p. 122; henceforth cited as *Freud/Zweig*.
24. George Viereck, *Glimpses of the Great* (London: Duckworth, 1930), p. 34.
25. *Letters*, p. 203.
26. Joseph Wortis, *Fragments of an Analysis with Freud* (New York: Simon and Schuster, 1954), p. 146.
27. *Freud/Zweig*, p. 40.
28. Leo Goldhammer, "Herzl and Freud," *Herzl Year Book* 1 (1958):196.
29. Ibid., p. 195.
30. Jones, *Life and Work*, p. 367.
31. Ibid., pp. 367–68.
32. Quoted in Costigan, *Sigmund Freud*, p. 265.
33. *S.E.*, 4:193.
34. *Letters*, pp. 339–40.
35. *Origins*, p. 170.
36. *S.E.*, 4:xxvi.
37. Roazen, *Freud and His Followers*, p. 78.
38. Jones, *Life and Work*, p. 239.
39. Ibid., p. 199.
40. *Origins*, p. 191.
41. *S.E.*, 4:136–45.
42. *S.E.*, 20:7.
43. *Letters*, p. 368.

44. Quoted in Costigan, *Sigmund Freud*, p. 270.
45. *S.E.*, 19:222.
46. Closer to home was the example of Martha's uncle Michael who had been baptized in order to gain a university professorship.
47. Heinrich Heine, *Heinrich Heine's Life Told in His Own Words*, ed. Gustav Karpeles, trans. Arthur Dexter (New York: Henry Holt, 1893), p. 130.
48. Ibid., p. 145.
49. *S.E.*, 4:194.
50. Ibid., pp. 194–95.
51. Ibid., p. 196.
52. Ibid., pp. 96–97.
53. Ibid., p. 136.
54. *Origins*, p. 342.
55. Ibid., p. 344.
56. Ibid.
57. Freud would always remain rather rigid and compulsive in his personal style.
58. Marthe Robert, *From Oedipus to Moses* (New York: Anchor Books, 1976), p. 11.
59. *S.E.* 4:208–18.
60. Chapter 7 will more fully explore the idea of psychoanalysis as an attack on gentile society.
61. *Freud/Abraham*, p. 146.
62. Jones, *Life and Work*, p. 198.
63. Ibid., p. 170.
64. Wortis, *Fragments*, p. 144.
65. Max Graf, "Reminiscences of Professor Sigmund Freud," *Psychoanalytic Quarterly* 11 (1942):473.
66. *S.E.*, 6:92–93.
67. Jones, *Life and Work*, p. 18.
68. *Origins*, p. 211.
69. Quoted in Costigan, *Sigmund Freud*, p. 267.
70. Jones, *Life and Work*, 3:182.
71. Letters, p. 368.
72. Ibid., pp. 366–67.
73. *S.E.*, 21:170.
74. Sigmund Freud and Oskar Pfister, *Psychoanalysis and Faith: The Letters of Sigmund Freud and Oskar Pfister* (New York: Basic Books: 1963), p. 63; henceforth cited as *Freud/Pfister*.
75. Letters, p. 365.
76. Ibid., p. 366.
77. Franz Alexander, Samuel Eisenstein, and Martin Gratjahn, eds., *Psychoanalytic Pioneers* (New York: Basic Books, 1966), p. 130.
78. It is of interest to note that it was from Popper-Lynkeus that Freud borrowed many of his ideas about dreams.
79. *S.E.*, 22:224.
80. Jones, *Life and Work*, p. 469.
81. Jones, *Life and Work*, 3:254.
82. *S.E.*, 20:9.
83. *S.E.*, 19:222.
84. *Freud/Abraham*, p. 9.

85. Wortis was a patient in analysis with Freud.
86. Wortis, *Fragments*, pp. 144–46.
87. *Letters*, p. 367.
88. Ibid., p. 428.
89. *Freuz/Abraham*, p. 34.
90. Ibid., p. 46.
91. *Freud/Zweig*, p. 40.
92. *S.E.*, 8:xv.
93. David Bakan, *Sigmund Freud and the Jewish Mystical Tradition* (New York: D. Van Nostrand, 1958), p. 137.
94. *S.E.*, 8:xv.
95. *Freud/Abraham*, p. 34.
96, Quoted in Rainey, *Freud as Student of Religion*, p. 77.
97. Jones, *Life and Work*, 2:353.
98. *Freud/Zweig*, p. 131. The last two lines of this quotation were omitted in the published correspondence. This is yet another example of selective editing of ethnically related material.
99. Jones, *Life and Work*, 2:360.
100. Jones, *Life and Work*, p. 289.
101. Ibid., p. 288.
102. Quoted in Costigan, *Sigmund Freud*, p. 185.
103. Jones, *Life and Work*, p. 288.
104. Costigan, *Sigmund Freud*, p. 186.
105. *S.E.*, 13:73.
106. Freud's vacillation and ambivalence about his ethnic identity as expressed in his work on religion would become even more marked in relation to his manuscript *Moses and Monotheism*.
107. *S.E.*, 8:157.
108. Ibid., p. 213.
109. Ibid., p. 233.
110. Ibid., p. 211.
111. Ibid., p. 233.
112. Jones, *Life and Work*, 2:233.
113. Jones, *Life and Work*, p. 471.
114. *Freud/Pfister*, p. 110.
115. Jones, *Life and Work*, pp. 501–2.
116. *Freud/Zweig*, p. 97.
117. *S.E.*, 23:58.
118. *Letters*, p. 307.
119. *S.E.*, 23:7.
120. Jones, *Life and Work*, p. 501.
121. *Freud/Zweig*, p. 98. Zweig had been sending Freud historical information on a regular basis since the inception of the Moses project.
122. Ibid., p. 106.
123. Ibid., p. 101.
124. This was during the period when Freud had begun to attribute an ever-increasing role to the ego in his theorizing.
125. *Freud/Zweig*, p. 178.
126. Jones, *Life and Work*, 3:242.
127. Such an outcome would have been too much to ask for, just as his self-analysis had not permanently resolved the same issues forty years earlier.

128. S.E., 23:136.
129. Ibid., p. 88.
130. Ibid.
131. Ibid., p. 90.
132. Ibid., p. 51.
133. S.E., 20:7.
134. S.E., 22:168.
135. Graf, "Reminiscences," pp. 474–25.
136. Kurt Eissler, *Medical Orthodoxy and the Future of Psychoanalysis* (New York: International University Press, 1965), p. 231.
137. S.E., 5:583.
138. Jones, *Life and Work*, 1:317.
139. S.E., 23:12.
140. S.E., 22:239.
141. Jones, *Life and Work*, 3:234.
142. Freud/Zweig, p. 163.
143. Letters, p. 448.

## Chapter 6. The Jews and Gentiles of Psychoanalysis

1. S.E., 5:483.
2. Jones, *Life and Work*, p. 112.
3. Letters, p. 202.
4. S.E., 3:261, editor's note.
5. Jones, *Life and Work*, p. 153.
6. Origins, p. 55.
7. Jones, *Life and Work*, p. 153.
8. Origins, p. 134.
9. Jones, *Life and Work*, 1:255.
10. S.E., 6:137–38.
11. Letter from Hannah Breuer to Ernest Jones, 21 April 1954 (Jones Archives.)
12. Letters, p. 49.
13. S.E., 19:280.
14. Jones, *Life and Work*, I:242.
15. S.E., 14:13–15.
16. Jones, *Life and Work*, p. 186.
17. This was reflected, for example, in the change from the formal *Sie* to the more informal *Du*.
18. Jones, *Life and Works*, p. 188.
19. The sister of Freud's friend Oskar Rie and one of Breuer's patients.
20. Fliess's side of the correspondence no longer remains extant.
21. Origins, p. 245.
22. Jones, *Life and Works*, p. 195.
23. Ibid., p. 169.
24. Quoted in Costigan, *Sigmund Freud*, p. 60.
25. Origins, p. 130.
26. Jones, *Life and Works*, p. 195.
27. Quoted in Costigan, *Sigmund Freud*, p. 59.

28. Roazen, *Freud and His Followers*, p. 89.
29. *Origins*, p. 60.
30. Jones, *Life and Works*, p. 193.
31. He had once told Jones that Fleiss was an "expert mathematician" and that by all manner of complex arithmatic "he would always arrive at the number he wanted."
32. Sigmund Freud and Carl Jung, *The Freud/Jung Letters*, ed. William McGuire (Princeton: Princeton University Press, 1974), p. 220; henceforth cited as *Freud/Jung*.
33. This took place during the summer of 1900 during one of their congresses.
34. Quoted Costigan, *Sigmund Freud*, p. 60.
35. Ibid., p. 63.
36. Jones, *Life and Works*, p. 187.
37. Sigmund Freud, "Untitled Statement to B'nai B'rith Wien," *B'nai Brith Millerlungen für Österreich* 35 (November and December 1935), p. 193.
38. Martin Freud, "Who Was Freud?" p. 204.
39. Quoted in Klein, *Jewish Origins*, p. 81.
40. His level of participation would lessen significantly with the establishment of the psychoanalytic study group in 1902.
41. Quoted in Klein, *Jewish Origins*, p. 81.
42. Henri Ellenberger, *The Discovery of the Unconscious* (New York: Basic Books, 1970), p. 424.
43. Quoted in Klein, *Jewish Origins*, p. 69.
44. *Origins*, p. 69.
45. Klein, *Jewish Origins*, p. 69.
46. Ibid., p. 82.
47. Ibid., p. 85.
48. *Letters*, p. 221.
49. Sigmund Freud, "Brief an Arthur Schnitzler," *Die Neue Rundschau* 66, 1 (1955):99–100.
50. Jones, *Life and Works*, 2:398.
51. Ibid., pp. 69–70.
52. Quoted in Roazen, *Freud and His Followers*, p. 183.
53. *S.E.*, 14:7.
54. Ibid., p. 52.
55. Roazen, *Freud and His Followers*, p. 178.
56. Quoted in Costigan, *Sigmund Freud*, p. 134.
57. Ibid., p. 135.
58. Hans Sachs, *Freud: Master and Friend* (Cambridge: Harvard University Press, 1944), p. 51.
59. Quoted in Roazen, *Freud and His Followers*, p. 207.
60. Fritz Wittels, *Sigmund Freud* (New York: Dodd and Mead, 1924), p. 225.
61. Sigmund Freud and Lou Andreas-Salomé, *Letters of Freud and Andreas-Salomé* (London: Hogarth, 1972), p. 19.
62. Sachs, *Master and Friend*, p. 115.
63. Jones, *Life and Works*, 2:137.
64. Ibid., p. 130.
65. *S.E.*, 14:51.

66. Jones, *Life and Works*, 3:208.
67. Adler's wife Raissa did not follow her husband's lead and convert.
68. Quoted in Ellenberger, *Discovery*, p. 584.
69. Ibid., p. 576.
70. Zurich's public mental hospital.
71. *S.E.*, 14:26.
72. Jones, *Life and Works*, 2:33.
73. Carl Jung, *Memories, Dreams, Reflections* (New York: Vintage Books, 1965), p. 361.
74. Wittels, *Sigmund Freud*, p. 138.
75. Jones, *Life and Works*, 2:33.
76. *Letters*, p. 302.
77. *Freud/Jung*, p. 457.
78. Ibid., p. 98.
79. *S.E.*, 14:61.
80. Ibid., p. 43.
81. Quoted in Nathan Hale, *Jones Jackson Putnam and Psychoanalysis* (Cambridge: Harvard University Press, 1971), p. 189.
82. Quoted in Costigan, *Sigmund Freud*, p. 127.
83. *Freud/Abraham*, p. 34.
84. Ibid., p. 46.
85. *S.E.*, 14:39–40.
86. *Freud/Abraham*, p. 64.
87. Ibid., p. 62.
88. Carl Jung, "Freud and Psychoanalysis," *Collected Works of Carl G. Jung*, 20 vols. (New York: Pantheon/Princeton, 1908), 4:107.
89. Ibid., pp. 164–65.
90. Quoted in Roazen, *Freud and His Followers*, p. 248. Letter from Lester Bernstein to Ernest Jones.
91. Jones, *Life and Works*, p. 325.
92. Quoted in Costigan, *Sigmund Freud*, p. 148.
93. Jones, *Life and Works*, 2:102.
94. Carl Jung, "The Freudian Theory of Hysteria," *Collected Works of Carl G. Jung*, 4:par. 53.
95. In her letters and diary she referred to the mythic child she wished to have with Jung as Siegfried after the character in Wagner. See Aldo Carotenuto, *A Secret Symmetry: Sabina Spielbein Between Jung and Freud* (New York: Pantheon Books, 1982), p. 86.
96. Ibid., pp. 116–17.
97. Ibid., p. 117.
98. Ibid., p. 118.
99. Ibid., p. 116.
100. Ibid., pp. 120–21.
101. Ibid., p. 121.
102. Ibid., pp. 122–23.
103. Ibid., p. xi.
104. Carl Jung, *Civilization in Transition* (London: Routledge and Kegan, 1964), pp. 165–66.
105. Clarence Karier, "The Ethics of a Therapeutic Man," *Psychoanalytic Review* 63, 1 (1976):353.

106. Jung, *Civilization*, p. 538.
107. Ibid., p. 539.
108. Costigan, *Sigmund Freud*, p. 158.
109. Jung, *Civilization*, p. 540.
110. Ibid., p. 541.
111. Quoted in Costigan, *Sigmund Freud*, p. 161.
112. Jones, *Life and Works*, p. 328.
113. *Freud/Abraham*, p. 160.
114. Quoted in Jones, *Life and Works*, p. 330.
115. Quoted in Peter Gay, *Freud: A Life for Our Time* (New York: W. W. Norton, 1988), p. 585.
116. Jones, *Life and Works*, p. 331.
117. Quoted in Costigan, *Sigmund Freud*, p. 171.
118. Jones, *Life and Works*, p. 401.
119. *S.E.*, 23:125.
120. Jones, *Life and Works*, p. 321.
121. *Freud/Jung*, p. 105.
122. Jones, *Life and Works*, p. 453.
123. Sacks, *Master and Friend*, pp. 166–67.
124. Jones, *Life and Works*, p. 333.
125. Quoted in Alexander, *Pioneers*, p. 130.
126. His biography was the only one written by an eminent analyst who had actually known Freud intimately.
127. Jones, *Life and Works*, p. 332.
128. Alexander, *Pioneers*, p. 188.
129. Freud was an exceptionally fast walker, and this analysis must have been a challenge physically as well as emotionally.
130. *Letters*, p. 300.
131. Eitingon at the time held a Polish passport.
132. Quoted in Alexander, *Pioneers*, p. 60.
133. *Letters*, p. 344.
134. Ludwig Binswanger, *Sigmund Freud: Reminescences of a Friendship* (New York and London: Grune and Stratton, 1957), pp. 78–79.
135. *Freud/Pfister*, pp. 61–62.
136. *Letters*, p. 390.
137. Quoted in Geofferey Cocks, *Psychotherapy in the Third Reich* (New York: Oxford University Press, 1985), pp. 87–88.
138. Ibid., p. 91.
139. The following account draws heavily on Ernest Jones's recounting of events in his biography of Freud.
140. Jones, *Life and Works*, pp. 512–13.
141. Ibid., p. 513.
142. Ibid., p. 514.
143. Ibid., pp. 514–5.
144. Ibid., p. 515.
145. Ibid.
146. Ibid., p. 517.
147. *Letters*, pp. 442–34.
148. Jones, *Life and Works*, p. 518.
149. Ibid., p. 530.

*Notes*

## Chapter 7. Psychoanalysis and Its Jewish Connection

1. Jung, *Civilization*, p. 166.
2. William McDougall, *Is America Safe for Democracy?* (New York: Ayer, 1977), p. 127.
3. Jones, *Life and Works*, p. 325.
4. Marc Lubin, "Study of the High Rate of Male Jewish Membership in the Profession of Psychoanalysis," *Proceedings*, 77th Annual Convention, American Psychological Association, (1969), pp. 527–28.
5. *Freud/Abraham*, p. 34.
6. *Letters*, p. 220.
7. Menninger, "Genius," p. 419.
8. Ibid., p. 420.
9. Ibid., p. 421.
10. Ibid., p. 422.
11. Ibid., pp. 421-22.
12. Ibid., p. 423.

# References

Alexander, Franz, Samuel Eisenstein and Martin Gratjahn. *Psychoanalytic Pioneers*. New York: Basic Books, 1966.

Aron, Willy. "Notes on Sigmund Freud's Ancestry and Jewish Contacts." *YIVO Annual of Jewish Social Sciences* 9 (1956–57): 286–95.

Bakan, David. *Sigmund Freud and the Jewish Mystical Tradition*. New York: D. Van Nostrand, 1958.

Bergmann, Martin. "Moses in the Evolution of Freud's Jewish Identity." *Israel Annals of Psychiatry and Related Sciences* 14 (March 1976): 3–26.

Bernays, Anna. "My Brother Sigmund Freud." *American Mercury* 51 (1940): 335–42.

Binswanger, Ludwig. *Sigmund Freud: Reminiscences of a Friendship*. New York and London: Grune and Stratton, 1957.

Carotenuto, Aldo. *A Secret Symmetry: Sabina Spielbein between Jung and Freud*. New York: Pantheon Books, 1982.

Cocks, Geoffrey. *Psychotherapy in the Third Reich*. New York: Oxford University Press, 1985.

Costigan, Giovanni. *Sigmund Freud: A Short Biography*. New York: Macmillan, 1965.

Cuddihy, John Murray. *The Ordeal of Civility: Freud, Marx, Levi-Strauss and the Jewish Struggle with Modernity*. New York: Basic Books, 1974.

Diamond, Stanley. "Kibbutz and Shtetl: The History of an Idea." *Social Forces* 5 (Fall 1957):71–99.

Ellenberger, Henri. *The Discovery of the Unconscious*. New York: Basic Books. 1970.

Eissler, Kurt. *Medical Orthodoxy and the Future of Psychoanalysis*. New York: International Universities Press, 1965.

Freud, Martin. *Sigmund Freud: Man and Father*. New York: Vanguard Press, 1958.

——— . "Who Was Freud?" In *The Jews of Austria: Essays on Their Life, History and Destruction*, edited by Josef Fraenkel. London: Vallentine & Mitchel, 1967.

Freud, Sigmund., "Briefe au Arthur Schnitzler." *Die Neue Rundschau* 66, no. 1 (1955): 95–106.

——— . *The Complete Letters of Sigmund Freud and Wilhelm Fliess, 1887–1904*. Translated and edited by Jeffrey Moussaieff Masson. Cambridge: Harvard University Press, 1985.

——— . *Letters of Sigmund Freud*. Edited by Ernst L. Freud. New York: Basic Books, 1960.

——— . *The Origins of Psychoanalysis: Letters to Wilhelm Fliess, Drafts and Notes, 1887–1902*. Edited by Marie Bonaparte, Anna Freud, and Ernst Kris. Translated by Eric Mosbacher and James Strachey. New York: Basic Books, 1954.

---. "Sieben Briefe und zwei Postkarten au Emil Fluss." *Psyche* 24 (1970): 766–84.

---. "Some Early Unpublished Letters of Freud." Edited by Ernst L. Freud. *International Journal of Psychoanalysis* 50 (1969): 419–427.

---. *The Standard Edition of the Complete Psychological Works of Sigmund Freud.* 24 vols. Translated under the general editorship of James Starchey in collaboration with Anna Freud. London: Hogarth Press and the Institute of Psychoanalysis, 1953–74.

---. "Untitled Statement to B'nai Brith Wien" *B'nai Brith Millerlungen für Osterreich* 26 (May 1926).

---. "Untitled Statement to B'nai Brith Wien." *B'nai Brith Millerlungen für Osterreich* 35 (November and December 1935.): 193.

Freud, Sigmund and Karl Abraham. *A Psycho-Analytic Dialogue: The Letters of Sigmund Freud and Karl Abraham, 1907–1926.* Edited by Hilda C. Abraham & Ernst L. Freud. Translated by Bernard Marsh and Hilda C. Abraham. New York: Basic Books, 1965.

Freud, Sigmund, and Len Andreas-Salomé. *Letters.* Edited by Ernst Pfeiffer. Translated by William and Elaine Robson-Scott. London: Hogarth Press, 1972.

Freud, Sigmund, and Carl G. Jung. *The Freud/Jung Letters.* Edited by William McGuire. Princeton: Princeton University Press, 1974.

Freud, Sigmund, and Oskar Pfister. (1963). *Psychoanalysis and Faith: The Letters of Sigmund Freud and Oskar Pfister.* Edited by Heinrich Meng and Ernst L. Freud. Translated by Eric Mosbacher. New York: Basic Books, 1953.

Freud, Sigmund, and Arnold Zweig. (1970). *The Letters of Sigmund Freud and Arnold Zweig.* Edited by Ernst L. Freud. Translated by Elaine and William Robson-Scott. New York: Harcourt Brace Jovanovich, 1970.

Fromm, Eric. *Sigmund Freud's Mission.* New York: Harper & Row, 1959.

Gay, Peter. *Freud: A Life for Our Time.* New York: W. W. Norton, 1988.

---. *Freud, Jews and Other Germans.* New York: Oxford University Press, 1978.

---. *A Godless Jew.* New Haven: Yale University Press, 1987.

Gicklhorn, Renée. "The Freiberg Period of the Freud Family." *Journal of the History of Medicine* 24 (1969): 37–43.

Goldhammer, Leo. "Herzl and Freud." In *Theodor Herzl Jahrbuch,* edited by Tulo Nussenblatt, pp. 266–68. Vienna: Victor Glanz, 1937.

Grinstein, Alexander. *The Index of Psychoanalytic Writings.* New York: International University Press, 1975.

Graf, Max. "Reminiscences of Professor Sigmund Freud." *Psychoanalytic Quarterly* 11 (1942): 465–76.

Grier, William, and Price Cobbs. *Black Rage.* New York: Basic Books, 1968.

Grunfeld, Frederic. *Prophets Without Honor.* New York: McGraw-Hill, 1979.

Hale, Nathan. *Jones Jackson Putnam and Psychoanalysis.* Cambridge: Harvard University Press, 1971.

Heine, Heinrich. *Heinrich Heine's Life Told in His Own Words.* Edited by Gustav Karpeles. New York: Henry Holt, 1893.

Heller, Judith. "Freud's Mother and Father." In *Freud as We Knew Him*, edited by Hendrik Ruitenbeek. Detroit: Wayne State University Press, 1973.
Jones, Ernst. *The Life and Work of Sigmund Freud*. Vols. 1–3. New York: Basic Books, 1953, 1955, 1957.
———. *The Life and Work of Sigmund Freud*. Abridged Edition. New York: Basic Books, 1961.
Jung, Carl G. *Civilization in Transition*. London: Routledge and Kegan, 1965.
———. "Freud and Psychoanalysis." In vol. 4, *Collected Works of Carl G. Jung*. 20 vols. New York: Pantheon/Princeton, 1953.
———. "The Freudian Theory of Hysteria." In vol. 4, *Collected Works of Carl G. Jung*. 20 vols. New York: Pantheon/Princeton, 1953.
———. *Memories, Dreams, Reflections*. New York: Vintage Books, 1965.
Karier, Clarence. "The Ethics of a Therapeutic Man." *Psychoanalytic Review* 63, no. 1 (1976): 15–46.
Klein, Dennis. *Jewish Origins of the Psychoanalytic Movement*. New York: Praeger, 1981.
Krull, Marianne. *Freud and His Father*. New York: W. W. Norton, 1986.
Lewis, Kurt. *Resolving Social Conflicts*. New York: Harper & Row, 1948.
Lewis, Theodore. "Freud, the Jews and Judaism." *The Jewish Spectator* (March 1958): 11–14.
Lubin, Marc. "Study of the High Rate of Male Jewish Membership in the Profession of Psychoanalysis." *Proceedings, 77th Annual Convention*. American Psychological Association (1969): 527–28.
Masson, Jeffrey Moussaieff. *The Assault on Truth*. New York: Farrar, Straus & Giroux, 1984.
Mayer, Sigmund. (1917). *Die Wiener Juden: Kommerz, Kultur, Politik 1700–1900*. Vienna and Berlin: Lowit Verlag, 1917.
McDougall, William. *Is America Safe for Democracy?* New York: Ayer, 1977.
Meadows, Arnold, and Harold Vetter. "Freudian Theory and the Judaic Value System." In *the Psychodynamics of American Jewish Life*, edited by Norman Kiell, pp. 151–68. New York: Twayne, 1967.
Menninger, Kurt. "The Genius of the Jew in Psychiatry." In *A Psychiatrist's World*, pp. 415–24. New York: Viking Press, 1959.
Mitchell, Juliet. *Psychoanalysis and Feminism*. New York: Vantage Books, 1974.
Myers, Hector, and Larry King. "Mental Health Issues in the Development of the Black American Child." In *The Psychosocial Development of Minority Children*, edited by Gloria Powell, pp. 275–306. New York: Brunner-Mazel, 1985.
Ostow, Mortimer. *Judaism and Psychoanalysis*. New York: KTAV, 1982.
Patterson, Orlando. *Ethnic Chauvinism, The Reactionary Impulse*. New York: Stein & Day, 1977.
Rainey, Reuben. *Freud as Student of Religion*. Missoula, Mont.: Scholars Press, 1975.
Reik, Theodor. "Years of Maturity." *Psychoanalysis* 4, no. 1 (1955): 68–74.
Roazen, Paul. *Freud and His Followers*. New York: Alfred A. Knopf, 1971.

Robert, Marthe. *From Oedipus to Moses.* New York: Anchor Books, 1976.

Rothman, Stanley, and Philip Isenberg. "Freud and Jewish Marginality." *Encounter* 43 (December 1974): 45–54.

Ruitenbeek, Hendrik. "The Professor." In *Freud as We Knew Him*, edited by Hendrik Ruitenbeek, pp. 17–21. Detroit: Wayne State University Press, 1973.

Sachs, Hans. *Freud: Master and Friend.* Cambridge: Harvard University Press, 1944.

Sajner, Jose. "Sigmund Freuds Beziehungen zu seinem Geburtsort Freiberg (Pribor) und zu Mahren." *Clio Medica* 3 (1968): 167–80.

Schorske, Carl. "Politics and Patricide in Freud's Interpretation of Dreams." *American History Review* 78 (1973): 328–47.

Simon, Ernst. "Sigmund Freud, the Jew." *Leo Baeck International Yearbook*, 2 (1957): 270–305.

Steadman, Ralph. *Sigmund Freud.* New York: Paddington Press, 1969.

Viereck, George. *Glimpses of the Great.* London: Duckworth, 1930.

Vitz, Paul. *Sigmund Freud's Christian Unconscious.* New York: Guilford Press, 1988.

Wittels, Fritz. *Sigmund Freud.* New York: Dodd and Mead, 1924.

Wortis, Joseph. *Fragments of an Analysis with Freud.* New York: Simon and Schuster, 1954.

Yarrow, Marian Radke. "Personality Development and Minority Group Membership." In *The Jews: Social Patterns of an American Group*, edited by Marshall Sklare, pp. 451–74. New York: Free Press, 1958.

Zilboorg, Gregory. *Freud and Religion: A Restatement of an Old Controversy.* Westminster: Newman Press, 1958.

# Index

Abraham, Karl, 21–22, 117, 122, 124, 143, 158, 171, 181–84, 186, 192, 196–98, 213
Adler, Alfred, 170, 171
Alexander, Franz, 196
Andreas-Salome, Lou, 203
Anna O. *See* Pappenheim, Bertha
Anti-Semitism, 18, 34. *See also* Vienna
Assimilation. *See* Jews: assimilated
Austria, 29–30, 35, 37–39; *See also* Galacia; Moravia; Vienna

Bakan, David, 165, 213
Bergmann, Martin, 210
Berlin, Isaiah, 87
Bernays, Eli (Sigmund Freud's brother-in-law), 83, 85
Bernays, Emmeline (Sigmund Freud's mother-in-law), 83, 85, 86
Bernays, Minna (later Schonberg, Sigmund Freud's sister-in-law), 83, 89
Binswanger, Ludwig, 170
Bisexuality, 159, 165–66
Bleuler, Eugen, 171, 178
B'nai B'rith, 119, 120, 121, 166–70
Bonaparte, Marie, 16, 93, 138, 166, 206, 207
Borne, Ludwig, 108–9, 154
Bragg, William, 207
Braun, Ludwig, 170
Breuer, Josef, 51, 72, 82, 88, 107, 150–58, 168–69
Breuer, Leopold, 72
Brill, Abraham A., 171
Brucke, Ernst, 81–82
Bullitt, W. C., 206

Carotenuto, Aldo, 185
Charcot, Jean, 153
Christianity. *See* Freud, Sigmund: and Christianity; Jews: assimilated
Costigan, Giovanni, 190
Cuddihy, John, 214, 215

Diamond, Stanley, 41
Dreyfus, Alfred, 158

Eder, David, 124
Eitingon, Max, 171, 192, 196, 200–201, 204
Ethnic group, 45–46, 50. *See also* Minority group
Ethnic identity, 26–27, 46. *See also* Jewishness

Ferenczi, Sandor, 172, 184, 191, 192–93, 198
Fleischl, Ernst, 151, 197
Fliess, Wilhelm, 21, 22, 107, 113, 114, 115, 118, 158–66, 175
Fluss, Gisela, 84
Freud, Adolfine (Sigmund Freud's sister), 61
Freud, Alexander (Sigmund Freud's brother), 61
Freud, Amalie Nathansohn (Sigmund Freud's mother), 53, 54, 59–60, 61, 63–64, 69, 71, 142
Freud, Anna (later Bernays; Sigmund Freud's sister), 61, 63
Freud, Anna (Sigmund Freud's daughter), 70, 71, 89, 96, 202; and flight from Vienna, 205, 206, 207, 208
Freud, Emmanuel (Sigmund Freud's step-brother), 56, 62, 73, 80–81, 144
Freud, Ernest (Sigmund Freud's son), 96, 100, 207
Freud, Jacob (Sigmund Freud's father), 37, 53, 55–59, 61, 106–7; and Sigmund Freud, 65–66, 69–70, 111–12, 115, 144, 145, 150, 169; tells story

238

of anti-Semitic incident, 91, 112, 157
Freud, John (Sigmund Freud's nephew), 149
Freud, Julius (Sigmund Freud's brother), 61, 66
Freud, Maria (Sigmund Freud's sister-in-law), 63
Freud, Marie (Sigmund Freud's sister), 61
Freud, Martha Bernays (Sigmund Freud's wife), 82–89, 92, 94, 97, 202, 205, 208
Freud, Martin (Sigmund Freud's son), 75, 96, 100, 194, 202, 205, 207; reminiscences by, 59, 61, 64, 68, 69, 75, 80, 93, 97, 167
Freud, Mathilde (Sigmund Freud's daughter), 96, 151, 185, 192
Freud, Oliver (Sigmund Freud's son), 81, 96
Freud, Paula (Sigmund Freud's sister), 61
Freud, Phillip (Sigmund Freud's stepbrother), 56, 62, 73, 80–81
Freud, Rosa (Sigmund Freud's sister), 61, 202
Freud, Sigmund
—and Acropolis, Athens, 144–45
—and Akhenaten in Egyptian religion, 143, 183–84, 197
—ancestors, 44, 56, 60
—and anti-Semitism: in "My Son the Myops," 98–99; reaction to, 14, 74–75, 79, 180–81, 198, 217; as a shared experience, 121; when raising children, 95
—and B'nai B'rith, 119, 120, 166–70
—and Catholic Church: as an advance over Judaism, 140; disapproval of *Moses and Monotheism*, 135; in "My Son the Myops," 98–100; and primal patricide, 139; and his works about, 126–27
—and Christianity, 16, 86, 92, 109–13, 214; and converts from Judaism, 117–18, 178; and marriage with adherents of, 123; and possibility of his conversion to, 116, 143, 144; in *Totem and Taboo*, 130
—and disciples, 131, 149

—dreams: "Count Thun," 116; of Theodor Herzl, 104; of Jewishness, 98, 112, 114; "My Son the Myops," 98–100, 104, 113; "People with Birds' Beaks," 142; of Rome, 110–12, 118; "The Uncle with the Yellow Beard," 109
—finances, 51, 95–96, 151, 155, 156, 202
—and gentiles, 26, 67, 116, 117, 123, 132, 167, 198, 210
—and Germanic culture, 25, 102
—and Hebrew language, 21, 72, 121
—and Hebrew University, Israel, 101, 121, 124
—Jewishness, 24, 209, 217; and his adjustment to, 16, 20, 48–49, 52–53, 90–91, 135, 137, 169, 178; biographers treatment of, 14–18, 22; described by him, 119–20; distorted impression given of, 21–22; in Eastern European Jews, 25, 77, 164; and Hebrew language, 21, 22, 99, 156, 159; and incident in the Biergarten, St. Barthomae, 97; and his name change, 110; positive aspects, 121–22, 140; reflected in Rome dreams, 111–13; in "The Uncle with the Yellow Beard," 109; and Yiddish language, 21, 72, 121. *See also* under Freud, Sigmund: and Jewish religion, and Moses; Psychoanalysis; Vienna
—and Jewish organizations, 119, 120, 121, 166–70
—and Jewish religion, 19–21, 140; antipathy toward, 76, 102; and Bible, 21, 69–70; in childhood, 55; and collecting ancient statuary, 92–93; and cremation, 93; education in, 72, 73–74; festivals and observances of, 77–78, 87–88; and his marriage ceremony, 88; mystical elements, influential, 165; and owning dogs, 92, 202; and Reformed Jews, 120; and refusal to admit primal patricide, 139; rejection of, 86, 91–93. *See also* Freud, Sigmund: Jewishness, and Moses; Psychoanalysis
—life (by chronology): birth, 54, 92;

name, 54; change of name, 110; circumcision, 54; specialness in family, 53, 62, 65, 66; early nursemaid, 63, 66–67, 91, 99, 142; depature from Freiberg, 67–68, 91, 110; to Vienna, 68–69; early education, 69; formal education before university, 70–71; religious education, 72, 73–74; militaristic interest, 74–75; infatuation with Gisela Fluss, 84; education at University of Vienna, 78; dueling, 75, 80; trip to England when student, 80–81; career choice of medicine, 78, 82; in physiological laboratory of Ernst Brucke, 81–84; engagement to Martha Bernays, 82–84; residency in General Hospital, Vienna, 82; work in psychiatric clinic of Theodor Meynert, 82; marriage, 84, 88; in-laws, 83, 85 (see also Bernays, Emmeline; Bernays, Eli; Schonberg, Ignaz; Schonberg, Martha); as parent, 93–97; begins medical practice, 88; lackluster progress in medical practice, 108; lack of promotion at University of Vienna, 108–9, 113–14; self-analysis, 20, 62, 107–8, 163, 165; middle career, 125; and inner committee of five, 191–92, 200; death of daughter (Sophia), 202; death of niece (Caecilie Graf), 202; death of grandson (Heinz Rudolph Halberstadt), 203; last years in Vienna, 201–8; cancer of the jaw and palate, 203–4; last months in England, 138, 146, 208; death, 208; cremation, 93, 208
—and Moses, 16, 49, 105, 112, 128, 179, 217; and his identification with, 49, 141, 144. See also Freud, Sigmund, works: *Moses and Monotheism*, "The Moses of Michelangelo"
—and Nazism, 25, 105, 106, 119, 135, 204–8
—personality traits: ambition and drive, 63, 71, 104, 105–6, 114, 157; anxiety neurosis, 107–8; daring, 157; death fear, 144–45; dependence on others, 155, 163, 179, 180; dominance, 157; emotionally reserved, 173, 176; "family romance" wish, 143–44; father figure himself, 116, 179, 192; father substitute search, 73, 75, 116, 150, 151–52, 155–56, 157, 161, 163; formal in manner, 173; friendships, 149–50; as a great man self-doubts, 104–5; health concerns, 108; homosexual overtones, 160; hypersensitivity, 53, 184, 217; independence of thought, 121–22, 157; inferiority feelings, 172; injustices opposed, 71; insecurity, 84; insular, 202; loss reaction, 67; narcissism, 53, 84, 150, 217; perception intuitive, 218; persistence, 157; personal habits well organized, 89, 173; *schnorrer* fantasies, 156; scientific aptitude, 78, 147–48; scientific objectivity, 147–49, 162, 165; self-confidence, 63; self-criticism, 137; self-doubt, 162; self-hating Jew, 17; speculative thoughts, 162, 163, 165; train phobia, 110; unpopular views courageously held, 121–22
—and persons known or admired: Karl Abraham, 21–22, 117, 122, 124, 143, 171, 181–84, 192, 196–98, 213; Alfred Adler, 170, 172–78; Lou Andreas-Salome, 203; Ludwig Binswanter, 170; Eugene Bleuler, 171, 178; Marie Bonaparte, 16, 93, 138, 206, 207; Ludwig Borne, 108–9, 154; Ludwig Braun, 170; Josef Breuer, 51, 82, 88, 107, 150–58, 168–69; Abraham A. Brill, 171; Ernst Brucke, 81–82; W. C. Bullitt, 206; Jean Charcot, 153; Alfred Dreyfus, 159; Max Eitingon, 171, 192, 200–201, 204; Sandor Ferenczi, 172, 184, 192–93; Ernst Fleischl, 151, 197; Wilhelm Fliess, 21, 22, 107, 113, 114, 115, 118, 158–66, 175; Max Graf, 117; Samuel Hammerschlag, 51, 72, 156; Hannibal, 74, 75, 111, 133, 143; Heinrich Heine, 109–10; Eduard Hitschmann, 170; Ernest Jones, 170, 171, 198–200, 205, 206; Carl Jung, 131, 164, 170, 178–91, break with

## Index

Freud, 23, 127–28, 131, 183–84, 186, designated successor, 23, 172, discusses Akhenaten, 143, 183–84; Max Kahane, 170; Paul Klemperer, 175; Carl Koller, 80; Leonard Konigstein, 170; Theodor Lessing, 117; Alphonse Maeder, 184; Thomas Mann, 128, 202; Marshal Andre Massena, 74; Theodor Meynert, 82, 153; Josef Paneth, 88; Anna O. (Bertha Pappenheim), 152–53, 154; Paul, the Apostle, 141; Elias Philipp, 88; Josep Popper-Lynkeus, 121; Otto Rank, 193–96; Rudolph Reitler, 170; Oscar Rie, 170; Romain Rolland, 144–45; Hanns Sachs, 137, 173–74, 192, 197, 199–200; Arthur Schnitzler, 106, 170; Eduard Silberstein, 71; Charles Singer, 136; Sabina Spielrein, 185–88; Wilhelm Stekel, 170, 172, 174, 175; Richard Sterba, 206; Rudolph Urbantschitsch, 170; Edoardo Weiss, 206; Chaim Weizman, 101; Joseph Wortis, 122–24; Arnold Zweig, 101, 124–25, 136, 137
—and politics, 105
—and religion, 15, 18, 19, 76. See also Freud, Sigmund: and Akhenaten, and Catholic Church, and Christianity, and Jewish religion
—and Rome, 110–13, 117
—self-analysis, 20, 62, 107–8, 163, 165
—vacations, 95, 110–13, 117
—views on: bisexuality, 165–66; human nature, 203; Jewish humor, 118–19; mysticism, 164; numerology, 164; Oedipal complex, 115; periodicity, 160, 164, 165; seduction theory, 115; self-hating Jews, 117
—works: *An Autobiographical Study*, 140; *Five Lectures on Psychoanalysis*, 25; *Future of an Illusion*, 141; *The Interpretation of Dreams*, 74; *Moses and Monotheism*, 14, 17, 21, 126, 135–45, 162, 195, 197, 217; "The Moses of Michelangelo," 131–34; *The Psychopathology of Everyday Life*, 118, 155, 164; *Studies in Hysteria*, 150, 154; *Totem and Taboo*, 127–30, 183; *Totem and Taboo* (Hebrew edition), 21, 101
—and Yiddish language, 21, 22, 99, 156, 159
—and Zionism, 22, 92–93, 100–102, 124
Freud, Sophie (later Halberstadt, Sigmund Freud's daughter), 96, 202, 203
Fromm, Erich, 84

Galacia: Jews in, 36–37, 59
Gay, Peter, 41
Gentiles. See Jews: and gentiles
Graf, Caecilie (Sigmund Freud's niece), 202
Graf, Max, 117, 141

Halberstadt, Heinz Rudolph (Sigmund Freud's grandson), 203
Halberstadt, Sophie Freud (Sigmund Freud's daughter), 96, 202, 203
Hammerschlag, Samuel, 51, 72, 156
Hannibal, 74, 75, 111, 133, 143
Hebrew language, 21, 72, 121
Hebrew University, 101, 121, 124, 201
Heine, Heinrich, 109–10
Heller, Judith, 58, 59, 60, 64
Herzl, Theodor, 21, 42–43, 103–5; *The New Ghetto*, 98–99, 103
Hitschmann, Eduard, 170
Hoare, Samuel, 207

Identity, 46. See also Jewishness; Minority group
Isenberg, Philip, 214, 215
Israel, 45, 142. See also Hebrew University

Jewishness, 32, 29, 45–46, 48–49. See also Ethnic identity; Jews: assimilated; Jews: personality traits of; Minority group
"Jewish Question," 18, 34–35
Jewish religion, 31–32, 37, 52, 55, 120. See also Freud, Sigmund: and Jewish religion
Jews
—assimilated, 20, 33–35, 37–38, 48–

49, 52, 169
—in Eastern Europe, 25, 77, 164
—emancipated, 24, 25–26, 28–29, 35, 72
—family life, 52
—in Galacia, 36–37, 59
—and gentiles, 16, 31, 41–42, 48, 168, 185–86, 188–89
—in ghettos, 31–36, 50–51
—Orthodox, 37
—personality traits of: aspirations, 52; concentration, 40; cynicism, 39; drive, 40, 52; egotism, 123; energy, 40; faith in future, 40; hypersensitivity, 39, 169; inner directedness, 43; intellectualism, 124, 140; irritability, 40; love of ideas, 43; love of words, 43; narcissistic childhood, 216; passiveness, 43; pragmatism, 171; pride in origins, 43; restlessness, 40; self-hatred, 17, 18, 20, 40–41, 48, 117; social skills, 123; specialness, 51– 52; suspiciousness, 39; work habits, 40; wounded self-esteem, 52. *See also* Jews: assimilated
—Reformed, 55, 120
—in Vienna, 20, 25, 36, 37, 43–44
Jones, Ernest, 22, 23, 170, 171, 191, 198–200, 205, 206; comments from his *The Life and Work of Sigmund Freud* mentioned, 65, 69, 74, 86, 88, 93, 94–95, 107–8, 158, 179
Jung, Carl, 23, 131, 164, 170, 178– 91, 210, 213; break with Freud, 23, 127–28, 131, 183–84, 186; designated successor, 23, 172; discusses Akhenaten, 143, 183–84

Kahane, Max, 170
Karier, Clarence, 189
Kibbutz (Israel), 41
Klein, Dennis, 15, 169
Klemperer, Paul, 175
Konigstein, Leonard, 170
Krull, Marianne, 64, 115, 145, 210

Lessing, Theodor, 117
Levi, Hermann, 40
Lewin, Kurt, 33
Lewis, Theodore, 17

McDougall, William, 210
Maeder, Alphonse, 184
Mahler, Margaret, 67
Mann, Thomas, 128, 202
Massena, Marshal Andre, 74
Masson, Jeffrey, 22, 115
Meadow, Arnold, 213
Menninger, Karl, 84, 52, 213, 215, 216, 217
Meynert, Theodor, 153
Minority group, 18, 45, 49–50. *See also* Ethnic group
Moravia: Jews in, 37
Mosbacker, Eric, 22

Nazism, 13–14, 25, 105, 106, 119, 135, 188–90, 204–5
Nova (television program), 14
Numerology, 164

O., Anna, 152–53, 154
Orthodox Jews. *See* Jews: Orthodox
Ostow, Mortimer, 17, 20–21, 213

Paneth, Josef, 88
Pappenheim, Bertha, 152–53, 154
Patterson, Orlando, 215
Paul, the Apostle, 141
Periodicity, 159, 160, 164, 165
Philipp, Elias, 88
Popper-Lynkeus, Josep, 121
Psychoanalysis: early days, 147–48, 170–73; exclusive domain of Freud's, 147; Freud's gift to world, 116; and gentiles in, 23, 170, 213 (*see also* Jung, Carl; Jones, Ernest); influenced by Freud's Jewishness, 211; influenced by Jewish culture, 74, 121, 148, 210, 213; and Jewish childhood as preparation for, 215–16; and its Jewishness not discussed, 21; and Nazism, 204; need to become non-Jewish, 14, 23–24, 184; a new religion, 141; practiced by Jews, 122, 127, 170, 212, 213; as response to Jewish marginality, 213, 215; universal applicability, 211–12; in Vienna, 135, 136, 171

Rado, Sandor, 196
Rainey, Reuben, 73

Rank, Otto, 191, 193–96
Reik, Theodor, 199
Reitler, Rudoph, 170
Rie, Oscar, 170
Roazen, Paul, 84, 183
Romain, Rolland, 144–45
Rosenthal, Mortiz, 65
Rothman, Stanley, 214, 215

Sachs, Hanns, 137, 173–74, 192, 196, 197, 199–200
Schnitzler, Arthur, 39, 106, 170
Schonberg, Ignaz (Sigmund Freud's brother-in-law), 83
Schonberg, Martha Bernays (Sigmund Freud's sister-in-law), 83
Schorske, Carl, 210, 215
Silberstein, Eduard, 71
Singer, Charles, 136
Spielrein, Sabina, 185–88

Stekel, Wilhelm, 170, 172, 174, 175
Sterba, Richard, 206
Strachey, James, 22

Urbantschitsch, Rudolph, 170

Vetter, Harold, 213
Vienna: anti-Semitism in, 15–16, 36, 25, 77, 79, 121, 153, 168; Jews in, 20, 25, 36, 37, 43–44; psychoanalysis in disfavor in, 135, 136, 171

Weininger, Otto, 41, 165
Weiss, Edoardo, 206
Weizman, Chaim, 101

Yiddish language, 21, 22, 99, 156, 159

Zilboorg, Gregory, 16–17, 48
Zweig, Arnold, 101, 124–25, 136, 137